Gloria Anzaldúa

Borderlands

La Frontera

The New Mestiza

25TH ANNIVERSARY
FOURTH EDITION

aunt lute books

SAN FRANCISCO

Fourth Edition

Aunt Lute Books
San Francisco, CA

"Holy Relics" first appeared in *Conditions Six*, 1980. "Cervicide" first appeared in *Labyris, A Feminist Arts Journal*, Vol. 4, No. 11, Winter 1983. *"En el nombre de todas las madres que han perdido sus hijos en la guerra"* first appeared in *IKON: Creativity and Change*, Second Series, No. 4, 1985.

First Edition: Cover and Text Design - Pamela Wilson Design Studio; Cover Art–Pamela Wilson (*Ehécatl*, The Wind)

Fourth Edition: Cover Re-design and Typesetting - Amy Woloszyn, Amymade Graphic Design

Printed in the U.S.A.

Library of Congress Cataloging-in-Publication Data

Anzaldúa, Gloria.
  Borderlands : the new mestiza = la frontera / by Gloria Anzaldúa. – 4th ed.
    p. cm.
  Includes bibliographical references.
  ISBN 978-1-879960-85-5 (alk. paper)
  1. Mexican American women–Poetry. 2. Mexican-American Border Region–Poetry. I. Title. II. Title: Frontera.
  PS3551.N95B6 2012
  811'.54–dc23
                      2012014640

15 14 13 12

Acknowledgments

To you who walked with me upon my path and who held out a hand when I stumbled;

to you who brushed past me at crossroads never to touch me again;

to you whom I never chanced to meet but who inhabit borderlands similar to mine;

to you for whom the borderlands is unknown territory;

to Kit Quan, for feeding me and listening to me rant and rave;

to Melanie Kaye/Kantrowitz, for believing in me and being there for me;

to Joan Pinkvoss, my editor and publisher, midwife extraordinaire, whose understanding, caring, and balanced mixture of gentle prodding and pressure not only helped me bring this "baby" to term, but helped to create it; these images and words are for you.

To the production staff at Spinsters/Aunt Lute who bore the pressure of impossible deadlines well: Martha Davis whose invaluable and excellent copy-editing has made the material more readable and cohesive; Debra DeBondt who worked long and hard to keep the book on schedule; Pam Wilson and Grace Harwood;

to Frances Doughty, Juanita Ramos, Judith Waterman, Irena Klepfisz, Randy Conner, Janet Aalphs, Mirtha N. Quintanales, Mandy Covey and Elana Dykewomon for their support and encouragement, as well as feedback, on various pieces; to my friends, students and colleagues in the ADP program in Vermont College, Women's Voices Writing Workshop, UCSC, and writers who participated in my writing workshops in NYC, New Haven, San Francisco, Berkeley, Oakland, and Austin, Texas, in particular: Pearl Olson, Paula Ross, Marcy Alancraig, Maya Valverde, Ariban, Tirsa Quiñones, Beth Brant, Chrystos, Elva Pérez -Treviño, Victoria Rosales, Christian McEwen, Roz Calvert, Nina Newington, and Linda Smuckler;

to Chela Sandoval, Rosa-María Villafane-Sosolak, Osa Hidalgo de la Riva, Lisa Carim, Sue Schwiek, Viviana Varela, Cindy Cleary, Papusa Molina, and Rusty Barcelo;

to Lisa Levin, Shelley Savren, Lisa Albrecht, Mary Pollock, Lea Arellano, Christine Weiland, Louise Rocha, Leon Fishman, Claude Talley;

to my family: my mother, Amalia; my sister, Hilda; my brothers, Urbano (Nune) and Oscar (Carito); my sisters-in-law, Janie and Sara; my niece, Missy, and my nephew, Urbie; Tío Pete *y* Tía Minga;

and especially to the memory of my father, Urbano, and my grandmothers, Eloisa (Locha) and Ramona;

gracias a toditos ustedes.

THIS BOOK

is dedicated *a todos mexicanos*

on both sides of the border.

G.E.A.

Contents

Breaking Borders/Constructing Bridges:
Twenty-Five Years of *Borderlands/La Frontera*

Introduction

In January 2012, twenty-five years after it was published, Gloria Anzaldúa's *Borderlands* was among the books banned by the Tucson Unified School System in Arizona as part of its enforcement of a new law banning Mexican American Studies in its public schools. As shocking as this action is, like all such bans, it affirms the value of the work even as it attempts to deny it; *Borderlands* is dangerous only because it has the power to change minds, to disturb complacencies. It is a power and relevance that has sustained and has provoked readers from a wide variety of constituencies since the book was first published in 1987. In the past twenty-five years, *Borderlands* has created an enduring foundation for scholarship and for activist and artistic engagement, significantly impacting not only Chican@ Studies, but Women's Studies, LGBT Studies, Postcolonial Studies, and other fields.

Because Gloria Anzaldúa wrote from her own lived experiences and honored every event in her life that helped her construct her own lens as she experienced the world, we begin this introduction by providing a short account of Gloria Anzaldúa's life. That short biography is followed by an overview of the major concepts proposed in *Borderlands* that were pathbreaking at the time of the first edition of the book and that persist in having a significant impact on a variety of academic disciplines, as well as among activists in various fields. We finish by outlining the worldwide significance of Gloria Anzaldúa's work in education and the various organizations, publications, and honors that sprung up after her passing. We hope this overview will situate Anzaldúa's life, the influences on her writing, the philosophical conceptual significance of her work, and the continuing importance of *Borderlands* inside and outside the academy.

Living in the Borderlands: The Life of Gloria Anzaldúa

> The U. S.-Mexican border *es una herida abierta* [it is a wound] where the Third World grates against the first and bleeds. And before a scab forms it hemorrhages again, the lifeblood of two worlds merging to form a third country—a border culture. (25)

Gloria Anzaldúa, a sixth generation Chicana, was born in 1942, less than twenty-five miles from the U.S.-Mexican border in Jesús María, a ranch settlement (a rancheria) in the Rio Grande Valley of South

Texas. Her early education was sporadic because her family worked as farm workers requiring them to migrate between Texas and the Midwest. To ensure a better education for his children, Anzaldúa's father chose to move the family to Hargill, a very small town near Anzaldúa's birthplace. She finished eighth grade in Hargill and was bused to attend high school at the larger nearby town of Edinburg, Texas. After graduation from high school, she stayed in Edinburg to attend Pan American University (now the University of Texas-Pan American), a state university with a predominantly Mexican American student body and a white professoriate, where she earned her bachelor's degree in English, art, and secondary education. After graduation, Anzaldúa worked as a teacher with migrant students in South Texas. As part of the migrant education program, Anzaldúa often traveled with her students' families between Texas and the Midwest. For a short period of time, she was the director of bilingual and migrant education in Indiana.

Anzaldúa eventually left her profession as a teacher and moved five hours away from her birthplace to pursue a master's degree in English and education at the University of Texas, Austin, which she completed in 1972. She returned to the Valley and taught English, and she then applied and was accepted to the doctoral program at UT Austin, but she grew increasingly frustrated because the program wouldn't allow her to pursue Chican@ literature as a legitimate subject of study. She left Texas and settled in California in 1977 where she supported herself through her writing and editorial work. During this time, Anzaldúa began work on the foundational anthology *This Bridge Called My Back: Writings by Radical Women of Color*, co-edited with Cherríe Moraga, which challenged white feminism for its exclusions and unmarked privilege. She also pursued her own writing as both an essayist and a poet, ultimately culminating in her definitive book *Borderlands/La Frontera: The New Mestiza*.

Anzaldúa's educational experiences in South Texas and in Austin had a profound effect on her writing and thinking. South Texas is an arid geographical area that begins in Brownsville, Texas, the south-most tip of the United States and runs up from the mouth of the Rio Grande, the river that divides Texas from Mexico, to Roma, Texas. El Valle, as it is commonly referred to by most Mexican Americans living in the area, is a unique blend of U.S. and Mexican culture, history, language, and ethos. It is also an area that is profoundly racist and isolated from the rest of the United States as well as from the rest of Mexico. The closest metropolitan cities, San Antonio, Texas and Monterrey, Mexico, are situated four hours north and south of El Valle respectively. For

Mexican Americans, El Valle is equivalent to the deep South for African Americans. Even today, the racism in the Valley is neither hidden nor apologized for by many of its white residents. At the time that Anzaldúa was attending schools in South Texas it was not uncommon for children to be physically punished for speaking Spanish in and outside of the classroom. Mexican culture was explicitly considered inferior to U.S. culture and the ethos was one of compulsory, complete and absolute assimilation to U.S. culture, language, and norms. The terrible irony was that in some areas of the Valley at least 85% of the residents were of Mexican descent whose families had, like Anzaldúa's, resided in the area before Texas was part of the United States.

The profound oppression experienced by Anzaldúa in her schooling, coupled with the sexism she experienced in the intimacy of her family, taught her to stand within and outside cultures, languages, and social structures. Her frequent visits to Mexico, just a few miles away, also made her keenly aware that oppression was not the exclusive province of one country or another, of one racial group or another, or even of one ethnic group or another. Nonetheless, Anzaldúa was always proudly Mexican, proudly Chicana, proudly American, and intensely loyal to her family of origin. In her own life she exemplified the core of the philosophy espoused in *Borderlands*—that it is possible to both understand and reject, to love and detest, to be loyal and question, and above all to continue to seek enlightenment out of the ambiguity and contradiction of all social existence.

Anzaldúa died of complications from diabetes in May of 2004 in Santa Cruz, California. Her body was flown to South Texas and is buried in the Valle de la Paz Cemetery in Hargill, Texas. It is a desolate place with a few mesquite trees that offer little shade. Under the relentless sun we can hear the cicadas and the centzontles—the wild birds of the area. Hardly a breeze blows. While her physical body lies under that hot Texas sun, her spirit lives on in her words.

The Impact of *Borderlands*

The academic field of Chicana Feminisms, which was in its early stages in the 1980s, readily embraced the work of Gloria Anzaldúa— writer, public intellectual, and one of the first Chicanas to publicly claim her lesbianism. Anzaldúa uses the geographical location of her birth as the source of her theorizing. She substantially developed Borderlands Theory, which expands W.E.B. Dubois' ideas on double consciousness to the experiences of Chicanas who have grown up in South Texas. In *Borderlands/La Frontera* Anzaldúa establishes the border between these two countries as a metaphor for all types of crossings—between geopolitical boundaries, sexual transgressions, social dislocations, and the crossings necessary to exist in multiple linguistic and cultural contexts. According to Anzaldúa, the history of conquest, which basically layered another country over a preexisting nation, created a political line dividing the United States from Mexico that did not correspond to the experiential existence on the border. Chicana feminists declare the border as the geographical location (lugar) that created the aperture for theorizing about subordination from an ethnically specific Chicana/mestiza consciousness.

La frontera (the border) is also the geographical area that is most susceptible to la mezcla (hybridity), neither fully of Mexico nor fully of the United States. Anzaldúa argues that living in the borderlands creates a third space between cultures and social systems. The word "borderlands" denotes that space in which antithetical elements mix, neither to obliterate each other nor to be subsumed by a larger whole, but rather to combine in unique and unexpected ways. As Anzaldúa claims, la frontera is where you "put chile in the borscht/eat whole wheat tortillas/speak Tex-Mex with a Brooklyn accent" (216). Anzaldúa's commitment to hybridity—that is the mixing that she proposes as central to living on the U.S.-Mexican border—is expressed in the actual construction of *Borderlands*. The first part of the book is a series of essays, with the last third of the text consisting of poetry. However, the essays both contain poetry and have a poetic and allusive quality to them, while the poetry in the latter half of the book records brutal "facts" about the oppression suffered by Chicanos/as throughout their history in the United States.

When *Borderlands* was published there was hardly a public discourse addressing multiculturalism. Anzaldúa's persistent mixing of cultures, languages, and even writing genres, as exemplified in the structure and content of *Borderlands,* was blasphemous. The "cultural wars" were in full force inside and outside the academy. The 1980s and early 1990s was the era of mainstream academics fighting to preserve the Western canon and of political mobilization by conservatives to add an amendment to the U.S. Constitution establishing English as the official language of the United States. This was also the era when Affirmative Action, which had begun to increase diversity in the institutions of higher education and in the workplace, was being dismantled state by state. Under these historical conditions, the publication of *Borderlands* was an act of courage as well an innovative intervention to continue advocating for cultural diversity, the inclusion of sexuality in all academic and political production, and a call to social justice based on inclusion rather than exclusion.

For Anzaldúa, the borderlands are important not only for the hybridity that occurs there, but also for the perspective they afford to their inhabitants. Living between two countries, two social systems, two languages, two cultures, results in understanding experientially the contingent nature of social arrangements. Thus, Anzaldúa asserts, living in the borderlands produces knowledge by being within a system while also retaining the knowledge of an outsider who comes from outside the system. This "outsider within" status gives Chicanas' sense of self a layered complexity that is captured in Anzaldúa's concept of mestiza consciousness (see Chapter 7, p. 102). It was at the border that Chicanas/mestizas learned the socially constructed nature of all social categories. By standing on the U.S. side of the river they saw Mexico and they saw home; by standing on the Mexican side of the border they saw the United States and they saw home. Yet they were not really accepted on either side. Their ability to "see" the arbitrary nature of all social categories but still take a stand challenges Chicana feminisms to exclude while including, to reject while accepting, and to struggle while negotiating. The basic concept involves the ability to hold multiple social perspectives while simultaneously maintaining a center that revolves around fighting against concrete material forms of oppression.

Although Anzaldúa developed Borderlands Theory by examining her experiences as the daughter of farmworkers living in extreme poverty in South Texas, the theory also applies to any kind of social, economic, sexual, and political dislocation. Her insights help us understand and theorize the experiences of individuals who are exposed to contradictory social systems and develop what Anzaldúa termed la facultad (ability or gift, see Chapter 3)—the notion that individuals (primarily women) who are exposed to multiple social worlds, as defined by cultures, languages, social classes, sexualities, nation states, and colonization, develop the agility to navigate and challenge monocultural and monolingual conceptions of social reality. Within Borderlands Theory, oppressions are not ranked nor are they conceptualized as static; rather they are recognized as fluid systems that take on different forms and nuances depending on the context.

Because Borderlands Theory allows for the articulation of mult- iple oppressions and forms of resistance to these oppressions, it has produced rich and unique analyses in various academic fields as well as among independent artists, community organizers, and professionals such as counselors, social workers, and public health workers. Borderlands Theory is particularly important for social action and coalition building. There are no absolute "sides" in conflict, but rather, contingent adversaries whose perceptions can be understood by examining (and empathizing with) their perspectives. Furthermore, no one is exempt from contributing to oppression in limited contexts. As such, self-reflexivity and seeing through the "eyes of others" becomes essential to gaining a deeper understanding than can be achieved by staying within one's social milieu. Anzaldúa explains:

> [I]t is not enough to stand on the opposite river bank, shouting questions, challenging patriarchal, white conventions. A counterstance locks one into a duel of oppressor and oppressed; locked in mortal combat, like the cop and the criminal, both are reduced to a common denominator of violence. The counterstance refutes the dominant culture's views and beliefs, and, for this, it is proudly defiant... But it is not a way of life. At some point, on our way to a new consciousness, we will have to leave the opposite bank, the split between the two mortal combatants somehow healed so that we are on both shores at once and, at once, see through serpent and eagle eyes... The possibilities are numerous once we decide to act and not react. (100)

Following the logic inherent in Borderlands Theory, stigmatized social identities based on sexuality, gender, race, class, ethnicity, and physical ableness are not additive; they do not result in increased oppression with an increased number of stigmatized group memberships. Instead, individuals' various sources of oppression are conceptualized as intersecting in a variety of ways depending on the social context. Developing a mestiza consciousness allows people to navigate these different social contexts and maintain knowledge of what it means to reside in these different social and political interstices. Through Borderlands Theory, Anzaldúa provided the experiential documentation to address how women may survive carrying the burden of their social and political stigma when they have no control over how others categorize them into social groups. Furthermore, Anzaldúa helped us understand how individuals cope with the incongruence between their private self-perceptions (say, as competent, intelligent, logical individuals) and others' negative perceptions of them. Anzaldúa proposes that one possibility among many is to use the contradiction to one's advantage and rise above the negative assignation to develop a complex view of the social self.

In many ways, Anzaldúa's work exemplifies the poetics of political resistance and rescues the potential of Chicanas (and other Latinas and women of color) from stigma, helping them survive and even thrive as writers, poets, artists, teachers and productive members of society. Anzaldúa readily recognizes that Chicanas are oppressed not only by their gender, but also by their class, ethnicity, race, and sexuality. Although the insight that women suffer from multiple oppressions currently seems commonsensical, twenty-five years ago it was a revolutionary statement. Feminism was not widely accepted or even recognized in academia. Women's Studies programs were becoming established as serious sites of intellectual work. Chicanas as well as other women of color were forced to choose between fighting for feminist causes or for their ethnic and racial communities. Anzaldúa's commitment to fight against *all* oppressions without ranking them was both innovative and radical in the fight for social justice.

The Worldwide Significance of Gloria Anzaldúa's Work

Anzaldúa's work created waves from the beginning of the publication of *This Bridge Called my Back*. Her followers anxiously awaited her next publication because everyone knew it would take us in different and unexpected directions. When *Borderlands* was published, it generated a tsunami of admiration, appreciation, and, for some, a real sense of spiritual connection; students and scholars found the work inspiring and transformative. It also provoked its share of controversy in some arenas. And, years later, expectations grew once again with the publication of one of the last pieces she wrote, *"Now let us shift...,"* knowing full well that a book-length manuscript based on this chapter would once again shake the scholarship of many of her followers. And then it all came to a distressing halt with her passing in 2004. And, as is the case in many instances, her reputation grew on the wave upon wave of grief as many mobilized spontaneously to recuperate what was being lost—the voice of a generation, or perhaps a lifetime.

Since its publication, scholars have taken up and worked with the concepts Anzaldúa introduced in *Borderlands*, presenting cutting edge work in professional association meetings and teaching new generations of scholars. Most notably, *Borderlands* lay the groundwork for critical interventions in the development of a Chicana Third Space Feminist approach in literary criticism as well as in popular culture and other disciplines. Since Sonia Saldívar-Hull presented one of the first papers on Anzaldúa's work at a meeting of the Modern Languages

Association, scholars have worked with the ideas from *Borderlands*. In fields as varied as Postcolonial Studies and Political Science, and in the perhaps predictable areas of philosophy and cultural studies, *Borderlands* created a vehicle for analysis and enhanced these fields even as it reshaped some of their tenets. Soon after its publication, *Borderlands* became a necessary source for scholars worldwide grappling with issues of globalization. Internationally, *Borderlands* has been the most cited of Anzaldúa's works, first, because the book resonated with many across the globe as they saw countries such as the Soviet Union and Yugoslavia disappear and new ones emerge— borders were erected, destroyed, and many times redrawn—and, more recently, as countries face demographic shifts due to immigration and emigration.

As we look back and take stock, we must also look forward and note the ways that *Borderlands* continues to shape newer scholarship. In the Czech Republic, Spain, France and Brazil and a number of other countries, scholars are working with Anzaldúa's ideas and applying them to their own socio-political realities. Scholars such as Tereza Kinĉlová, María Henriquez-Betancor, Maria Antonia Oliver-Rotger, Romana Radlwimmer, and Carolina Nuñez applied Anzaldúan concepts to the contemporary situation in Europe. For instance, in her work on immigration in Spain, Henriquez-Betancor mobilizes Anzaldúa's conceptualization of the borderlands to illuminate the situation of immigrant populations into Spain, especially to the Canary Islands with its rich and diverse population. Such immigrants often feel "at home" neither in their former country of origin nor in their new homeland, Spain. Furthermore, Spain, like the southern United States, also has a border where death is rampant; the Mediterranean that Northern African immigrants must cross is the site of a violence and racism similar to that found in the geopolitical site that is the subject of Anzaldúa's *Borderlands*. Similarly, Tereza Kinĉlová's work examines the immigrant's plight in her own country, The Czech Republic, through a Border Theory lens.

Furthermore, the new genre of life-writing Anzaldúa first practiced in *Borderlands* has led to new explorations and new epistemologies as Anzaldúan concepts such as spiritual mestizaje and auto-historia teoría, become keys to exploring the philosophical interrogations of Border Theory. Anzaldúan scholarship in this mode extends widely across geographies and disciplines from the Israeli-Palestinian conflict to issues of epistemological foundations in Third Space Chicana Feminism. Literary critic Theresa Delgadillo applies an Anzaldúan lens to what can be called a spritiual mestizaje that is also a spiritual activism; her book titled, *Spiritual Mestizaje: Religion, Gender, Race and Nation in Contemporary Chicana Narrative* alongside anthropologist Brenda Sendejo's work weaves Anzaldúa's theories into a framework for examining the spirituality of Chicanas.

Borderlands as a Pedagogical Tool

Borderlands continues to be taught in classrooms all over the United States and internationally. In the United States, *Borderlands* took off like wild fire. Stories abound of how *Borderlands* influenced young people to stay in school, to pursue Chican@ or Women's Studies as a field of study. In college classrooms across the country, *Borderlands* appeared on course syllabi in Women's Studies, Chican@ Literature, Mexican American Studies, and eventually in disciplines all across the humanities and the social sciences. Anzaldúa scholar Patricia Pedroza applies the concepts from *Borderlands* to her teaching and in her performance, and in her presentations at the El Mundo Zurdo Conferences, she reiterates the power of teaching *Borderlands* in her classes. While not always entirely accessible to non-Spanish speakers, the students who struggle through with a dictionary in hand will often say that it was worth the effort. Teachers have successfully used *Borderlands* outside the U.S. as well. At the symposium on Anzaldúa in 2007, Mexican scholar Papusa Molina spoke of using *Borderlands* with Mayan students in Merida. Italian professor Paola Zaccharia similarly reads *Borderlands* in Italy to help her students discern the situation in Italy vis-à-vis immigrant and disenfranchised populations. In fact she produced, wrote and directed a documentary film, *ALTAR: Crossing Borders/Building Bridges*, that includes extensive interviews with key figures in El Valle, in San Antonio, and in California. Two scholars at the Universidad Autónoma de México, Claire Joysmith of the Centro de Investigaciones Sobre Norte America (CISAN) and Marisa Belausteguigoitia, Director of the Programa Universitario de Estudios de Genero (PUEG), use *Borderlands* with their students to interrogate the difficult situation along the U.S. Mexico border, that "herida abierta" or open wound as Anzaldúa names it.

Maintaining Anzaldúa's Legacy

To continue Anzaldúa's life work, the Society for the Study of Gloria Anzaldúa, affiliated with the Society for the Study of American Women Writers, was founded in 2005 with the goal of bringing together scholars, students, artists and activists who are working with her ideas. The organization held its first symposium on Anzaldúa in November 2007 to commemorate the 20th anniversary of the publication of *Borderlands*. A full-fledged conference followed in May of 2009, on the anniversary of her passing; subsequent conferences were held in November 2010, and May 2012. The conference remains a site for continued discussion of Anzaldúan thought, with students and scholars eager and hungry not only to discuss Anzaldúa and her work, but also to build on that work, creating new avenues to advance social justice movements. The Society for the Study of Gloria Anzaldúa and the conferences exist because it was apparent that there was enough interest to warrant a venue, a place to share ideas and to honor Anzaldúa's life's work. Another site of activity that supports the continued research exists in the Anzaldúa Archives, housed at The Nettie Lee Benson Library at the University of Texas, Austin, as it allows scholars to mine the rich materials of her papers, photographs and artifacts. The archive is one of the most visited at the Benson.

In the aftermath of her death, various groups instituted awards and prizes in Anzaldúa's name. The University of California at Santa Cruz offered a prize, the Gloria E. Anzaldúa Distinguished Lecture Award, presented by the Chicana/o Latina/o Research Center (CLRC). The American Studies Association Women's Committee Gloria E. Anzaldúa Award for Independent Scholars, Contingent or Community College Faculty honors Anzaldúa's outstanding career as an independent scholar, as contingent faculty, along with her groundbreaking contributions to scholarship on women of color and to queer theory. The National Women's Studies Association book prize recognizes "groundbreaking scholarship in women's studies that makes significant multicultural feminist contributions to women of color/transnational scholarship." These awards and prizes affirm the importance of Anzaldúa's work to the academic world, but her work, especially *Borderlands*, impacted artists as well as scholars and activists who see in her candid portrayal of one woman's life a pattern worth emulating. In El Mundo Zurdo 2010, artists Deborah "Kuetzpalin" Vasquez, Santa Barraza, and Liliana Wilson, Anzaldúa's friends and collaborators, spoke of Anzaldúa's support of Chicana artists and of her insistence on the integration of art and scholarship. Similarly, community activists like Graciela Sánchez share Anzaldúa's passion for social change, for righting wrongs, and find solace and comfort in *Borderlands*. But everyone, old friends and young students and scholars who just discover her work, lament her early demise and the contributions she didn't get to make.

It would be nice to be able to claim, twenty-five years later, that Gloria Anzaldúa's work can now be considered a monument to truths now taken for granted, perspectives widely shared, values thoroughly embraced. However, because inequities persist, because the wounding violence of exclusion and subordination persists in all its insidious forms, Anzaldúa's *Borderlands* persists as inspiration and impels scholars and writers to write, artists to create, community activists to continue the struggle to bring about radical social change. In the next twenty-five years, it will no doubt gain new readers and offer insight and tools for reading the increasingly globalized world and the racist and homophobic manifestations that occur across the globe.

Norma Élia Cantú
San Antonio, 2012

Aída Hurtado
Santa Barbara, 2012

Editor's Note

Gloria and I first talked about doing a book together after I'd heard her read her poetry at a 1985 conference on racism in Iowa City, Iowa. I'd explained that we probably would not be able to do well with a book that was only poetry, even poetry as important as hers; did she have anything else? Yes, she said. She had these essays she'd been wanting to work on. I had no idea what that work would mean until we were well into the book. But we were off—not running, because the essay work was in fits and starts—but definitely moving towards a book. I would go over to Oakland once or twice a week and read her latest output while she continued to work. And we'd discuss and discuss.

I came away from these meetings profoundly changed, the recipient of many lessons. Raised on dialectic materialism, I was left speechless by Gloria's destruction of that way of understanding. Gloria was *not* saying: well here are these two opposites and out of this contradiction comes a new, third way. No, *no*...she was saying that these opposites had to be kicked out from under—they were not a foundation, but only got in the way of creating what she was after. There was no linear combination of two contradictions to create a third; rather Gloria saw that between the contradictions was a place of the untethered possibility. A place that she, in her very act of writing into it, would learn how to occupy.

Working with Gloria I came to realize that I was in the presence of a writer's courage that I'd never seen before...or would experience again. For me, the legacy of *Borderlands* will always be the courage that it took for Gloria to confront every possible demon she would ever face in order to rise back out of the ashes she'd created—the burnt offerings in which she volunteered herself as the sacrifice. In so doing, she plumbed every possible resource—psychically and spiritually—her history, her dreams, her nightmares, her physical strength *and* collapse. (She wrote deep into the night and rested in short spurts during the day, barely able to feed herself. Her friend Kit Quan, then working at Aunt Lute, would take meals to her that were her major sustenance.)

Being midwife to her creation was difficult. My role was to push and cajole, ask the relevant and sometimes difficult questions, help to tease and force the work out, knowing the pain it was causing, unable to relieve it, only to bear witness. And really I was just the assistant midwife. It was Gloria who reached down into herself with her own bloodied hands to wrench out what would become her defining work.

Gloria often talked about and wrote about a near drowning episode she'd had as a young child on one of the trips she took to the seaside with her parents. No one else in the family was aware of her struggle inside the water. Only she saw her lonely death approaching and then receding. It was a formative experience for her, the extremity of those moments. And in a way, I think she repeated that experience many times during the writing of the essays. She wrote as though her life depended on it, and as she got further into the work, I think she saw that it did.

This is why *Borderlands* remains as important today as it was the day she finished it. Her lesson to each of us: that one takes oneself and one's life into one's own hands and gives it the possibility of existence. That difficult...but also that simple. She did not set out to write a great book or to be a great writer, she set out to write a book that showed the way and therein lies her greatness.

When it was all done, I don't think she understood for some time the magnitude of what she'd created. She continually expressed to me her amazement at the reception she and the book were receiving and, in her unparalleled humility, was—again more than any writer I've met—willing to acknowledge the role Aunt Lute played in helping her voice come to fruition.

In the year *Borderlands* was published it was picked by *Library Journal* for its prestigious "Best Books of 1987" list. It was the only book from a small press that was chosen—an example of Gloria's compelling and timely voice, how she spoke to a needed change. But it would be three more years before her work really caught on, was widely distributed and seen. Then came the many awards, the honorary chair at U.C. Santa Cruz, and national and international recognition.

Gloria went on to write many other important essays that expanded her theories, gave lectures and lengthy interviews, collected the work of others into published books, and started myriad projects—all the while giving herself over and over to the community she had helped create. But it is in the work between these two covers where she did for herself what she has done, and continues to do, for so many, many others. She struggled through unyielding waves, up towards the shimmering light, broke through the surface gasping for air, and saw land—new land, uninhabited, newly possible. *Borderlands/La Frontera* is the work in which Gloria set herself free.

Joan Pinkvoss
San Francisco, 2007

Borderlands
La Frontera

Preface to the First Edition

The actual physical borderland that I'm dealing with in this book is the Texas-U.S Southwest/Mexican border. The psychological borderlands, the sexual borderlands and the spiritual borderlands are not particular to the Southwest. In fact, the Borderlands are physically present wherever two or more cultures edge each other, where people of different races occupy the same territory, where under, lower, middle and upper classes touch, where the space between two individuals shrinks with intimacy.

I am a border woman. I grew up between two cultures, the Mexican (with a heavy Indian influence) and the Anglo (as a member of a colonized people in our own territory). I have been straddling that *tejas*-Mexican border, and others, all my life. It's not a comfortable territory to live in, this place of contradictions. Hatred, anger and exploitation are the prominent features of this landscape.

However, there have been compensations for this *mestiza,* and certain joys. Living on borders and in margins, keeping intact one's shifting and multiple identity and integrity, is like trying to swim in a new element, an "alien" element. There is an exhilaration in being a participant in the further evolution of humankind, in being "worked" on. I have the sense that certain "faculties"— not just in me but in every border resident, colored or non-colored—and dormant areas of consciousness are being activated, awakened. Strange, huh? And yes, the "alien" element has become familiar—never comfortable, not with society's clamor to uphold the old, to rejoin the flock, to go with the herd. No, not comfortable but home.

This book, then, speaks of my existence. My preoccupations with the inner life of the Self, and with the struggle of that Self amidst adversity and violation; with the confluence of primordial images; with the unique positionings consciousness takes at these confluent streams; and with my almost instinctive urge to communicate, to speak, to write about life on the borders, life in the shadows.

Books saved my sanity, knowledge opened the locked places in me and taught me first how to survive and then how to soar. *La madre naturaleza* succored me, allowed me to grow roots that anchored me to the earth. My love of images—mesquite flowering, the wind, *Ehécatl*, whispering its secret knowledge, the fleeting images of the soul in fantasy—and words, my passion for the daily struggle to render them concrete in the world and on paper, to render them flesh, keeps me alive.

The switching of "codes" in this book from English to Castillian Spanish to the North Mexican dialect to Tex-Mex to a sprinkling of Nahuatl to a mixture of all of these, reflects my language, a new language—the language of the Borderlands. There, at the juncture of cultures, languages cross-pollinate and are revitalized; they die and are born. Presently this infant language, this bastard language, Chicano Spanish, is not approved by any society. But we Chicanos no longer feel that we need to beg entrance, that we need always to make the first overture—to translate to Anglos, Mexicans and Latinos, apology blurting out of our mouths with every step. Today we ask to be met halfway. This book is our invitation to you—from the new *mestizas*.

Atravesando Fronteras

Crossing Borders

1

The Homeland, Aztlán

El otro México

*El otro México que acá hemos construído
el espacio es lo que ha sido
territorio nacional.
Este es el esfuerzo de todos nuestros hermanos
y latinoamericanos que han sabido
progressar.*

—Los Tigres del Norte[1]

"The *Aztecas del norte* . . . compose the largest single tribe
or nation of Anishinabeg (Indians) found in the United States
today . . . . Some call themselves Chicanos and see themselves
as people whose true homeland is Aztlán [the U.S. Southwest]."[2]

Wind tugging at my sleeve
feet sinking into the sand
I stand at the edge where earth touches ocean
where the two overlap
a gentle coming together
at other times and places a violent clash.

Across the border in Mexico
stark silhouette of houses gutted by waves,
cliffs crumbling into the sea,
silver waves marbled with spume
gashing a hole under the border fence.

Miro el mar atacar
la cerca en Border Field Park
con sus buchones de agua,
an Easter Sunday resurrection
of the brown blood in my veins.

Oigo el llorido del mar, el respiro del aire,
my heart surges to the beat of the sea.
In the gray haze of the sun
the gulls' shrill cry of hunger,
the tangy smell of the sea seeping into me.

I walk through the hole in the fence
to the other side.
Under my fingers I feel the gritty wire
rusted by 139 years
of the salty breath of the sea.

Beneath the iron sky
Mexican children kick their soccer ball across,
run after it, entering the U.S.

I press my hand to the steel curtain—
chainlink fence crowned with rolled barbed wire—
rippling from the sea where Tijuana touches San Diego
unrolling over mountains
and plains
and deserts,
this "Tortilla Curtain" turning into *el río Grande*
flowing down to the flatlands
of the Magic Valley of South Texas
its mouth emptying into the Gulf.

1,950 mile-long open wound
dividing a *pueblo*, a culture,
running down the length of my body,
staking fence rods in my flesh,
splits me   splits me
me raja   me raja

This is my home
this thin edge of
barbwire.

But the skin of the earth is seamless.
The sea cannot be fenced,
el mar does not stop at borders.
To show the white man what she thought of his
arrogance,
Yemayá blew that wire fence down.

This land was Mexican once,
was Indian always
and is.
And   will be again.

Yo soy un puente tendido
del mundo gabacho al del mojado,
lo pasado me estira pa' 'trás
y lo presente pa' 'delante,
Que la Virgen de Guadalupe me cuide
Ay ay ay, soy mexicana de este lado.

The U.S.-Mexican border *es una herida abierta* where the
Third World grates against the first and bleeds. And before a scab
forms it hemorrhages again, the lifeblood of two worlds merging
to form a third country—a border culture. Borders are set up to
define the places that are safe and unsafe, to distinguish *us* from
them. A border is a dividing line, a narrow strip along a steep
edge. A borderland is a vague and undetermined place created by
the emotional residue of an unnatural boundary. It is in a constant state of transition. The prohibited and forbidden are its
inhabitants. *Los atravesados* live here: the squint-eyed, the per-
verse, the queer, the troublesome, the mongrel, the mulato, the
half-breed, the half dead; in short, those who cross over, pass
over, or go through the confines of the "normal." Gringos in the
U.S. Southwest consider the inhabitants of the borderlands trans-
gressors, aliens—whether they possess documents or not,
whether they're Chicanos, Indians or Blacks. Do not enter, tres-
passers will be raped, maimed, strangled, gassed, shot. The only
"legitimate" inhabitants are those in power, the whites and those

who align themselves with whites. Tension grips the inhabitants of the borderlands like a virus. Ambivalence and unrest reside there and death is no stranger.

In the fields, *la migra.* My aunt saying, *"No corran,* don't run. They'll think you're *del otro lao."* In the confusion, Pedro ran, terrified of being caught. He couldn't speak English, couldn't tell them he was fifth generation American. *Sin papeles*—he did not carry his birth certificate to work in the fields. *La migra* took him away while we watched. *Se lo llevaron.* He tried to smile when he looked back at us, to raise his fist. But I saw the shame pushing his head down, I saw the terrible weight of shame hunch his shoulders. They deported him to Guadalajara by plane. The furthest he'd ever been to Mexico was Reynosa, a small border town opposite Hidalgo, Texas, not far from McAllen. Pedro walked all the way to the Valley. *Se lo llevaron sin un centavo al pobre. Se vino andando desde Guadalajara.*

During the original peopling of the Americas, the first inhabitants migrated across the Bering Straits and walked south across the continent. The oldest evidence of humankind in the U.S.— the Chicanos' ancient Indian ancestors—was found in Texas and has been dated to 35000 B.C.[3] In the Southwest United States archeologists have found 20,000-year-old campsites of the Indians who migrated through, or permanently occupied, the Southwest, Aztlán—land of the herons, land of whiteness, the Edenic place of origin of the Azteca.

In 1000 B.C., descendants of the original Cochise people migrated into what is now Mexico and Central America and became the direct ancestors of many of the Mexican people. (The Cochise culture of the Southwest is the parent culture of the Aztecs. The Uto-Aztecan languages stemmed from the language of the Cochise people.)[4] The Aztecs (the Nahuatl word for people of Aztlán) left the Southwest in 1168 A.D.

Now let us go.
Tihueque, tihueque,
Vámonos, vámonos.
Un pájaro cantó.

Con sus ocho tribus salieron
de la "cueva del origen."
los aztecas siguieron al dios
Huitzilopochtli.

Huitzilopochtli, the God of War, guided them to the place (that later became Mexico City) where an eagle with a writhing serpent in its beak perched on a cactus. The eagle symbolizes the spirit (as the sun, the father); the serpent symbolizes the soul (as the earth, the mother). Together, they symbolize the struggle between the spiritual/celestial/male and the underworld/earth/feminine. The symbolic sacrifice of the serpent to the "higher" masculine powers indicates that the patriarchal order had already vanquished the feminine and matriarchal order in pre-Columbian America.

At the beginning of the 16th century, the Spaniards and Hernán Cortés invaded Mexico and, with the help of tribes that the Aztecs had subjugated, conquered it. Before the Conquest, there were twenty-five million Indian people in Mexico and the Yucatán. Immediately after the Conquest, the Indian population had been reduced to under seven million. By 1650, only one-and-a-half-million pure-blooded Indians remained. The *mestizos* who were genetically equipped to survive small pox, measles, and typhus (Old World diseases to which the natives had no immunity), founded a new hybrid race and inherited Central and South America.[5] *En 1521 nació una nueva raza, el mestizo, el mexicano* (people of mixed Indian and Spanish blood), a race that had never existed before. Chicanos, Mexican-Americans, are the offspring of those first matings.

Our Spanish, Indian, and *mestizo* ancestors explored and settled parts of the U.S. Southwest as early as the sixteenth century. For every gold-hungry *conquistador* and soul-hungry missionary who came north from Mexico, ten to twenty Indians and *mestizos* went along as porters or in other capacities.[6] For the Indians, this constituted a return to the place of origin, Aztlán, thus making Chicanos originally and secondarily indigenous to the Southwest. Indians and *mestizos* from central Mexico intermarried with North American Indians. The continual intermarriage between Mexican and American Indians and Spaniards formed an even greater *mestizaje*.

El destierro / The Lost Land

> *Entonces corre la sangre*
> *no sabe el indio que hacer,*
> *le van a quitar su tierra,*
> *la tiene que defender,*
> *el indio se cae muerto,*
> *y el afuerino de pie.*
> *Levántate, Manquilef.*
>
> *Arauco tiene una pena*
> *más negra que su chamal,*
> *ya no son los españoles*
> *los que le hacen llorar,*
> *hoy son los propios chilenos*
> *los que le quitan su pan.*
> *Levántate, Pailahuan.*
> —Violeta Parra, *"Arauco tiene una pena"*[7]

In the 1800s, Anglos migrated illegally into Texas, which was then part of Mexico, in greater and greater numbers and gradually drove the *tejanos* (native Texans of Mexican descent) from their lands, committing all manner of atrocities against them. Their illegal invasion forced Mexico to fight a war to keep its Texas territory. The Battle of the Alamo, in which the Mexican forces vanquished the whites, became, for the whites, the symbol for the cowardly and villainous character of the Mexicans. It became (and still is) a symbol that legitimized the white imperialist takeover. With the capture of Santa Anna later in 1836, Texas became a republic. *Tejanos* lost their land and, overnight, became the foreigners.

> *Ya la mitad del terreno*
> *les vendió el traidor Santa Anna,*
> *con lo que se ha hecho muy rica*
> *la nación americana.*
>
> *¿Qué acaso no se conforman*
> *con el oro de las minas?*
> *Ustedes muy elegantes*
> *y aquí nosotros en ruinas.*
> —from the Mexican corrido,
> *"Del peligro de la Intervención"*[8]

In 1846, the U.S. incited Mexico to war. U.S. troops invaded and occupied Mexico, forcing her to give up almost half of her nation, what is now Texas, New Mexico, Arizona, Colorado and California. With the victory of the U.S. forces over the Mexican in the U.S.-Mexican War, *los norteamericanos* pushed the Texas border down 100 miles, from *el río Nueces* to *el río Grande*. South Texas ceased to be part of the Mexican state of Tamaulipas. Separated from Mexico, the Native Mexican-Texan no longer looked toward Mexico as home; the Southwest became our homeland once more. The border fence that divides the Mexican people was born on February 2, 1848 with the signing of the Treaty of Guadalupe-Hidalgo. It left 100,000 Mexican citizens on this side, annexed by conquest along with the land. The land established by the treaty as belonging to Mexicans was soon swindled away from its owners. The treaty was never honored and restitution, to this day, has never been made.

> The justice and benevolence of God
> will forbid that . . . Texas should again
> become a howling wilderness
> trod only by savages, or . . . benighted
> by the ignorance and superstition,
> the anarchy and rapine of Mexican misrule.
> The Anglo-American race are destined
> to be forever the proprietors of
> this land of promise and fulfillment.
> Their laws will govern it,
> their learning will enlighten it,
> their enterprise will improve it.
> Their flocks range its boundless pastures,
> for them its fertile lands will yield . . .
> luxuriant harvests . . .
> The wilderness of Texas has been redeemed
> by Anglo-American blood & enterprise.
> —William H. Wharton[9]

The Gringo, locked into the fiction of white superiority, seized complete political power, stripping Indians and Mexicans of their land while their feet were still rooted in it. *Con el destierro y el exilio fuimos desuñados, destroncados, destripa-*

dos—we were jerked out by the roots, truncated, disemboweled, dispossessed, and separated from our identity and our history. Many, under the threat of Anglo terrorism, abandoned homes and ranches and went to Mexico. Some stayed and protested. But as the courts, law enforcement officials, and government officials not only ignored their pleas but penalized them for their efforts, *tejanos* had no other recourse but armed retaliation.

After Mexican-American resisters robbed a train in Brownsville, Texas on October 18, 1915, Anglo vigilante groups began lynching Chicanos. Texas Rangers would take them into the brush and shoot them. One hundred Chicanos were killed in a matter of months, whole families lynched. Seven thousand fled to Mexico, leaving their small ranches and farms. The Anglos, afraid that the *mexicanos*[10] would seek independence from the U.S., brought in 20,000 army troops to put an end to the social protest movement in South Texas. Race hatred had finally fomented into an all out war.[11]

> My grandmother lost all her cattle,
> they stole her land.

"Drought hit South Texas," my mother tells me. *"La tierra se puso bien seca y los animales comenzaron a morirse de se'. Mi papá se murió de un* heart attack *dejando a mamá* pregnant *y con ocho huercos*, with eight kids and one on the way. *Yo fui la mayor, tenía diez años.* The next year the drought continued *y el ganado* got hoof and mouth. *Se cayeron* in droves *en las pastas y el* brushland, *panzas blancas* ballooning to the skies. *El siguiente año* still no rain. *Mi pobre madre viuda perdió* two-thirds of her *ganado*. A smart *gabacho* lawyer took the land away *mamá* hadn't paid taxes. *No hablaba inglés*, she didn't know how to ask for time to raise the money." My father's mother, Mama Locha, also lost her *terreno*. For a while we got $12.50 a year for the "mineral rights" of six acres of cemetery, all that was left of the ancestral lands. Mama Locha had asked that we bury her there beside her husband. *El cementerio estaba cercado*. But there was a fence around the cemetery, chained and padlocked by the ranch owners of the surrounding land. We couldn't even get in to visit the graves, much less bury her there. Today, it is still padlocked. The sign reads: "Keep out. Trespassers will be shot."

In the 1930s, after Anglo agribusiness corporations cheated the small Chicano landowners of their land, the corporations hired gangs of *mexicanos* to pull out the brush, chaparral and cactus and to irrigate the desert. The land they toiled over had once belonged to many of them, or had been used communally by them. Later the Anglos brought in huge machines and root plows and had the Mexicans scrape the land clean of natural vegetation. In my childhood I saw the end of dryland farming. I witnessed the land cleared; saw the huge pipes connected to underwater sources sticking up in the air. As children, we'd go fishing in some of those canals when they were full and hunt for snakes in them when they were dry. In the 1950s I saw the land, cut up into thousands of neat rectangles and squares, constantly being irrigated. In the 340-day growth season, the seeds of any kind of fruit or vegetable had only to be stuck in the ground in order to grow. More big land corporations came in and bought up the remaining land.

To make a living my father became a sharecropper. Rio Farms Incorporated loaned him seed money and living expenses. At harvest time, my father repaid the loan and forked over 40% of the earnings. Sometimes we earned less than we owed, but always the corporations fared well. Some had major holdings in vegetable trucking, livestock auctions and cotton gins. Altogether we lived on three successive Rio farms; the second was adjacent to the King Ranch and included a dairy farm; the third was a chicken farm. I remember the white feathers of three thousand Leghorn chickens blanketing the land for acres around. My sister, mother and I cleaned, weighed and packaged eggs. (For years afterwards I couldn't stomach the sight of an egg.) I remember my mother attending some of the meetings sponsored by well-meaning whites from Rio Farms. They talked about good nutrition, health, and held huge barbecues. The only thing salvaged for my family from those years are modern techniques of food canning and a food-stained book they printed made up of recipes from Rio Farms' Mexican women. How proud my mother was to have her recipe for *enchiladas coloradas* in a book.

El cruzar del mojado/Illegal Crossing

> *"Ahora si ya tengo una tumba para llorar,"*
> *dice Conchita,* upon being reunited with

her unknown mother just before the mother dies.
—from Ismael Rodriguez' film,
Nosotros los pobres[12]

La crisis. Los gringos had not stopped at the border. By the
end of the nineteenth century, powerful landowners in Mexico,
in partnership with U.S. colonizing companies, had dispossessed
millions of Indians of their lands. Currently, Mexico and her
eighty million citizens are almost completely dependent on the
U.S. market. The Mexican government and wealthy growers are
in partnership with such American conglomerates as American
Motors, IT&T and Du Pont which own factories called
maquiladoras. One-fourth of all Mexicans work at *maquiladoras*; most are young women. Next to oil, *maquiladoras* are
Mexico's second greatest source of U.S. dollars. Working eight to
twelve hours a day to wire in backup lights of U.S. autos or sol-
der minuscule wires in TV sets is not the Mexican way. While the
women are in the *maquiladoras,* the children are left on their
own. Many roam the street, become part of *cholo* gangs. The
infusion of the values of the white culture, coupled with the
exploitation by that culture, is changing the Mexican way of life.

The devaluation of the *peso* and Mexico's dependency on
the U.S. have brought on what the Mexicans call *la crisis. No
hay trabajo*. Half of the Mexican people are unemployed. In the
U.S. a man or woman can make eight times what they can in
Mexico. By March, 1987, 1,088 *pesos* were worth one U.S. dollar. I remember when I was growing up in Texas how we'd cross
the border at Reynosa or Progreso to buy sugar or medicines
when the dollar was worth eight *pesos* and fifty *centavos*.

La travesía. For many *mexicanos del otro lado,* the choice
is to stay in Mexico and starve or move north and live. *Dicen que
cada mexicano siempre sueña de la conquista en los brazos de
cuatro gringas rubias, la conquista del país poderoso del norte,
los Estados Unidos. En cada Chicano y mexicano vive el mito
del tesoro territorial perdido.* North Americans call this return to
the homeland the silent invasion.

"A la cueva volverán"
—El Puma *en la canción "Amalia"*

South of the border, called North America's rubbish dump by Chicanos, *mexicanos* congregate in the plazas to talk about the best way to cross. Smugglers, *coyotes, pasadores, enganchadores* approach these people or are sought out by them. *"¿Qué dicen muchachos a echársela de mojado?"*

> "Now among the alien gods with
> weapons of magic am I."
> —Navajo protection song,
> sung when going into battle.[13]

We have a tradition of migration, a tradition of long walks. Today we are witnessing *la migración de los pueblos mexicanos,* the return odyssey to the historical/mythological Aztlán. This time, the traffic is from south to north.

El retorno to the promised land first began with the Indians from the interior of Mexico and the *mestizos* that came with the *conquistadores* in the 1500s. Immigration continued in the next three centuries, and, in this century, it continued with the *braceros* who helped to build our railroads and who picked our fruit. Today thousands of Mexicans are crossing the border legally and illegally; ten million people without documents have returned to the Southwest.

Faceless, nameless, invisible, taunted with "Hey cucaracho" (cockroach). Trembling with fear, yet filled with courage, a courage born of desperation. Barefoot and uneducated, Mexicans with hands like boot soles gather at night by the river where two worlds merge creating what Reagan calls a frontline, a war zone. The convergence has created a shock culture, a border culture, a third country, a closed country.

Without benefit of bridges, the *"mojados"* (wetbacks) float on inflatable rafts across *el río Grande,* or wade or swim across naked, clutching their clothes over their heads. Holding onto the grass, they pull themselves along the banks with a prayer to *Virgen de Guadalupe* on their lips: *Ay virgencita morena, mi madrecita, dame tu bendición.*

The Border Patrol hides behind the local McDonalds on the outskirts of Brownsville, Texas or some other border town. They set traps around the river beds beneath the bridge.[14] Hunters in army-green uniforms stalk and track these economic refugees by the powerful nightvision of electronic sensing devices planted in the ground or mounted on Border Patrol vans. Cornered by flashlights, frisked while their arms stretch over their heads, *los mojados* are handcuffed, locked in jeeps, and then kicked back across the border.

One out of every three is caught. Some return to enact their rite of passage as many as three times a day. Some of those who make it across undetected fall prey to Mexican robbers such as those in Smugglers' Canyon on the American side of the border near Tijuana. As refugees in a homeland that does not want them, many find a welcome hand holding out only suffering, pain, and ignoble death.

Those who make it past the checking points of the Border Patrol find themselves in the midst of 150 years of racism in Chicano *barrios* in the Southwest and in big northern cities. Living in a no-man's-borderland, caught between being treated as criminals and being able to eat, between resistance and deportation, the illegal refugees are some of the poorest and the most exploited of any people in the U.S. It is illegal for Mexicans to work without green cards. But big farming combines, farm bosses and smugglers who bring them in make money off the "wetbacks'" labor—they don't have to pay federal minimum wages, or ensure adequate housing or sanitary conditions.

The Mexican woman is especially at risk. Often the *coyote* (smuggler) doesn't feed her for days or let her go to the bathroom. Often he rapes her or sells her into prostitution. She cannot call on county or state health or economic resources because she doesn't know English and she fears deportation. American employers are quick to take advantage of her helplessness. She can't go home. She's sold her house, her furniture, borrowed from friends in order to pay the *coyote* who charges her four or five thousand dollars to smuggle her to Chicago. She may work as a live-in maid for white, Chicano or Latino households for as little as $15 a week. Or work in the garment industry, do hotel work. Isolated and worried about her family back home, afraid of getting caught and deported, living with as many as fifteen people in one room, the *mexicana* suffers serious health problems. *Se enferma de los nervios, de alta presión.*[15]

La mojada, la mujer indocumentada, is doubly threatened in this country. Not only does she have to contend with sexual violence, but like all women, she is prey to a sense of physical helplessness. As a refugee, she leaves the familiar and safe home-ground to venture into unknown and possibly dangerous terrain.

> This is her home
>> this thin edge of
>> barbwire.

2

Movimientos de rebeldía y las culturas que traicionan

Esos movimientos de rebeldía que tenemos en la sangre nosotros los mexicanos surgen como ríos desbocanados en mis venas. Y como mi raza que cada en cuando deja caer esa esclavitud de obedecer, de callarse y aceptar, en mi está la rebeldía encimita de mi carne. Debajo de mi humillada mirada está una cara insolente lista para explotar. Me costó muy caro mi rebeldía—acalambrada con desvelos y dudas, sintiéndome inútil, estúpida, e impotente.

Me entra una rabia cuando alguien—sea mi mamá, la Iglesia, la cultura de los anglos—me dice haz esto, haz eso sin considerar mis deseos.

Repele. Hable pa' 'tras. Fui muy hocicona. Era indiferente a muchos valores de mi culture. No me dejé de los hombres. No fui buena ni obediente.

Pero he crecido. Ya no sólo paso toda mi vida botando las costumbres y los valores de mi cultura que me traicionan. También recojo las costumbres que por el tiempo se han probado y las costumbres de respeto a las mujeres. But despite my growing tolerance, for this Chicana *la guerra de independencia* is a constant.

The Strength of My Rebellion

I have a vivid memory of an old photograph: I am six years old. I stand between my father and mother, head cocked to the right, the toes of my flat feet gripping the ground. I hold my mother's hand.

To this day I'm not sure where I found the strength to leave the source, the mother, disengage from my family, *mi tierra, mi gente,* and all that picture stood for. I had to leave home so I could find myself, find my own intrinsic nature buried under the personality that had been imposed on me.

I was the first in six generations to leave the Valley, the only one in my family to ever leave home. But I didn't leave all the parts of me: I kept the ground of my own being. On it I walked away, taking with me the land, the Valley, Texas. *Gané mi camino y me largué. Muy andariega mi hija.* Because I left of my own accord *me dicen, "¿Cómo te gusta la mala vida?"*

At a very early age I had a strong sense of who I was and what I was about and what was fair. I had a stubborn will. It tried constantly to mobilize my soul under my own regime, to live life on my own terms no matter how unsuitable to others they were. *Terca.* Even as a child I would not obey. I was "lazy." Instead of ironing my younger brothers' shirts or cleaning the cupboards, I would pass many hours studying, reading, painting, writing. Every bit of self-faith I'd painstakingly gathered took a beating daily. Nothing in my culture approved of me. *Había agarrado malos pasos.* Something was "wrong" with me. *Estaba más allá de la tradición.*

There is a rebel in me—the Shadow-Beast. It is a part of me that refuses to take orders from outside authorities. It refuses to take orders from my conscious will, it threatens the sovereignty of my rulership. It is that part of me that hates constraints of any kind, even those self-imposed. At the least hint of limitations on my time or space by others, it kicks out with both feet. Bolts.

Cultural Tyranny

Culture forms our beliefs. We perceive the version of reality that it communicates. Dominant paradigms, predefined concepts that exist as unquestionable, unchallengeable, are transmitted to us through the culture. Culture is made by those in power—men. Males make the rules and laws; women transmit them. How many times have I heard mothers and mothers-in-law tell their sons to beat their wives for not obeying them, for being *hociconas* (big mouths), for being *callejeras* (going to visit and gossip with neighbors), for expecting their husbands to help with the rearing of children and the housework, for wanting to be something other than housewives?

The culture expects women to show greater acceptance of, and commitment to, the value system than men. The culture and the Church insist that women are subservient to males. If a woman rebels she is a *mujer mala*. If a woman doesn't renounce herself in favor of the male, she is selfish. If a woman remains a *virgen* until she marries, she is a good woman. For a woman of my culture there used to be only three directions she could turn: to the Church as a nun, to the streets as a prostitute, or to the home as a mother. Today some of us have a fourth choice: entering the world by way of education and career and becoming self-autonomous persons. A very few of us. As a working class people our chief activity is to put food in our mouths, a roof over our heads and clothes on our backs. Educating our children is out of reach for most of us. Educated or not, the onus is still on woman to be a wife/mother—only the nun can escape motherhood. Women are made to feel total failures if they don't marry and have children. *"¿Y cuándo te casas, Gloria? Se te va a pasar el tren."* Y yo les digo, "*Pos si me caso, no va ser con un hombre." Se quedan calladitas. Sí, soy hija de la Chingada.* I've always been her daughter. *No 'tés chingando.*

Humans fear the supernatural, both the undivine (the animal impulses such as sexuality, the unconscious, the unknown, the alien) and the divine (the superhuman, the god in us). Culture and religion seek to protect us from these two forces. The female, by virtue of creating entities of flesh and blood in her stomach (she bleeds every month but does not die), by virtue of being in tune with nature's cycles, is feared. Because, according to Christianity and most other major religions, woman is carnal, animal, and closer to the undivine, she must be protected. Protected from herself. Woman is the stranger, the other. She is man's recognized nightmarish pieces, his Shadow-Beast. The sight of her sends him into a frenzy of anger and fear.

La gorra, el rebozo, la mantilla are symbols of my culture's "protection" of women. Culture (read males) professes to protect women. Actually it keeps women in rigidly defined roles. It keeps the girlchild from other men—don't poach on my preserves, only I can touch my child's body. Our mothers taught us well, *"Los hombres nomás quieren una cosa";* men aren't to be trusted, they are selfish and are like children. Mothers made sure we didn't walk into a room of brothers or fathers or uncles in nightgowns or shorts. We were never alone with men, not even those of our own family.

Through our mothers, the culture gave us mixed messages: *No voy a dejar que ningún pelado desgraciado maltrate a mis hijos.* And in the next breath it would say, *La mujer tiene que hacer lo que le diga el hombre.* Which was it to be—strong, or submissive, rebellious or conforming?

Tribal rights over those of the individual insured the survival of the tribe and were necessary then, and, as in the case of all indigenous peoples in the world who are still fighting off intentional, premeditated murder (genocide), they are still necessary.

Much of what the culture condemns focuses on kinship relationships. The welfare of the family, the community, and the tribe is more important than the welfare of the individual. The individual exists first as kin—as sister, as father, as *padrino*— and last as self.

In my culture, selfishness is condemned, especially in women; humility and selflessness, the absence of selfishness, is considered a virtue. In the past, acting humble with members outside the family ensured that you would make no one *envidioso* (envious); therefore he or she would not use witchcraft against you. If you get above yourself, you're an *envidiosa.* If you don't behave like everyone else, *la gente* will say that you think you're better than others, *que te crees grande.* With ambition (condemned in the Mexican culture and valued in the Anglo) comes envy. *Respeto* carries with it a set of rules so that social categories and hierarchies will be kept in order: respect is reserved for *la abuela, papá, el patrón,* those with power in the community. Women are at the bottom of the ladder one rung above the deviants. The Chicano, *mexicano,* and some Indian cultures have no tolerance for deviance. Deviance is whatever is condemned by the community. Most societies try to get rid of their deviants. Most cultures have burned and beaten their homosexuals and others who deviate from the sexual common.[1] The queer are the mirror reflecting the heterosexual tribe's fear: being different, being other and therefore lesser, therefore subhuman, in-human, non-human.

Half and Half

There was a *muchacha* who lived near my house. *La gente del pueblo* talked about her being *una de las otras*, "of the Others." They said that for six months she was a woman who had a vagina that bled once a month, and that for the other six months she was a man, had a penis and she peed standing up. They called her half and half, *mita' y mita'*, neither one nor the other but a strange doubling, a deviation of nature that horrified, a work of nature inverted. But there is a magic aspect in abnormality and so-called deformity. Maimed, mad, and sexually different people were believed to possess supernatural powers by primal cultures' magico-religious thinking. For them, abnormality was the price a person had to pay for her or his inborn extraordinary gift.

There is something compelling about being both male and female, about having an entry into both worlds. Contrary to some psychiatric tenets, half and halfs are not suffering from a confusion of sexual identity, or even from a confusion of gender. What we are suffering from is an absolute despot duality that says we are able to be only one or the other. It claims that human nature is limited and cannot evolve into something better. But I, like other queer people, am two in one body, both male and female. I am the embodiment of the *hieros gamos:* the coming together of opposite qualities within.

Fear of Going Home: Homophobia

⌈For the lesbian of color, the ultimate rebellion she can make against her native culture is through her sexual behavior.⌋She goes against two moral prohibitions: sexuality and homosexuality. Being lesbian and raised Catholic, indoctrinated as straight, I *made the choice to be queer* (for some it is genetically inherent). It's an interesting path, one that continually slips in and out of the white, the Catholic, the Mexican, the indigenous, the instincts. In and out of my head. It makes for *loquería*, the crazies. It is a path of knowledge—one of knowing (and of learning) the history of oppression of our *raza*. It is a way of balancing, of mitigating duality.

In a New England college where I taught, the presence of a few lesbians threw the more conservative heterosexual students and faculty into a panic. The two lesbian students and we two lesbian instructors met with them to discuss their fears. One of the students said, "I thought homophobia meant fear of going home after a residency."

And I thought, how apt. Fear of going home. And of not being taken in. We're afraid of being abandoned by the mother, the culture, *la Raza,* for being unacceptable, faulty, damaged. Most of us unconsciously believe that if we reveal this unacceptable aspect of the self our mother/culture/race will totally reject us. To avoid rejection, some of us conform to the values of the culture, push the unacceptable parts into the shadows. Which leaves only one fear—that we will be found out and that the Shadow-Beast will break out of its cage. Some of us take another route. We try to make ourselves conscious of the Shadow-Beast, stare at the sexual lust and lust for power and destruction we see on its face, discern among its features the undershadow that the reigning order of heterosexual males project on our Beast. Yet still others of us take it another step: we try to waken the Shadow-Beast inside us. Not many jump at the chance to confront the Shadow-Beast in the mirror without flinching at her lidless serpent eyes, her cold clammy moist hand dragging us underground, fangs bared and hissing. How does one put feathers on this particular serpent? But a few of us have been lucky—on the face of the Shadow-Beast we have seen not lust but tenderness; on its face we have uncovered the lie.

Intimate Terrorism: Life in the Borderlands

The world is not a safe place to live in. We shiver in separate cells in enclosed cities, shoulders hunched, barely keeping the panic below the surface of the skin, daily drinking shock along with our morning coffee, fearing the torches being set to our buildings, the attacks in the streets. Shutting down. Woman does not feel safe when her own culture, and white culture, are critical of her; when the males of all races hunt her as prey.

Alienated from her mother culture, "alien" in the dominant culture, the woman of color does not feel safe within the inner life of her Self. Petrified, she can't respond, her face caught between *los intersticios,* the spaces between the different worlds she inhabits.

The ability to respond is what is meant by responsibility, yet our cultures take away our ability to act—shackle us in the name of protection. Blocked, immobilized, we can't move forward, can't move backwards. That writhing serpent movement, the very movement of life, swifter than lightning, frozen.

We do not engage fully. We do not make full use of our faculties. We abnegate. And there in front of us is the crossroads and choice: to feel a victim where someone else is in control and therefore responsible and to blame (being a victim and transferring the blame on culture, mother, father, ex-lover, friend, absolves me of responsibility), or to feel strong, and, for the most part, in control.

My Chicana identity is grounded in the Indian woman's history of resistance. The Aztec female rites of mourning were rites of defiance protesting the cultural changes which disrupted the equality and balance between female and male, and protesting their demotion to a lesser status, their denigration. Like *la Llorona*, the Indian woman's only means of protest was wailing.

So *mamá, Raza,* how wonderful, *no tener que rendir cuentas a nadie.* I feel perfectly free to rebel and to rail against my culture. I fear no betrayal on my part because, unlike Chicanas and other women of color who grew up white or who have only recently returned to their native cultural roots, I was totally immersed in mine. It wasn't until I went to high school that I "saw" whites. Until I worked on my master's degree I had not gotten within an arm's distance of them. I was totally immersed *en lo mexicano,* a rural, peasant, isolated, *mexicanismo.* To separate from my culture (as from my family) I had to feel competent enough on the outside and secure enough inside to live life on my own. Yet in leaving home I did not lose touch with my origins because *lo mexicano* is in my system. I am a turtle, wherever I go I carry "home" on my back.

Not me sold out my people but they me. So yes, though "home" permeates every sinew and cartilage in my body, I too am afraid of going home. Though I'll defend my race and culture when they are attacked by non-*mexicanos, conozco el malestar de mi cultura.* I abhor some of my culture's ways, how it cripples its women, *como burras,* our strengths used against us, lowly *burras* bearing humility with dignity. The ability to serve, claim the males, is our highest virtue. I abhor how my culture makes *macho* caricatures of its men. No, I do not buy all the myths of the tribe into which I was born. I can understand why the more tinged with Anglo blood, the more adamantly my colored and colorless sisters glorify their colored culture's values—to offset the extreme devaluation of it by the white culture. It's a legitimate reaction. But I will not glorify those aspects of my culture which have injured me and which have injured me in the name of protecting me.

So, don't give me your tenets and your laws. Don't give me your lukewarm gods. What I want is an accounting with all three cultures—white, Mexican, Indian. I want the freedom to carve and chisel my own face, to staunch the bleeding with ashes, to fashion my own gods out of my entrails. And if going home is denied me then I will have to stand and claim my space, making a new culture—*una cultura mestiza*—with my own lumber, my own bricks and mortar and my own feminist architecture.

The Wounding of the *india*-Mestiza

> *Estas carnes indias que despreciamos nosotros los mexicanos así como despreciamos condenamos a nuestra madre, Malinali. Nos condenamos a nosotros mismos. Esta raza vencida, enemigo cuerpo.*

Not me sold out my people but they me. *Malinali Tenepat,* or *Malintzín,* has become known as *la Chingada*—the fucked one. She has become the bad word that passes a dozen times a day from the lips of Chicanos. Whore, prostitute, the woman who sold out her people to the Spaniards are epithets Chicanos spit out with contempt.

The worst kind of betrayal lies in making us believe that the Indian woman in us is the betrayer. We, *indias y mestizas,* police the Indian in us, brutalize and condemn her. Male culture has done a good job on us. *Son las costumbres que traicionan. La india en mí es la sombra: La Chingada, Tlazolteotl, Coatlicue. Son ellas que oyemos lamentando a sus hijas perdidas.*

Not me sold out my people but they me. Because of the color of my skin they betrayed me. The dark-skinned woman has been silenced, gagged, caged, bound into servitude with marriage, bludgeoned for 300 years, sterilized and castrated in the twentieth century. For 300 years she has been a slave, a force of cheap labor, colonized by the Spaniard, the Anglo, by her own people (and in Mesoamerica her lot under the Indian patriarchs was not free of wounding). For 300 years she was invisible, she was not heard. Many times she wished to speak, to act, to protest, to challenge. The odds were heavily against her. She hid her feelings; she hid her truths; she concealed her fire; but she kept stoking the inner flame. She remained faceless and voiceless, but a light shone through her veil of silence. And though she was unable to spread her limbs and though for her right now the sun has sunk under the earth and there is no moon, she continues to tend the flame. The spirit of the fire spurs her to fight for her own skin and a piece of ground to stand on, a ground from which to view the world—a perspective, a homeground where she can plumb the rich ancestral roots into her own ample *mestiza* heart. She waits till the waters are not so turbulent and the mountains not so slippery with sleet. Battered and bruised she waits, her bruises throwing her back upon herself and the rhythmic pulse of the feminine. *Coatlalopeuh* waits with her.

> *Aquí en la soledad prospera su rebeldía.*
> *En la soledad Ella prospera.*

3

Entering Into the Serpent

Sueño con serpientes, con serpientes del mar,
Con cierto mar, ay de serpientes sueño yo.
Largas, transparentes, en sus barrigas llevan
Lo que puedan arebatarle al amor.
Oh, oh, oh, la mató y aparece una mayor.
Oh, con mucho más infierno en digestión.

I dream of serpents, serpents of the sea,
A certain sea, oh, of serpents I dream.
Long, transparent, in their bellies they carry
All that they can snatch away from love.
Oh, oh, oh, I kill one and a larger one appears.
Oh, with more hellfire burning inside!
—Silvio Rodriguez, *"Sueño Con Serpientes"*[1]

In the predawn orange haze, the sleepy crowing of roosters atop the trees. *No vayas al escusado en lo oscuro.* Don't go to the outhouse at night, Prieta, my mother would say. *No se te vaya a meter algo por allá.* A snake will crawl into your *nalgas,*[2] make you pregnant. They seek warmth in the cold. *Dicen que las culebras* like to suck *chiches,*[3] can draw milk out of you.

En el escusado in the half-light spiders hang like gliders. Under my bare buttocks and the rough planks the deep yawning tugs at me. I can see my legs fly up to my face as my body falls through the round hole into the sheen of swarming maggots below. Avoiding the snakes under the porch I walk back into the kitchen, step on a big black one slithering across the floor.

Ella tiene su tono[4]

Once we were chopping cotton in the fields of Jesus Maria Ranch. All around us the woods. *Quelite*[5] towered above me, choking the stubby cotton that had outlived the deer's teeth.

I swung *el azadón*[6] hard. *El quelite* barely shook, showered nettles on my arms and face. When I heard the rattle the world froze.

I barely felt its fangs. Boot got all the *veneno.*[7] My mother came shrieking, swinging her hoe high, cutting the earth, the writhing body.

I stood still, the sun beat down. Afterwards I smelled where fear had been: back of neck, under arms, between my legs; I felt its heat slide down my body. I swallowed the rock it had hardened into.

When Mama had gone down the row and was out of sight, I took out my pocketknife. I made an X over each prick. My body followed the blood, fell onto the soft ground. I put my mouth over the red and sucked and spit between the rows of cotton.

I picked up the pieces, placed them end on end. *Culebra de cascabel.*[8] I counted the rattlers: twelve. It would shed no more. I buried the pieces between the rows of cotton.

That night I watched the window sill, watched the moon dry the blood on the tail, dreamed rattler fangs filled my mouth, scales covered my body. In the morning I saw through snake eyes, felt snake blood course through my body. The serpent, *mi tono,* my animal counterpart. I was immune to its venom. Forever immune.

Snakes, *víboras:* since that day I've sought and shunned them. Always when they cross my path, fear and elation flood my body. I know things older than Freud, older than gender. She—that's how I think of *la Víbora,* Snake Woman. Like the ancient Olmecs, I know Earth is a coiled Serpent. [Forty years it's taken me to enter into the Serpent, to acknowledge that I have a body, that I am a body and to assimilate the animal body, the animal soul.]

Coatlalopeuh, She Who Has Dominion Over Serpents

Mi mamagrande Ramona toda su vida mantuvo un altar pequeño en la esquina del comedor. Siempre tenía las velas prendidas. Allí hacía promesas a la Virgen de Guadalupe. My family, like most Chicanos, did not practice Roman Catholicism but a folk Catholicism with many pagan elements. *La Virgen de Guadalupe's* Indian name is *Coatlalopeuh.* She is the central deity connecting us to our Indian ancestry.

Coatlalopeuh is descended from, or is an aspect of, earlier Mesoamerican fertility and Earth goddesses. The earliest is *Coatlicue,* or "Serpent Skirt." She had a human skull or serpent for a head, a necklace of human hearts, a skirt of twisted serpents and taloned feet. As creator goddess, she was mother of the celestial deities, and of *Huitzilopochtli* and his sister, *Coyolxauhqui,* She With Golden Bells, Goddess of the Moon, who was decapitated by her brother. Another aspect of *Coatlicue* is *Tonantsi.*[9] The Totonacs, tired of the Aztec human sacrifices to the male god, *Huitzilopochtli,* renewed their reverence for *Tonantsi* who preferred the sacrifice of birds and small animals.[10]

The male-dominated Azteca-Mexica culture drove the powerful female deities underground by giving them monstrous attributes and by substituting male deities in their place, thus splitting the female Self and the female deities. They divided her who had been complete, who possessed both upper (light) and underworld (dark) aspects. *Coatlicue,* the Serpent goddess, and her more sinister aspects, *Tlazolteotl* and *Cihuacoatl,* were "darkened" and disempowered much in the same manner as the Indian *Kali.*

Tonantsi—split from her dark guises, *Coatlicue, Tlazolteotl,* and *Cihuacoatl*—became the good mother. The Nahuas, through ritual and prayer, sought to oblige *Tonantsi* to ensure their health and the growth of their crops. It was she who gave *México* the cactus plant to provide her people with milk and pulque. It was she who defended her children against the wrath of the Christian God by challenging God, her son, to produce mother's milk (as she had done) to prove that his benevolence equaled his disciplinary harshness.[11]

After the Conquest, the Spaniards and their Church continued to split *Tonantsi/Guadalupe.* They desexed *Guadalupe,* taking *Coatlalopeuh,* the serpent/sexuality, out of her. They completed the split begun by the Nahuas by making *la Virgen de Guadalupe/Virgen María* into chaste virgins and *Tlazolteotl/Coatlicue/la Chingada* into *putas;* into the Beauties and the Beasts. They went even further; they made all Indian deities and religious practices the work of the devil.

Thus *Tonantsi* became *Guadalupe,* the chaste protective mother, the defender of the Mexican people.

> *El nueve de diciembre del año 1531*
> *a las cuatro de la madrugada*
> *un pobre indio que se llamaba Juan Diego*
> *iba cruzando el cerro de Tepeyác*
> *cuando oyó un canto de pájaro.*
> *Alzó la cabeza vío que la cima del cerro*
> *estaba cubierta con una brillante nube blanca.*
> *Parada en frente del sol*
> *sobre una luna creciente*
> *sostenida por un ángel*
> *estaba una azteca*
> *vestida en ropa de india.*
> *Nuestra Señora María de Coatlalopeuh*
> *se le apareció.*
> *"Juan Dieguito, El-que-habla-como-un-águila,"*
> *la Virgen le dijo en el lenguaje azteca.*
> *"Para hacer mi altar este cerro elijo.*
> *Dile a tu gente que yo soy la madre de Dios,*
> *a los indios yo les ayudaré."*
> *Estó se lo contó a Juan Zumárraga*
> *pero el obispo no le creyó.*
> *Juan Diego volvió, llenó su tilma*[12]
> *con rosas de castilla*
> *creciendo milagrosamente en la nieve.*
> *Se las llevó al obispo,*
> *y cuando abrió su tilma*
> *el retrato de la Virgen*
> *ahí estaba pintado.*

Guadalupe appeared on December 9, 1531, on the spot where the Aztec goddess, *Tonantsi* ("Our Lady Mother"), had been worshipped by the Nahuas and where a temple to her had stood. Speaking Nahuatl, she told Juan Diego, a poor Indian crossing Tepeyác Hill, whose Indian name was *Cuautlaohuac* and who belonged to the *mazehual* class, the humblest within the Chichimeca tribe, that her name was *María Coatlalopeuh*. *Coatl* is the Nahuatl word for serpent. *Lopeuh* means "the one who has dominion over serpents." I interpret this as "the one who is at one with the beasts." Some spell her name *Coatlaxopeuh* (pronounced *"Cuatlashupe"* in Nahuatl) and say that *xopeuh* means "crushed or stepped on with disdain." Some say it means "she who crushed the serpent," with the serpent as the symbol of the indigenous religion, meaning that her religion was to take the place of the Aztec religion.[13] Because *Coatlalopeuh* was homophonous to the Spanish *Guadalupe,* the Spanish identified her with the dark Virgin, *Guadalupe,* patroness of West Central Spain.[14]

From that meeting, Juan Diego walked away with the image of *la Virgen* painted on his cloak. Soon after, Mexico ceased to belong to Spain, and *la Virgen de Guadalupe* began to eclipse all the other male and female religious figures in Mexico, Central America and parts of the U.S. Southwest. *"Desde entonces para el mexicano ser Guadalupano es algo esencial/*since then for the Mexican, to be a *Guadalupano* is something essential."[15]

Mi Virgen Morena	My brown virgin
Mi Virgen Ranchera	my country virgin
Eres nuestra Reina	you are our queen
México es tu tierra	Mexico is your land
Y tú su bandera.	and you its flag.

—*"La Virgen Ranchera"*[16]

In 1660 the Roman Catholic Church named her Mother of God, considering her synonymous with *la Virgen María;* she became *la Santa Patrona de los mexicanos.* The role of defender (or patron) has traditionally been assigned to male gods. During the Mexican Revolution, Emiliano Zapata and Miguel Hidalgo used her image to move *el pueblo mexicano* toward freedom. During the 1965 grape strike in Delano, California and in subsequent Chicano farmworkers' marches in Texas and other parts of the Southwest, her image on banners heralded and united the farmworkers. *Pachucos* (zoot suiters) tattoo her image on their bodies. Today, in Texas and Mexico she is more venerated than Jesus or God the Father. In the Lower Rio Grande Valley of south

Texas it is *la Virgen de San Juan de los Lagos* (an aspect of *Guadalupe*) that is worshipped by thousands every day at her shrine in San Juan. In Texas she is considered the patron saint of Chicanos. *Cuando Carito, mi hermanito,* was missing in action and, later, wounded in Viet Nam, *mi mamá* got on her knees *y le prometió a Ella que si su hijito volvía vivo* she would crawl on her knees and light novenas in her honor.

Today, *la Virgen de Guadalupe* is the single most potent religious, political and cultural image of the Chicano/*mexicano*. She, like my race, is a synthesis of the old world and the new, of the religion and culture of the two races in our psyche, the conquerors and the conquered. She is the symbol of the *mestizo* true to his or her Indian values. *La cultura chicana* identifies with the mother (Indian) rather than with the father (Spanish). Our faith is rooted in indigenous attributes, images, symbols, magic and myth. Because *Guadalupe* took upon herself the psychological and physical devastation of the conquered and oppressed *indio,* she is our spiritual, political and psychological symbol. As a symbol of hope and faith, she sustains and insures our survival. The Indian, despite extreme despair, suffering and near genocide, has survived. To Mexicans on both sides of the border, *Guadalupe* is the symbol of our rebellion against the rich, upper and middleclass; against their subjugation of the poor and the *indio.*

Guadalupe unites people of different races, religions, languages: Chicano protestants, American Indians and whites. *"Nuestra abogada siempre serás/*Our *mediatrix* you will always be." She mediates between the Spanish and the Indian cultures (or three cultures as in the case of *mexicanos* of African or other ancestry) and between Chicanos and the white world. She mediates between humans and the divine, between this reality and the reality of spirit entities. *La Virgen de Guadalupe* is the symbol of ethnic identity and of the tolerance for ambiguity that Chicanos-*mexicanos,* people of mixed race, people who have Indian blood, people who cross cultures, by necessity possess.

La gente Chicana tiene tres madres. All three are mediators: *Guadalupe,* the virgin mother who has not abandoned us, *la Chingada (Malinche),* the raped mother whom we have abandoned, and *la Llorona,* the mother who seeks her lost children and is a combination of the other two.

Ambiguity surrounds the symbols of these three "Our Mothers." *Guadalupe* has been used by the Church to mete out institutionalized oppression: to placate the Indians and *mexicanos* and Chicanos. In part, the true identity of all three has been subverted—*Guadalupe* to make us docile and enduring, *la Chingada* to make us ashamed of our Indian side, and *la Llorona* to make us long-suffering people. This obscuring has encouraged the *virgen/puta* (whore) dichotomy.

Yet we have not all embraced this dichotomy. In the U.S. Southwest, Mexico, Central and South America the *indio* and the *mestizo* continue to worship the old spirit entities (including *Guadalupe*) and their supernatural power, under the guise of Christian saints.[17]

Las invoco diosas mías, ustedes las indias
sumergidas en mi carne que son mis sombras.
Ustedes que persisten mudas en sus cuevas.
Ustedes Señoras que ahora, como yo,
        están en desgracia.

For Waging War Is My Cosmic Duty: The Loss of the Balanced Oppositions and the Change to Male Dominance

> Therefore I decided to leave
> The country (Aztlán),
> Therefore I have come as one charged with a
>   special duty,
> Because I have been given arrows and shields,
> For waging war is my duty,
> And on my expeditions I
> Shall see all the lands,
> I shall wait for the people and meet them
> In all four quarters and I shall give them
> Food to eat and drinks to quench their thirst,
> For here I shall unite all the different peoples!
>   —*Huitzilopochtli*
>   speaking to the Azteca-Mexica[18]

Before the Aztecs became a militaristic, bureaucratic state where male predatory warfare and conquest were based on patrilineal nobility, the principle of balanced opposition between the sexes existed.[19] The people worshipped the Lord and Lady of

Duality, *Ometecuhtli* and *Omecihuatl*. Before the change to male dominance, *Coatlicue,* Lady of the Serpent Skirt, contained and balanced the dualities of male and female, light and dark, life and death.

The changes that led to the loss of the balanced oppositions began when the Azteca, one of the twenty Toltec tribes, made the last pilgrimage from a place called Aztlán. The migration south began about the year A.D. 820. Three hundred years later the advance guard arrived near Tula, the capital of the declining Toltec empire. By the 11th century, they had joined with the Chichimec tribe of Mexitin (afterwards called Mexica) into one religious and administrative organization within Aztlán, the Aztec territory. The Mexitin, with their tribal god *Tetzauhteotl Huitzilopochtli* (Magnificent Humming Bird on the Left), gained control of the religious system.[20] (In some stories *Huitzilopochtli* killed his sister, the moon goddess *Malinalxoch,* who used her supernatural power over animals to control the tribe rather than wage war.)

Huitzilopochtli assigned the Azteca-Mexica the task of keeping the human race (the present cosmic age called the Fifth Sun, *El Quinto Sol*) alive. They were to guarantee the harmonious preservation of the human race by unifying all the people on earth into one social, religious and administrative organ. The Aztec people considered themselves in charge of regulating all earthly matters.[21] Their instrument: controlled or regulated war to gain and exercise power.

After 100 years in the central plateau, the Azteca-Mexica went to Chapultepec, where they settled in 1248 (the present site of the park on the outskirts of Mexico City). There, in 1345, the Azteca-Mexica chose the site of their capital, Tenochtitlán.[22] By 1428, they dominated the Central Mexican lake area.

The Aztec ruler, *Itzcoatl,* destroyed all the painted documents (books called codices) and rewrote a mythology that validated the wars of conquest and thus continued the shift from a tribe based on clans to one based on classes. From 1429-1440, the Aztecs emerged as a militaristic state that preyed on neighboring tribes for tribute and captives.[23] The "wars of flowers" were encounters between local armies with a fixed number of warriors, operating within the Aztec World, and, according to set rules, fighting ritual battles at fixed times and on predetermined battlefields. The religious purpose of these wars was to procure prisoners of war who could be sacrificed to the deities of the capturing party. For if one "fed" the gods, the human race would be saved from total extinction. The social purpose was to enable males of noble families and warriors of low descent to win honor, fame and administrative offices, and to prevent social and cultural decadence of the elite. The Aztec people were free to have their own religious faith, provided it did not conflict too much with the three fundamental principles of state ideology: to fulfill the special duty set forth by *Huitzilopochtli* of unifying all peoples, to participate in the wars of flowers, and to bring ritual offerings and do penance for the purpose of preventing decadence.[24]

Matrilineal descent characterized the Toltecs and perhaps early Aztec society. Women possessed property, and were curers as well as priestesses. According to the codices, women in former times had the supreme power in Tula, and in the beginning of the Aztec dynasty, the royal blood ran through the female line. A council of elders of the Calpul headed by a supreme leader, or *tlactlo,* called the father and mother of the people, governed the tribe. The supreme leader's vice-emperor occupied the position of "Snake Woman" or *Cihuacoatl,* a goddess.[25] Although the high posts were occupied by men, the terms referred to females, evidence of the exalted role of women before the Aztec nation became centralized. The final break with the democratic Calpul came when the four Aztec lords of royal lineage picked the king's successor from his siblings or male descendants.[26]

La Llorona's wailing in the night for her lost children has an echoing note in the wailing or mourning rites performed by women as they bade their sons, brothers and husbands good-bye before they left to go to the "flowery wars." Wailing is the Indian, Mexican and Chicana woman's feeble protest when she has no other recourse. These collective wailing rites may have been a sign of resistance in a society which glorified the warrior and war and for whom the women of the conquered tribes were booty.[27]

In defiance of the Aztec rulers, the *mazehuales* (the common people) continued to worship fertility, nourishment and agricultural female deities, those of crops and rain. They venerated *Chalchiuhtlicue* (goddess of sweet or inland water), *Chicomecoatl* (goddess of food) and *Huixtocihuatl* (goddess of salt).

Nevertheless, it took less than three centuries for Aztec society to change from the balanced duality of their earlier times and from the egalitarian traditions of a wandering tribe to those of a predatory state. The nobility kept the tribute, the commoner got nothing, resulting in a class split. The conquered tribes hated the Aztecs because of the rape of their women and the heavy taxes levied on them. The Tlaxcalans were the Aztecs' bitter enemies and it was they who helped the Spanish defeat the Aztec rulers, who were by this time so unpopular with their own common people that they could not even mobilize the populace to defend the city. Thus the Aztec nation fell not because *Malinali (la Chingada)* interpreted for and slept with Cortés, but because the ruling elite had subverted the solidarity between men and women and between noble and commoner.[28]

Sueño con serpientes

Coatl. In pre-Columbian America the most notable symbol was the serpent. The Olmecs associated womanhood with the Serpent's mouth which was guarded by rows of dangerous teeth, a sort of *vagina dentata.* They considered it the most sacred place on earth, a place of refuge, the creative womb from which all things were born and to which all things returned. Snake people had holes, entrances to the body of the Earth Serpent; they followed the Serpent's way, identified with the Serpent deity, with the mouth, both the eater and the eaten. The destiny of humankind is to be devoured by the Serpent.[29]

Dead,
the doctor by the operating table said.
I passed between the two fangs,
the flickering tongue.
Having come through the mouth of the serpent,
swallowed,
I found myself suddenly in the dark,
sliding down a smooth wet surface
down down into an even darker darkness.
Having crossed the portal, the raised hinged mouth,
having entered the serpent's belly,
now there was no looking back, no going back.

Why do I cast no shadow?
Are there lights from all sides shining on me?
Ahead, ahead.

> curled up inside the serpent's coils,
> the damp breath of death on my face.
> I knew at that instant: something must change
> or I'd die.
> *Algo tenía que cambiar.*

After each of my four bouts with death I'd catch glimpses of an otherworld Serpent. Once, in my bedroom, I saw a cobra the size of the room, her hood expanding over me. When I blinked she was gone. I realized she was, in my psyche, the mental picture and symbol of the instinctual in its collective impersonal, pre-human. She, the symbol of the dark sexual drive, the chthonic (underworld), the feminine, the serpentine movement of sexuality, of creativity, the basis of all energy and life.

The Presences

> She appeared in white, garbed in white,
> standing white, pure white.
> —Bernardino de Sahagún[30]

On the gulf where I was raised, *en el Valle del Río Grande* in South Texas—that triangular piece of land wedged between the river *y el golfo* which serves as the Texas-U.S./Mexican border— is a Mexican *pueblito* called Hargill (at one time in the history of this one-grocery-store, two-service-stations town there were thirteen churches and thirteen *cantinas*). Down the road, a little ways from our house, was a deserted church. It was known among the *mexicanos* that if you walked down the road late at night you would see a woman dressed in white floating about, peering out the church window. She would follow those who had done something bad or who were afraid. *Los mexicanos* called her *la Jila.* Some thought she was *la Llorona.* She was, I think, *Cihuacoatl,* Serpent Woman, ancient Aztec goddess of the earth, of war and birth, patron of midwives, and antecedent of *la Llorona.* Covered with chalk, *Cihuacoatl* wears a white dress with a decoration half red and half black. Her hair forms two little horns (which the Aztecs depicted as knives) crossed on her forehead. The lower part of her face is a bare jawbone, signifying death. On her back she carries a cradle, the knife of sacrifice swaddled as if it were her papoose, her child.[31] Like *la Llorona,* *Cihuacoatl* howls and weeps in the night, screams as if demented.

She brings mental depression and sorrow. Long before it takes place, she is the first to predict something is to happen.

Back then, I, an unbeliever, scoffed at these Mexican super-stitions as I was taught in Anglo school. Now, I wonder if this story and similar ones were the culture's attempts to "protect" members of the family, especially girls, from "wandering." Stories of the devil luring young girls away and having his way with them discouraged us from going out. There's an ancient Indian tradi-tion of burning the umbilical cord of an infant girl under the house so she will never stray from it and her domestic role.

> *A mis ancas caen los cueros de culebra,*
> *cuatro veces por año los arrastro,*
> *me tropiezo y me caigo*
> *y cada vez que miro una culebra le pregunto*
> *¿Qué traes conmigo?*

Four years ago a red snake crossed my path as I walked through the woods. The direction of its movement, its pace, its colors, the "mood" of the trees and the wind and the snake—they all "spoke" to me, told me things. [I look for omens everywhere, everywhere catch glimpses of the patterns and cycles of my life.] Stones "speak" to Luisah Teish, a Santera; trees whisper their secrets to Chrystos, a Native American. I remember listening to the voices of the wind as a child and understanding its messages. *Los espíritus* that ride the back of the south wind. I remember their exhalation blowing in through the slits in the door during those hot Texas afternoons. A gust of wind raising the linoleum under my feet, buffeting the house. Everything trembling.

We're not supposed to remember such otherworldly events. We're supposed to ignore, forget, kill those fleeting images of the soul's presence and of the spirit's presence. We've been taught that the spirit is outside our bodies or above our heads some-where up in the sky with God. We're supposed to forget that every cell in our bodies, every bone and bird and worm has spir-it in it.

Like many Indians and Mexicans, I did not deem my psychic experiences real. I denied their occurrences and let my inner senses atrophy. I allowed white rationality to tell me that the existence of the "other world" was mere pagan superstition. I accepted their reality, the "official" reality of the rational, reasoning mode which is connected with external reality, the upper world, and is considered the most developed consciousness—the consciousness of duality.

The other mode of consciousness facilitates images from the soul and the unconscious through dreams and the imagination. Its work is labeled "fiction," make-believe, wish-fulfillment. White anthropologists claim that Indians have "primitive" and therefore deficient minds, that we cannot think in the higher mode of consciousness—rationality. They are fascinated by what they call the "magical" mind, the "savage" mind, the *participation mystique* of the mind that says the world of the imagination—the world of the soul—and of the spirit is just as real as physical reality.[32] In trying to become "objective," Western culture made "objects" of things and people when it distanced itself from them, thereby losing "touch" with them. This dichotomy is the root of all violence.

Not only was the brain split into two functions but so was reality. Thus people who inhabit both realities are forced to live in the interface between the two, forced to become adept at switching modes. Such is the case with the *india* and the *mestiza.*

Institutionalized religion fears trafficking with the spirit world and stigmatizes it as witchcraft. It has strict taboos against this kind of inner knowledge. It fears what Jung calls the Shadow, the unsavory aspects of ourselves. But even more it fears the supra-human, the god in ourselves.

"The purpose of any established religion . . . is to glorify, sanction and bless with a superpersonal meaning all personal and interpersonal activities. This occurs through the 'sacraments,' and indeed through most religious rites."[33] But it sanctions only its own sacraments and rites. Voodoo, Santeria, Shamanism and other native religions are called cults and their beliefs are called mythologies. In my own life, the Catholic Church fails to give meaning to my daily acts, to my continuing encounters with the "other world." It and other institutionalized religions impoverish all life, beauty, pleasure.

The Catholic and Protestant religions encourage fear and distrust of life and of the body; they encourage a split between the body and the spirit and totally ignore the soul; they encourage us to kill off parts of ourselves. We are taught that the body is an ignorant animal; intelligence dwells only in the head. But the body is smart. It does not discern between external stimuli and stimuli from the imagination. It reacts equally viscerally to events from the imagination as it does to "real" events.

So I grew up in the interface trying not to give countenance to *el mal aigre*,[34] evil non-human, non-corporeal entities riding the wind, that could come in through the window, through my nose with my breath. I was not supposed to believe in *susto*, a sudden shock or fall that frightens the soul out of the body. And growing up between such opposing spiritualities how could I reconcile the two, the pagan and the Christian?

No matter to what use my people put the supranatural world, it is evident to me now that the spirit world, whose existence the whites are so adamant in denying, does in fact exist. This very minute I sense the presence of the spirits of my ancestors in my room. And I think *la Jila* is *Cihuacoatl*, Snake Woman; she is *la Llorona*, Daughter of Night, traveling the dark terrains of the unknown searching for the lost parts of herself. I remember *la Jila* following me once, remember her eerie lament. I'd like to think that she was crying for her lost children, *los* Chicanos/*mexicanos*.

La facultad

La facultad is the capacity to see in surface phenomena the meaning of deeper realities, to see the deep structure below the surface. It is an instant "sensing," a quick perception arrived at without conscious reasoning. It is an acute awareness mediated by the part of the psyche that does not speak, that communicates in images and symbols which are the faces of feelings, that is, behind which feelings reside/hide. The one possessing this sensitivity is excruciatingly alive to the world.

Those who are pushed out of the tribe for being different are likely to become more sensitized (when not brutalized into insensitivity). Those who do not feel psychologically or physically safe in the world are more apt to develop this sense. Those who are pounced on the most have it the strongest—the females, the homosexuals of all races, the darkskinned, the outcast, the persecuted, the marginalized, the foreign.

When we're up against the wall, when we have all sorts of oppressions coming at us, we are forced to develop this faculty so that we'll know when the next person is going to slap us or lock us away. We'll sense the rapist when he's five blocks down the street. Pain makes us acutely anxious to avoid more of it, so we hone that radar. It's a kind of survival tactic that people, caught between the worlds, unknowingly cultivate. It is latent in all of us.

I walk into a house and I know whether it is empty or occupied. I feel the lingering charge in the air of a recent fight or love-making or depression. I sense the emotions someone near is emitting—whether friendly or threatening. Hate and fear—the more intense the emotion, the greater my reception of it. I feel a tingling on my skin when someone is staring at me or thinking about me. I can tell how others feel by the way they smell, where others are by the air pressure on my skin. I can spot the love or greed or generosity lodged in the tissues of another. Often I sense the direction of and my distance from people or objects—in the dark, or with my eyes closed, without looking. It must be a vestige of a proximity sense, a sixth sense that's lain dormant from long-ago times.

Fear develops the proximity sense aspect of *la facultad*. But there is a deeper sensing that is another aspect of this faculty. [It *does the book do this?* is anything that breaks into one's everyday mode of perception, that causes a break in one's defenses and resistance, anything that takes one from one's habitual grounding, causes the depths to open up, causes a shift in perception.] This shift in perception deepens the way we see concrete objects and people; the senses become so acute and piercing that we can see through things, view events in depth, a piercing that reaches the underworld (the realm of the soul). As we plunge vertically, the break, with its accompanying new seeing, makes us pay attention to the soul, and we are thus carried into awareness—an experiencing of soul (Self).

We lose something in this mode of initiation, something is taken from us: our innocence, our unknowing ways, our safe and easy ignorance. There is a prejudice and a fear of the dark, chthonic (underworld), material such as depression, illness, death and the violations that can bring on this break. Confronting anything that tears the fabric of our everyday mode of consciousness and that thrusts us into a less literal and more psychic sense of reality increases awareness and *la facultad*.

4

La herencia de Coatlicue

The *Coatlicue* State

protean being

dark   dumb   windowless   no moon glides
across the stone   the nightsky   alone   alone
no lights just mirrorwalls   obsidian   smoky   in the
  mirror she sees   a woman with four heads   the heads
turning round and round   spokes of a wheel   her neck
is an axle   she stares at each face   each wishes the
other not there   the obsidian knife in the air   the
building   so high   should she jump   would she feel
the breeze   fanning her face   tumbling down the steps
  of the temple   heart offered up to the sun   wall
  growing thin   thinner   she is eyeless   a mole
burrowing deeper   tunneling here   tunneling there
tunneling through the air   in the photograph a double
image   a ghost arm alongside the flesh one   inside her
       head   the cracks ricocheting   bisecting
crisscrossing   she hears the rattlesnakes   stirring in
  a jar   being fed with her flesh   she listens to the
seam between dusk and dark   they are talking she hears
  their frozen thumpings   the soul encased   in black
obsidian   smoking   smoking   she bends to catch a
    feather of herself   as she falls   lost in the
silence   of the empty air   turning   turning
at midnight   turning into a wild pig   how to get back
all the feathers   put them in the jar   the rattling

full circle and back   dark   windowless   no moon
   glides across the nightsky   nightsky   night

Enfrentamientos con el alma

When my father died, my mother put blankets over the mirrors. Consciously, she had no idea why. Perhaps a part of her knew that a mirror is a door through which the soul may "pass" to the other side and she didn't want us to "accidentally" follow our father to the place where the souls of the dead live.

The mirror is an ambivalent symbol. Not only does it reproduce images (the twins that stand for thesis and antithesis);[1] it contains and absorbs them. In ancient times the Mexican Indians made mirrors of volcanic glass known as obsidian. Seers would gaze into a mirror until they fell into a trance. Within the black, glossy surface, they saw clouds of smoke which would part to reveal a vision concerning the future of the tribe and the will of the gods.[2]

There is another quality to the mirror and that is the act of seeing. Seeing and being seen. Subject and object, I and she. The eye pins down the object of its gaze, scrutinizes it, judges it. A glance can freeze us in place; it can "possess" us. It can erect a barrier against the world. But in a glance also lies awareness, knowledge. These seemingly contradictory aspects—the act of being seen, held immobilized by a glance, and "seeing through" an experience—are symbolized by the underground aspects of *Coatlicue, Cihuacoatl,* and *Tlazolteotl* which cluster in what I call the *Coatlicue* state.

El secreto terrible y la rajadura

> Shame is a wound felt from the inside, dividing
> us both from ourselves and from one another.
> —Gershen Kaufman[3]

I was two or three years old the first time *Coatlicue* visited my psyche, the first time she "devoured" me (and I "fell" into the underworld). By the worried look on my parents' faces I learned early that something was fundamentally wrong with me. When I was older I would look into the mirror, afraid of *mi secreto terrible,* the secret sin I tried to conceal—*la seña,* the mark of the Beast. I was afraid it was in plain sight for all to see. The secret

I tried to conceal was that I was not normal, that I was not like the others. I felt alien, I knew I was alien. I was the mutant stoned out of the herd, something deformed with evil inside.

She has this fear   that she has no names   that she has many names   that she doesn't know her names   She has this fear   that she's an image   that comes and goes clearing and darkening   the fear that she's the dreamwork inside someone else's skull   She has this fear   that if she takes off her clothes   shoves her brain aside peels off her skin   that if she drains   the blood vessels   strips the flesh from the bone   flushes out the marrow   She has this fear   that when she does reach herself   turns around to embrace herself   a lion's or witch's or serpent's head   will turn around swallow her and grin   She has this fear that if she digs into herself   she won't find anyone   that when she gets "there"   she won't find her notches on the trees   the birds will have eaten all the crumbs   She has this fear that she won't find the way back

She felt shame for being abnormal. The bleeding distanced her from others. Her body had betrayed her. She could not trust her instincts, her "horses," because they stood for her core self, her dark Indian self. *La consentida, la rancherita que se avergonzaba de su cuerpo* tried not to show pain but the kids could read her face.

Her soft belly exposed to the sharp eyes of everyone; they see, they see. Their eyes penetrate her; they slit her from head to belly. *Rajada.* She is at their mercy, she can do nothing to defend herself. And she is ashamed that they see her so exposed, so vulnerable. She has to learn to push their eyes away. She has to still her eyes from looking at their feelings—feelings that can catch her in their gaze, bind her to them.

> *"Oh, silencio, silencio . . . en torno de mi cama*
> *Tu boca bien amada dulcemente me llama."*
> —Alfonsina Storni, *"Silencio"*[4]

Internada en mi cuarto con mi intocada piel, en el oscuro velo con la noche. Embrazada en

---

pesadillas, escarbando el hueso de la ternura me envejezco. Ya verás, tan bajo que me he caído.

Días enteros me la paso atrancada con candado. Esa Gloria, ¿qué estará haciendo en su cuarto con la santa y la perversa? Mosquita muerta, ¿por qué 'tas tan quietecita? Por que la vida me arremolina pa' ca y pa' ya como hoja seca, me araña y me golpea, me deshuesa— mi culpa por que me desdeño. Ay mamá, tan bajo que me he caído.

Esa Gloria, la que niega, la que teme correr desenfrenada, la que tiene miedo renegar al papel de víctima. Esa, la que voltea su cara a la pared descascarada. Mira, tan bajo que se ha caído.

Despierta me encuentra la madrugada, una desconocida aullando profecías entre cenizas, sangrando mi cara con las uñas, escarbando la desgracia debajo de mi máscara. Ya vez, tan bajo que me he caído.

Se enmudecen mis ojos al saber que la vida no se entrega. Mi pecado no es la rebeldía ni el anajamiento. Es que no amé mucho, que anduve indecisa y a la prisa, que tuve poca fe y no fui dispuesta de querer ser lo que soy. Traicioné a mi camino.

Ya verás, tan bajo que me he caído. Aquí nomás encerrada en mi cuarto, sangrándome la cara con las uñas. Esa Gloria que rechaza entregarse a su destino. Quiero contenerme, no puedo y desbordo. Vas a ver lo alto que voy a subir, aquí vengo.

I locked the door, kept the world out; I vegetated, hibernated, remained in stasis, idled. No telephone, no television, no radio. Alone with the presence in the room. Who? Me, my psyche, the Shadow-Beast?

During the dark side of the moon something in the mirror catches my gaze, I seem all eyes and nose. Inside my skull something shifts. I "see" my face. Gloria, the everyday face; Prieta and Prietita, my childhood faces; Gaudi, the face my mother and sister and brothers know. And there in the black, obsidian mirror of the Nahuas is yet another face, a stranger's face. *Simultáneamente me miraba la cara desde distintos ángulos. Y mi cara, como la realidad, tenía un caracter multíplice.*

The gaping mouth slit heart from mind. Between the two eyes in her head, the tongueless magical eye and the loquacious rational eye, was *la rajadura,* the abyss that no bridge could span. Separated, they could not visit each other and each was too far away to hear what the other was saying. Silence rose like a river and could not be held back, it flooded and drowned everything.

Nopal de castilla

Soy nopal de castilla like the spineless and therefore defenseless cactus that Mamagrande Ramona grew in back of her shed. I have no protection. So I cultivate needles, nettles, razor-sharp spikes to protect myself from others.

There are many defense strategies that the self uses to escape the agony of inadequacy and I have used all of them. I have split from and disowned those parts of myself that others rejected. I have used rage to drive others away and to insulate myself against exposure. I have reciprocated with contempt for those who have roused shame in me. I have internalized rage and contempt, one part of the self (the accusatory, persecutory, judgmental) using defense strategies against another part of the self (the object of contempt). As a person, I, as a people, we, Chicanos, blame ourselves, hate ourselves, terrorize ourselves. Most of this goes on unconsciously; we only know that we are hurting, we suspect that there is something "wrong" with us, something fundamentally "wrong."

In order to escape the threat of shame or fear, one takes on a compulsive, repetitious activity as though to busy oneself, to distract oneself, to keep awareness at bay. One fixates on drinking, smoking, popping pills, acquiring friend after friend who betrays; repeating, repeating, to prevent oneself from "seeing."

Held in thrall by one's obsession, by the god or goddess symbolizing that addiction, one is not empty enough to become possessed by anything or anyone else. One's attention cannot be captured by something else, one does not "see" and awareness does not happen. One remains ignorant of the fact that one is afraid, and that it is fear that holds one petrified, frozen in stone. If we can't see the face of fear in the mirror, then fear must not be there. The feeling is censored and erased before it registers in our consciousness.

An addiction (a repetitious act) is a ritual to help one through a trying time; its repetition safeguards the passage, it becomes one's talisman, one's touchstone. If it sticks around after having outlived its usefulness, we become "stuck" in it and it takes possession of us. But we need to be arrested. Some past experience or condition has created this need. This stopping is a survival mechanism, but one which must vanish when it's no longer needed if growth is to occur.

We need *Coatlicue* to slow us up so that the psyche can assimilate previous experiences and process the changes. If we don't take the time, she'll lay us low with an illness, forcing us to "rest." Come, little green snake. Let the wound caused by the serpent be cured by the serpent. The soul uses everything to further its own making. Those activities or *Coatlicue* states which disrupt the smooth flow (complacency) of life are exactly what propel the soul to do its work: make soul, increase consciousness of itself. Our greatest disappointments and painful experiences—if we can make meaning out of them—can lead us toward becoming more of who we are. Or they can remain meaningless. The *Coatlicue* state can be a way station or it can be a way of life.

The *Coatlicue* State

Coatlicue da luz a todo y a todo devora. Ella es el monstruo que se tragó todos los seres vivientes y los astros, es el monstruo que se traga al sol cada tarde y le da luz cada mañana. *Coatlicue* is a rupture in our everyday world. As the Earth, she opens and swallows us, plunging us into the underworld where the soul resides, allowing us to dwell in darkness.

Coatlicue[5] is one of the powerful images, or "archetypes,"[6] that inhabits, or passes through, my psyche. For me, *la Coatlicue* is the consuming internal whirlwind,[7] the symbol of the underground aspects of the psyche. *Coatlicue* is the mountain, the Earth Mother who conceived all celestial beings out of her cavernous womb.[8] Goddess of birth and death, *Coatlicue* gives and takes away life; she is the incarnation of cosmic processes.

Simultaneously, depending on the person, she represents: duality in life, a synthesis of duality, and a third perspective—something more than mere duality or a synthesis of duality.

I first saw the statue[9] of this life-in-death and death-in-life, headless "monster" goddess (as the *Village Voice* dubbed her) at the Museum of Natural History in New York City. She has no head. In its place two spurts of blood gush up, transfiguring into enormous twin rattlesnakes facing each other, which symbolize the earth-bound character of human life. She has no hands. In their place are two more serpents in the form of eagle-like claws, which are repeated at her feet: claws which symbolize the digging of graves into the earth as well as the sky-bound eagle, the masculine force. Hanging from her neck is a necklace of open hands alternating with human hearts. The hands symbolize the act of giving life; the hearts, the pain of Mother Earth giving birth to all her children, as well as the pain that humans suffer throughout life in their hard struggle for existence. The hearts also represent the taking of life through sacrifice to the gods in exchange for their preservation of the world. In the center of the collar hangs a human skull with living eyes in its sockets. Another identical skull is attached to her belt. These symbolize life and death together as parts of one process.

Coatlicue depicts the contradictory. In her figure, all the symbols important to the religion and philosophy of the Aztecs are integrated. Like Medusa, the Gorgon, she is a symbol of the fusion of opposites: the eagle and the serpent, heaven and the underworld, life and death, mobility and immobility, beauty and horror.

When pain, suffering and the advent of death become intolerable, there is *Tlazolteotl* hovering at the crossroads of life to lure a person away from his or her seemingly appointed destination and we are held *embrujadas*, kept from our destiny, our soul arrested. We are not living up to our potentialities and thereby impeding the evolution of the soul—or worse, *Coatlicue,* the Earth, opens and plunges us into its maw, devours us. By keeping the conscious mind occupied or immobile, the germination work takes place in the deep, dark earth of the unconscious.

> Frozen in stasis, she perceives a slight
> movement—a thousand slithering serpent hairs,
> *Coatlicue.* It is activity (not immobility) at its
> most dynamic stage, but it is an underground
> movement requiring all her energy. It brooks no
> interference from the conscious mind.

The *Coatlicue* State Is A Prelude To Crossing

Voy cagándome de miedo, buscando lugares acuevados. I don't want to know, I don't want to be seen. My resistance, my refusal to know some truth about myself brings on that paralysis, depression—brings on the *Coatlicue* state. At first I feel exposed and opened to the depth of my dissatisfaction. Then I feel myself closing, hiding, holding myself together rather than allowing myself to fall apart.

Sweating, with a headache, unwilling to communicate, frightened by sudden noises, *estoy asustada.* In the Mexican culture it is called *susto,* the soul frightened out of the body. The afflicted one is allowed to rest and recuperate, to withdraw into the "underworld" without drawing condemnation.

I descend into *mictlán,* the underworld. In the "place of the dead" I wallow, sinking deeper and deeper. When I reach bottom, something forces me to push up, walk toward the mirror, confront the face in the mirror. But I dig in my heels and resist. I don't want to see what's behind *Coatlicue's* eyes, her hollow sockets. I can't confront her face to face; I must take small sips of her face through the corners of my eyes, chip away at the ice a sliver at a time.

Behind the ice mask I see my own eyes. They will not look at me. *Miro que estoy encabronada, miro la resistencia*—resistance to knowing, to letting go, to that deep ocean where once I dived into death. I am afraid of drowning. Resistance to sex, intimate touching, opening myself to the alien other where I am out of control, not on patrol. The outcome on the other side unknown, the reins failing and the horses plunging blindly over the crumbling path rimming the edge of the cliff, plunging into its thousand foot drop.

Every increment of consciousness, every step forward is a *travesía,* a crossing. I am again an alien in new territory. And again, and again. But if I escape conscious awareness, escape "knowing," I won't be moving. Knowledge makes me more aware, it makes me more conscious. "Knowing" is painful because after "it" happens I can't stay in the same place and be comfortable. I am no longer the same person I was before.

No, it isn't enough that she is female—a second-class member of a conquered people who are taught to believe they are inferior because they have indigenous blood, believe in the supernatural and speak a deficient language. Now she beats herself over the head for her "inactivity," a stage that is as necessary as breathing. But that means being Mexican. All her life she's been told that Mexicans are lazy. She has had to work twice as hard as others to meet the standards of the dominant culture which have, in part, become her standards.

Why does she have to go and try to make "sense" of it all? Every time she makes "sense" of something, she has to "cross over," kicking a hole out of the old boundaries of the self and slipping under or over, dragging the old skin along, stumbling over it. It hampers her movement in the new territory, dragging the ghost of the past with her. It is a dry birth, a breech birth, a screaming birth, one that fights her every inch of the way. It is only when she is on the other side and the shell cracks open and the lid from her eyes lifts that she sees things in a different perspective. It is only then that she makes the connections, formulates the insights. It is only then that her consciousness expands a tiny notch, another rattle appears on the rattlesnake tail and the added growth slightly alters the sounds she makes. Suddenly the repressed energy rises, makes decisions, connects with conscious energy and a new life begins. It is her reluctance to cross over, to make a hole in the fence and walk across, to cross the river, to take that flying leap into the dark, that drives her to escape, that forces her into the fecund cave of her imagination where she is cradled in the arms of *Coatlicue,* who will never let her go. If she doesn't change her ways, she will remain a stone forever. *No hay más que cambiar.*

The one who watches, Darkness, my night. There is darkness and there is darkness. Though darkness was "present" before the world and all things were created, it is equated with matter, the maternal, the germinal, the potential. The dualism of light/darkness did not arise as a symbolic formula for morality until primordial darkness had been split into light and dark.[10] Now Darkness, my night, is identified with the negative, base and evil forces—the masculine order casting its dual shadow— and all these are identified with darkskinned people.

In attending to this first darkness I am led back to the mystery of the Origin. The one who watches, the one who whispers in a slither of serpents. Something is trying to tell me. That voice at the edge of things. But I know what I want and I stamp ahead, arrogance edging my face. I tremble before the animal, the alien, the sub- or suprahuman, the me that has something in common with the wind and the trees and the rocks, that possesses a demon determination and ruthlessness beyond the human.

That Which Abides

En esta tarde gris me siento entre dos aguas, el calor de mi casa y el frío de afuera. Los dos arbitran por el cuadro de vidrio de la ventana. I can sense the premonition of cold in the way the wind stirs the leaves in the trees, in the gray slate square of sky that frames my window. Winter's coming.

I sit between warmth and cold never knowing which is my territory, domesticated as I am by human warmth and the peck peck of my keyboard. Having lived my whole life in an ignorant shadow, under the sight of hunger shuffling its little child feet, whimpering, lost. Pain is the way of life. Now I sense a warm breath on my face, see the shadow of a giant bird, her huge wings folding over me. *Ella.*

I spent the first half of my life learning to rule myself, to grow a will, and now at midlife I find that autonomy is a boulder on my path that I keep crashing into. I can't seem to stay out of my own way. I've always been aware that there is a greater power than the conscious I. That power is my inner self, the entity that is the sum total of all my reincarnations, the godwoman in me I call *Antigua, mi Diosa,* the divine within, *Coatlicue-Cihuacoatl-Tlazolteotl-Tonantzin-Coatlalopeuh-Guadalupe*— they are one. When to bow down to Her and when to allow the limited conscious mind to take over—that is the problem.

Let the wound caused by the serpent be cured by the serpent. For a few minutes, *Antigua, mi Diosa,* I'm going to give up my control to you. I'm going to pull it out. I plunge my hands into my solar plexus, pull. Plop. Out comes the handle with a dial face, dripping blood, unblinking eyes, watching. Eagle eyes, my mother calls me. Looking, always looking, only I don't have enough eyes. My sight is limited. Here, *Antigua,* take this lever-shaped handle with needles that measure the temperature, the air pressure, danger. You hold it for a while. Promise to give it back. Please, *Antigua.*

I'll take over now, she tells me. The alarm will go off if you're in danger. I imagine its shrill peel when danger walks around the corner, the insulating walls coming down around me.

Suddenly, I feel like I have another set of teeth in my mouth. A tremor goes through my body from my buttocks to the roof of my mouth. On my palate I feel a tingling ticklish sensation, then something seems to be falling on me, over me, a curtain of rain or light. Shock pulls my breath out of me. The sphincter muscle tugs itself up, up, and the heart in my cunt starts to beat. A light is all around me—so intense it could be white or black or at that juncture where extremes turn into their opposites. It passes through my body and comes out of the other side. I collapse into myself—a delicious caving into myself—imploding, the walls like matchsticks softly folding inward in slow motion.

I see *oposición e insurrección*. I see the crack growing on the rock. I see the fine frenzy building. I see the heat of anger or rebellion or hope split open that rock, releasing *la Coatlicue*. And someone in me takes matters into our own hands, and eventually, takes dominion over serpents—over my own body, my sexual activity, my soul, my mind, my weaknesses and strengths. Mine. Ours. Not the heterosexual white man's or the colored man's or the state's or the culture's or the religion's or the parents'—just ours, mine.

And suddenly I feel everything rushing to a center, a nucleus. All the lost pieces of myself come flying from the deserts and the mountains and the valleys, magnetized toward that center. *Completa*.

Something pulsates in my body, a luminous thin thing that grows thicker every day. Its presence never leaves me. I am never alone. That which abides: my vigilance, my thousand sleepless serpent eyes blinking in the night, forever open. And I am not afraid.

5

How to Tame a Wild Tongue

"We're going to have to control your tongue," the dentist says, pulling out all the metal from my mouth. Silver bits plop and tinkle into the basin. My mouth is a motherlode.

The dentist is cleaning out my roots. I get a whiff of the stench when I gasp. "I can't cap that tooth yet, you're still draining," he says.

"We're going to have to do something about your tongue," I hear the anger rising in his voice. My tongue keeps pushing out the wads of cotton, pushing back the drills, the long thin needles. "I've never seen anything as strong or as stubborn," he says. And I think, how do you tame a wild tongue, train it to be quiet, how do you bridle and saddle it? How do you make it lie down?

> "Who is to say that robbing a people of
> its language is less violent than war?"
> —Ray Gwyn Smith[1]

I remember being caught speaking Spanish at recess—that was good for three licks on the knuckles with a sharp ruler. I remember being sent to the corner of the classroom for "talking back" to the Anglo teacher when all I was trying to do was tell her how to pronounce my name. "If you want to be American, speak 'American.' If you don't like it, go back to Mexico where you belong."

"I want you to speak English. *Pa' hallar buen trabajo tienes que saber hablar el inglés bien. Qué vale toda tu educación si todavía hablas inglés con un* 'accent,'" my mother would say, mortified that I spoke English like a Mexican. At Pan American University, I, and all Chicano students were required to take two speech classes. Their purpose: to get rid of our accents.

Attacks on one's form of expression with the intent to censor are a violation of the First Amendment. *El Anglo con cara de inocente nos arrancó la lengua.* Wild tongues can't be tamed, they can only be cut out.

Overcoming the Tradition of Silence

> *Ahogadas, escupimos el oscuro.*
> *Peleando con nuestra propia sombra*
> *el silencio nos sepulta.*

En boca cerrada no entran moscas. "Flies don't enter a closed mouth" is a saying I kept hearing when I was a child. *Ser habladora* was to be a gossip and a liar, to talk too much. *Muchachitas bien criadas,* well-bred girls don't answer back. *Es una falta de respeto* to talk back to one's mother or father. I remember one of the sins I'd recite to the priest in the confession box the few times I went to confession: talking back to my mother, *hablar pa' 'trás, repelar. Hocicona, repelona, chismosa,* having a big mouth, questioning, carrying tales are all signs of being *mal criada.* In my culture they are all words that are derogatory if applied to women—I've never heard them applied to men.

The first time I heard two women, a Puerto Rican and a Cuban, say the word *"nosotras,"* I was shocked. I had not known the word existed. Chicanas use *nosotros* whether we're male or female. We are robbed of our female being by the masculine plural. Language is a male discourse.

> And our tongues have become
> dry   the wilderness has
> dried out our tongues   and
> we have forgotten speech.
>   —Irena Klepfisz[2]

Even our own people, other Spanish speakers *nos quieren poner candados en la boca.* They would hold us back with their bag of *reglas de academia.*

Oyé como ladra: el lenguaje de la frontera

Quien tiene boca se equivoca.
—Mexican saying

"*Pocho,* cultural traitor, you're speaking the oppressor's language by speaking English, you're ruining the Spanish language," I have been accused by various Latinos and Latinas. Chicano Spanish is considered by the purist and by most Latinos deficient, a mutilation of Spanish.

But Chicano Spanish is a border tongue which developed naturally. Change, *evolución, enriquecimiento de palabras nuevas por invención o adopción* have created variants of Chicano Spanish, *un nuevo lenguaje. Un lenguaje que corresponde a un modo de vivir.* Chicano Spanish is not incorrect, it is a living language.

For a people who are neither Spanish nor live in a country in which Spanish is the first language; for a people who live in a country in which English is the reigning tongue but who are not Anglo; for a people who cannot entirely identify with either standard (formal, Castillian) Spanish nor standard English, what recourse is left to them but to create their own language? A language which they can connect their identity to, one capable of communicating the realities and values true to themselves—a language with terms that are neither *español ni inglés,* but both. We speak a patois, a forked tongue, a variation of two languages.

Chicano Spanish sprang out of the Chicanos' need to identify ourselves as a distinct people. We needed a language with which we could communicate with ourselves, a secret language. For some of us, language is a homeland closer than the Southwest—for many Chicanos today live in the Midwest and the East. And because we are a complex, heterogeneous people, we speak many languages. Some of the languages we speak are:

1. Standard English
2. Working class and slang English
3. Standard Spanish
4. Standard Mexican Spanish
5. North Mexican Spanish dialect
6. Chicano Spanish (Texas, New Mexico, Arizona and California have regional variations)
7. Tex-Mex
8. *Pachuco* (called *caló*)

My "home" tongues are the languages I speak with my sister and brothers, with my friends. They are the last five listed, with 6 and 7 being closest to my heart. From school, the media and job situations, I've picked up standard and working class English. From Mamagrande Locha and from reading Spanish and Mexican literature, I've picked up Standard Spanish and Standard Mexican Spanish. From *los recién llegados,* Mexican immigrants, and *braceros,* I learned the North Mexican dialect. With Mexicans I'll try to speak either Standard Mexican Spanish or the North Mexican dialect. From my parents and Chicanos living in the Valley, I picked up Chicano Texas Spanish, and I speak it with my mom, younger brother (who married a Mexican and who rarely mixes Spanish with English), aunts and older relatives.

With Chicanas from *Nuevo México* or *Arizona* I will speak Chicano Spanish a little, but often they don't understand what I'm saying. With most California Chicanas I speak entirely in English (unless I forget). When I first moved to San Francisco, I'd rattle off something in Spanish, unintentionally embarrassing them. Often it is only with another Chicana *tejana* that I can talk freely.

Words distorted by English are known as anglicisms or *pochismos.* The *pocho* is an anglicized Mexican or American of Mexican origin who speaks Spanish with an accent characteristic of North Americans and who distorts and reconstructs the language according to the influence of English.[3] Tex-Mex, or Spanglish, comes most naturally to me. [I may switch back and forth from English to Spanish in the same sentence or in the same word.] With my sister and my brother Nune and with Chicano *tejano* contemporaries I speak in Tex-Mex.

From kids and people my own age I picked up *Pachuco. Pachuco* (the language of the zoot suiters) is a language of rebellion, both against Standard Spanish and Standard English. It is a secret language. Adults of the culture and outsiders cannot understand it. It is made up of slang words from both English and Spanish. *Ruca* means girl or woman, *vato* means guy or dude, *chale* means no, *simón* means yes, *churo* is sure, talk is *periquiar, pigionear* means petting, *que gacho* means how nerdy, *ponte águila* means watch out, death is called *la pelona.* Through lack of practice and not having others who can speak it, I've lost most of the *Pachuco* tongue.

Chicano Spanish

Chicanos, after 250 years of Spanish/Anglo colonization have developed significant differences in the Spanish we speak. We collapse two adjacent vowels into a single syllable and sometimes shift the stress in certain words such as *maíz/maiz, cohete/cuete*. We leave out certain consonants when they appear between vowels: *lado/lao, mojado/mojao*. Chicanos from South Texas pronounced *f* as *j* as in *jue (fue)*. Chicanos use "archaisms," words that are no longer in the Spanish language, words that have been evolved out. We say *semos, truje, haiga, ansina*, and *naiden*. We retain the "archaic" *j*, as in *jalar,* that derives from an earlier *h*, (the French *halar* or the Germanic *halon* which was lost to standard Spanish in the 16th century), but which is still found in several regional dialects such as the one spoken in South Texas. (Due to geography, Chicanos from the Valley of South Texas were cut off linguistically from other Spanish speakers. We tend to use words that the Spaniards brought over from Medieval Spain. The majority of the Spanish colonizers in Mexico and the Southwest came from Extremadura—Hernán Cortés was one of them—and Andalucía. Andalucians pronounce *ll* like a *y*, and their *d*'s tend to be absorbed by adjacent vowels: *tirado* becomes *tirao*. They brought *el lenguaje popular, dialectos y regionalismos.*[4])

Chicanos and other Spanish speakers also shift *ll* to *y* and *z* to *s*.[5] We leave out initial syllables, saying *tar* for *estar, toy* for *estoy, hora* for *ahora* (*cubanos* and *puertorriqueños* also leave out initial letters of some words.) We also leave out the final syllable such as *pa* for *para*. The intervocalic *y*, the *ll* as in *tortilla, ella, botella*, gets replaced by *tortia* or *tortiya, ea, botea*. We add an additional syllable at the beginning of certain words: *atocar* for *tocar, agastar* for *gastar.* Sometimes we'll say *lavaste las vacijas*, other times *lavates* (substituting the *ates* verb endings for the *aste*).

We use anglicisms, words borrowed from English: *bola* from ball, *carpeta* from carpet, *máchina de lavar* (instead of *lavadora*) from washing machine. Tex-Mex argot, created by adding a Spanish sound at the beginning or end of an English word such as *cookiar* for cook, *watchar* for watch, *parkiar* for park, and *rapiar* for rape, is the result of the pressures on Spanish speakers to adapt to English.

We don't use the word *vosotros/as* or its accompanying verb form. We don't say *claro* (to mean yes), *imagínate*, or *me emociona,* unless we picked up Spanish from Latinas, out of a book, or in a classroom. Other Spanish-speaking groups are going through the same, or similar, development in their Spanish.

Linguistic Terrorism

> *Deslenguadas. Somos los del español deficiente.* We are your linguistic nightmare, your linguistic aberration, your linguistic *mestizaje,* the subject of your *burla.* Because we speak with tongues of fire we are culturally crucified. Racially, culturally and linguistically *somos huérfanos—*we speak an orphan tongue.

Chicanas who grew up speaking Chicano Spanish have internalized the belief that we speak poor Spanish. It is illegitimate, a bastard language. And because we internalize how our language has been used against us by the dominant culture, we use our language differences against each other.

Chicana feminists often skirt around each other with suspicion and hesitation. For the longest time I couldn't figure it out. Then it dawned on me. To be close to another Chicana is like looking into the mirror. We are afraid of what we'll see there. *Pena.* Shame. Low estimation of self. In childhood we are told that our language is wrong. Repeated attacks on our native tongue diminish our sense of self. The attacks continue throughout our lives.

Chicanas feel uncomfortable talking in Spanish to Latinas, afraid of their censure. Their language was not outlawed in their countries. They had a whole lifetime of being immersed in their native tongue; generations, centuries in which Spanish was a first language, taught in school, heard on radio and TV, and read in the newspaper.

If a person, Chicana or Latina, has a low estimation of my native tongue, she also has a low estimation of me. Often with *mexicanas y latinas* we'll speak English as a neutral language. Even among Chicanas we tend to speak English at parties or conferences. Yet, at the same time, we're afraid the other will think we're *agringadas* because we don't speak Chicano Spanish. We oppress each other trying to out-Chicano each other, vying to be the "real" Chicanas, to speak like Chicanos. There is no one Chicano language just as there is no one Chicano experience. A monolingual Chicana whose first language is English or Spanish is just as much a Chicana as one who speaks several variants of Spanish. A Chicana from Michigan or Chicago or Detroit is just as much a Chicana as one from the Southwest. Chicano Spanish is as diverse linguistically as it is regionally.

By the end of this century, Spanish speakers will comprise the biggest minority group in the U.S., a country where students in high schools and colleges are encouraged to take French classes because French is considered more "cultured." But for a language to remain alive it must be used.[6] By the end of this century English, and not Spanish, will be the mother tongue of most Chicanos and Latinos.

So, if you want to really hurt me, talk badly about my language. Ethnic identity is twin skin to linguistic identity—I am my language. Until I can take pride in my language, I cannot take pride in myself. Until I can accept as legitimate Chicano Texas Spanish, Tex-Mex and all the other languages I speak, I cannot accept the legitimacy of myself. Until I am free to write bilingually and to switch codes without having always to translate, while I still have to speak English or Spanish when I would rather speak Spanglish, and as long as I have to accommodate the English speakers rather than having them accommodate me, my tongue will be illegitimate.

I will no longer be made to feel ashamed of existing. I will have my voice: Indian, Spanish, white. I will have my serpent's tongue—my woman's voice, my sexual voice, my poet's voice. I will overcome the tradition of silence.

> My fingers
> move sly against your palm
> Like women everywhere, we speak in code . . . .
> —Melanie Kaye/Kantrowitz[7]

"Vistas," corridos, y comida: My Native Tongue

In the 1960s, I read my first Chicano novel. It was *City of Night* by John Rechy, a gay Texan, son of a Scottish father and a Mexican mother. For days I walked around in stunned amazement that a Chicano could write and could get published. When I read *I Am Joaquín*[8] I was surprised to see a bilingual book by a Chicano in print. When I saw poetry written in Tex-Mex for the first time, a feeling of pure joy flashed through me. I felt like we really existed as a people. In 1971, when I started teaching High School English to Chicano students, I tried to supplement the required texts with works by Chicanos, only to be reprimanded and forbidden to do so by the principal. He claimed that I was supposed to teach "American" and English literature. At the risk of being fired, I swore my students to secrecy and slipped in Chicano short stories, poems, a play. In graduate school, while working toward a Ph.D., I had to "argue" with one advisor after the other, semester after semester, before I was allowed to make Chicano literature an area of focus.

Even before I read books by Chicanos or Mexicans, it was the Mexican movies I saw at the drive-in—the Thursday night special of $1.00 a carload—that gave me a sense of belonging. *"Vámonos a las vistas,"* my mother would call out and we'd all—grandmother, brothers, sister and cousins—squeeze into the car. We'd wolf down cheese and bologna white bread sandwiches while watching Pedro Infante in melodramatic tear-jerkers like *Nosotros los pobres,* the first "real" Mexican movie (that was not an imitation of European movies). I remember seeing *Cuando los hijos se van* and surmising that all Mexican movies played up the love a mother has for her children and what ungrateful sons and daughters suffer when they are not devoted to their mothers. I remember the singing-type "westerns" of Jorge Negrete and Miguel Aceves Mejía. When watching Mexican movies, I felt a sense of homecoming as well as alienation. People who were to amount to something didn't go to Mexican movies, or *bailes* or tune their radios to *bolero, rancherita,* and *corrido* music.

The whole time I was growing up, there was *norteño* music sometimes called North Mexican border music, or Tex-Mex music, or Chicano music, or *cantina* (bar) music. I grew up listening to *conjuntos,* three- or four-piece bands made up of folk musicians playing guitar, *bajo sexto,* drums and button accordion, which Chicanos had borrowed from the German immigrants who had come to Central Texas and Mexico to farm and build breweries. In the Rio Grande Valley, Steve Jordan and Little Joe Hernández were popular, and Flaco Jiménez was the accordion king. The rhythms of Tex-Mex music are those of the polka, also adapted from the Germans, who in turn had borrowed the polka from the Czechs and Bohemians.

I remember the hot, sultry evenings when *corridos*—songs of love and death on the Texas-Mexican borderlands—reverberated out of cheap amplifiers from the local *cantinas* and wafted in through my bedroom window.

Corridos first became widely used along the South Texas/ Mexican border during the early conflict between Chicanos and Anglos. The *corridos* are usually about Mexican heroes who do valiant deeds against the Anglo oppressors. Pancho Villa's song, *"La cucaracha,"* is the most famous one. *Corridos* of John F. Kennedy and his death are still very popular in the Valley. Older Chicanos remember Lydia Mendoza, one of the great border *corrido* singers who was called *la Gloria de Tejas*. Her *"El tango negro,"* sung during the Great Depression, made her a singer of the people. The everpresent *corridos* narrated one hundred years of border history, bringing news of events as well as entertaining. These folk musicians and folk songs are our chief cultural mythmakers, and they made our hard lives seem bearable.

I grew up feeling ambivalent about our music. Country-western and rock-and-roll had more status. In the 50s and 60s, for the slightly educated and *agringado* Chicanos, there existed a sense of shame at being caught listening to our music. Yet I couldn't stop my feet from thumping to the music, could not stop humming the words, nor hide from myself the exhilaration I felt when I heard it.

There are more subtle ways that we internalize identification, especially in the forms of images and emotions. For me food and certain smells are tied to my identity, to my homeland. Woodsmoke curling up to an immense blue sky; woodsmoke perfuming my grandmother's clothes, her skin. The stench of cow manure and the yellow patches on the ground; the crack of a .22 rifle and the reek of cordite. Homemade white cheese sizzling in a pan, melting inside a folded *tortilla*. My sister Hilda's hot, spicy *menudo, chile colorado* making it deep red, pieces of *panza* and hominy floating on top. My brother Carito barbecuing *fajitas* in the backyard. Even now and 3,000 miles away, I can see my mother spicing the ground beef, pork and venison with *chile*. My mouth salivates at the thought of the hot steaming *tamales* I would be eating if I were home.

Si le preguntas a mi mamá, "¿Qué eres?"

> "Identity is the essential core of who
> we are as individuals, the conscious
> experience of the self inside."
> —Kaufman[9]

Nosotros los Chicanos straddle the borderlands. On one side of us, we are constantly exposed to the Spanish of the Mexicans, on the other side we hear the Anglos' incessant clamoring so that we forget our language. Among ourselves we don't say *nosotros los americanos, o nosotros los españoles, o nosotros los hispanos.* We say *nosotros los mexicanos* (by *mexicanos* we do not mean citizens of Mexico; we do not mean a national identity, but a racial one). We distinguish between *mexicanos del otro lado* and *mexicanos de este lado.* Deep in our hearts we believe that being Mexican has nothing to do with which country one lives in. Being Mexican is a state of soul—not one of mind, not one of citizenship. Neither eagle nor serpent, but both. And like the ocean, neither animal respects borders.

> *Dime con quien andas y te diré quien eres.*
> (Tell me who your friends are and I'll tell you who
> you are.)
> —Mexican saying

Si le preguntas a mi mamá, "¿Qué eres?" te dirá, "Soy mexicana." My brothers and sister say the same. I sometimes will answer *"soy mexicana"* and at others will say *"soy Chicana" o "soy tejana."* But I identified as *"Raza"* before I ever identified as *"mexicana"* or "Chicana."

As a culture, we call ourselves Spanish when referring to ourselves as a linguistic group and when copping out. It is then that we forget our predominant Indian genes. We are 70 to 80% Indian.[10] We call ourselves Hispanic[11] or Spanish-American or Latin American or Latin when linking ourselves to other Spanish-speaking peoples of the Western hemisphere and when copping out. We call ourselves Mexican-American[12] to signify we are neither Mexican nor American, but more the noun "American" than the adjective "Mexican" (and when copping out).

Chicanos and other people of color suffer economically for not acculturating. This voluntary (yet forced) alienation makes for psychological conflict, a kind of dual identity—we don't identify with the Anglo-American cultural values and we don't totally identify with the Mexican cultural values. We are a synergy of two cultures with various degrees of Mexicanness or Angloness. I have so internalized the borderland conflict that sometimes I feel like one cancels out the other and we are zero, nothing, no one. *A veces no soy nada ni nadie. Pero hasta cuando no lo soy, lo soy.*

When not copping out, when we know we are more than nothing, we call ourselves Mexican, referring to race and ancestry; *mestizo* when affirming both our Indian and Spanish (but we hardly ever own our Black ancestry); Chicano when referring to a politically aware people born and/or raised in the U.S.; *Raza* when referring to Chicanos; *tejanos* when we are Chicanos from Texas.

Chicanos did not know we were a people until 1965 when Cesar Chavez and the farmworkers united and *I Am Joaquín* was published and *la Raza Unida* party was formed in Texas. With that recognition, we became a distinct people. Something momentous happened to the Chicano soul—we became aware of our reality and acquired a name and a language (Chicano Spanish) that reflected that reality. Now that we had a name, some of the fragmented pieces began to fall together—who we were, what we were, how we had evolved. We began to get glimpses of what we might eventually become.

Yet the struggle of identities continues, the struggle of borders is our reality still. One day the inner struggle will cease and a true integration take place. In the meantime, *tenemos que hacerla lucha. ¿Quién está protegiendo los ranchos de mi gente? ¿Quién está tratando de cerrar la fisura entre la india y el blanco en nuestra sangre? El Chicano, sí, el Chicano que anda como un ladrón en su propia casa.*

Los Chicanos, how patient we seem, how very patient. There is the quiet of the Indian about us.[13] We know how to survive. When other races have given up their tongue, we've kept ours. We know what it is to live under the hammer blow of the dominant *norteamericano* culture. But more than we count the blows, we count the days the weeks the years the centuries the eons until the white laws and commerce and customs will rot in the deserts they've created, lie bleached. *Humildes* yet proud, *quietos* yet wild, *nosotros los mexicanos*-Chicanos will walk by the crumbling ashes as we go about our business. Stubborn, persevering, impenetrable as stone, yet possessing a malleability that renders us unbreakable, we, the *mestizas* and *mestizos,* will remain.

6

Tlilli, Tlapalli

The Path of the Red and Black Ink

"Out of poverty, poetry;
out of suffering, song."
—a Mexican saying

When I was seven, eight, nine, fifteen, sixteen years old, I
would read in bed with a flashlight under the covers, hiding
my self-imposed insomnia from my mother. I preferred the
world of the imagination to the death of sleep. My sister,
Hilda, who slept in the same bed with me, would threaten
to tell my mother unless I told her a story.

I was familiar with *cuentos*—my grandmother told stories
like the one about her getting on top of the roof while down
below rabid coyotes were ravaging the place and wanting to
get at her. My father told stories about a phantom giant dog
that appeared out of nowhere and sped along the side of the
pickup no matter how fast he was driving.

Nudge a Mexican and she or he will break out with a story.
So, huddling under the covers, I made up stories for my
sister night after night. After a while she wanted two stories
per night. I learned to give her installments, building up
the suspense with convoluted complications until the story
climaxed several nights later. It must have been then that
I decided to put stories on paper. It must have been then
that working with images and writing became connected
to night.

Invoking Art

In the ethno-poetics and performance of the shaman, my people, the Indians, did not split the artistic from the functional, the sacred from the secular, art from everyday life. The religious, social and aesthetic purposes of art were all intertwined. Before the Conquest, poets gathered to play music, dance, sing and read poetry in open-air places around the *Xochicuahuitl, el Árbol Florido,* Tree-in-Flower. (The *Coaxihuitl* or morning glory is called the snake plant and its seeds, known as *ololiuhqui,* are hallucinogenic.[1]) The ability of story (prose and poetry) to transform the storyteller and the listener into something or someone else is shamanistic. The writer, as shape-changer, is a *nahual,* a shaman.

In looking at this book that I'm almost finished writing, I see a mosaic pattern (Aztec-like) emerging, a weaving pattern, thin here, thick there. I see a preoccupation with the deep structure, the underlying structure, with the gesso underpainting that is red earth, black earth. I can see the deep structure, the scaffolding. If I can get the bone structure right, then putting flesh on it proceeds without too many hitches. The problem is that the bones often do not exist prior to the flesh, but are shaped after a vague and broad shadow of its form is discerned or uncovered during beginning, middle and final stages of the writing. Numerous overlays of paint, rough surfaces, smooth surfaces make me realize I am preoccupied with texture as well. Too, I see the barely contained color threatening to spill over the boundaries of the object it represents and into other "objects" and over the borders of the frame. I see a hybridization of metaphor, different species of ideas popping up here, popping up there, full of variations and seeming contradictions, though I believe in an ordered, structured universe where all phenomena are interrelated and imbued with spirit. This almost finished product seems an assemblage, a montage, a beaded work with several leitmotifs and with a central core, now appearing, now disappearing in a crazy dance. The whole thing has had a mind of its own, escaping me and insisting on putting together the pieces of its own puzzle with minimal direction from my will. It is a rebellious, willful entity, a precocious girl-child forced to grow up too quickly, rough, unyielding, with pieces of feather sticking out here and there, fur, twigs, clay. My child, but not for much longer. This female being is angry, sad, joyful, is *Coatlicue,* dove, horse, serpent, cactus. Though it is a flawed thing—a clumsy, complex, groping blind thing—for me it is alive, infused with spirit. I talk to it; it talks to me.

I make my offerings of incense and cracked corn, light my candle. In my head I sometimes will say a prayer—an affirmation and a voicing of intent. Then I run water, wash the dishes or my underthings, take a bath, or mop the kitchen floor. This "induction" period sometimes takes a few minutes, sometimes hours. But always I go against a resistance. Something in me does not want to do this writing. Yet once I'm immersed in it, I can go fifteen to seventeen hours in one sitting and I don't want to leave it.

My "stories" are acts encapsulated in time, "enacted" every time they are spoken aloud or read silently. I like to think of them as performances and not as inert and "dead" objects (as the aesthetics of Western culture think of art works). Instead, the work has an identity; it is a "who" or a "what" and contains the presences of persons, that is, incarnations of gods or ancestors or natural and cosmic powers. The work manifests the same needs as a person, it needs to be "fed," *la tengo que bañar y vestir.*

When invoked in rite, the object/event is "present"; that is, enacted," it is both a physical thing and the power that infuses it. It is metaphysical in that it "spins its energies between gods and humans" and its task is to move the gods. This type of work dedicates itself to managing the universe and its energies. I'm not sure what it is when it is at rest (not in performance). It may or may not be a "work" then. A mask may only have the power of presence during a ritual dance and the rest of the time it may merely be a "thing." Some works exist forever invoked, always in performance. I'm thinking of totem poles, cave paintings. Invoked art is communal and speaks of everyday life. It is dedicated to the validation of humans; that is, it makes people hopeful, happy, secure, and it can have negative effects as well, which propel one towards a search for validation.[2]

The aesthetic of virtuosity, art typical of Western European cultures, attempts to manage the energies of its own internal system such as conflicts, harmonies, resolutions and balances. It bears the presences of qualities and internal meanings. It is dedicated to the validation of itself. Its task is to move humans by means of achieving mastery in content, technique, feeling. Western art is always whole and always "in power." It is individual (not communal). It is "psychological" in that it spins its energies between itself and its witness.[3]

Western cultures behave differently toward works of art than do tribal cultures. The "sacrifices" Western cultures make are in housing their art works in the best structures designed by the best architects; and in servicing them with insurance, guards to protect them, conservators to maintain them, specialists to mount and display them, and the educated and upper classes to "view" them. Tribal cultures keep art works in honored and sacred places in the home and elsewhere. They attend them by making sacrifices of blood (goat or chicken), libations of wine. They bathe, feed, and clothe them. The works are treated not just as objects, but also as persons. The "witness" is a participant in the enactment of the work in a ritual, and not a member of the privileged classes.[4]

Ethnocentrism is the tyranny of Western aesthetics. An Indian mask in an American museum is transposed into an alien aesthetic system where what is missing is the presence of power invoked through performance ritual. It has become a conquered thing, a dead "thing" separated from nature and, therefore, its power.

Modern Western painters have "borrowed," copied, or otherwise extrapolated the art of tribal cultures and called it cubism, surrealism, symbolism. The music, the beat of the drum, the Blacks' jive talk. All taken over. Whites, along with a good number of our own people, have cut themselves off from their spiritual roots, and they take our spiritual art objects in an unconscious attempt to get them back. If they're going to do it, I'd like them to be aware of what they are doing and to go about doing it the right way. Let's all stop importing Greek myths and the Western Cartesian split point of view and root ourselves in the mythological soil and soul of this continent. White America has only attended to the body of the earth in order to exploit it, never to succor it or to be nurtured in it. Instead of surreptitiously ripping off the vital energy of people of color and putting it to commercial use, whites could allow themselves to share and exchange and learn from us in a respectful way. By taking up *curanderismo,* Santeria, shamanism, Taoism, Zen and otherwise delving into the spiritual life and ceremonies of multi-colored people, Anglos would perhaps lose the white sterility they have in their kitchens, bathrooms, hospitals, mortuaries and missile bases. Though in the conscious mind, black and dark may be associated with death, evil and destruction, in the subconscious mind and in our dreams, white is associated with disease, death and hopelessness. Let us hope that the left hand, that of darkness, of femaleness, of "primitiveness," can divert the indifferent, right-handed, "rational" suicidal drive that, unchecked, could blow us into acid rain in a fraction of a millisecond.

Ni cuicani: I, the Singer

For the ancient Aztecs, *tlilli, tlapalli, la tinta negra y roja de sus códices* (the black and red ink painted on codices) were the colors symbolizing *escritura y sabiduría* (writing and wisdom).[5] They believed that through metaphor and symbol, by means of poetry and truth, communication with the Divine could be attained, and *topan* (that which is above—the gods and spirit world) could be bridged with *mictlán* (that which is below—the underworld and the region of the dead).

Poet: she pours water from the mouth of the pump, lowers the handle then lifts it, lowers, lifts. Her hands begin to feel the pull from the entrails, the live animal resisting. A sigh rises up from the depths, the handle becomes a wild thing in her hands, the cold sweet water gushes out, splashing her face, the shock of nightlight filling the bucket.

An image is a bridge between evoked emotion and conscious knowledge; words are the cables that hold up the bridge. Images are more direct, more immediate than words, and closer to the unconscious. Picture language precedes thinking in words; the metaphorical mind precedes analytical consciousness.

The Shamanic State

When I create stories in my head, that is, allow the voices and scenes to be projected in the inner screen of my mind, I "trance." I used to think I was going crazy or that I was having hallucinations. But now I realize it is my job, my calling, to traffic in images. Some of these film-like narratives I write down; most are lost, forgotten. When I don't write the images down for several days or weeks or months, I get physically ill. Because writing invokes images from my unconscious, and because some of the images are residues of trauma which I then have to reconstruct, I sometimes get sick when I *do* write. I can't stomach it, become nauseous, or burn with fever, worsen. But, in reconstructing the traumas behind the images, I make "sense" of them, and once they have "meaning" they are changed, transformed. It is then that writing heals me, brings me great joy.

To facilitate the "movies" with soundtracks, I need to be alone, or in a sensory-deprived state. I plug up my ears with wax, put on my black cloth eye-shades, lie horizontal and unmoving, in a state between sleeping and waking, mind and body locked into my fantasy. I am held prisoner by it. My body is experiencing events. In the beginning it is like being in a movie theater, as pure spectator. Gradually I become so engrossed with the activities, the conversations, that I become a participant in the drama. I have to struggle to "disengage" or escape from my "animated story," I have to get some sleep so I can write tomorrow. Yet I am gripped by a story which won't let me go. Outside the frame, I am film director, screenwriter, camera operator. Inside the frame, I am the actors—male and female—I am desert sand, mountain, I am dog, mosquito. I can sustain a four- to six-hour "movie." Once I am up, I can sustain several "shorts" of anywhere between five and thirty minutes. Usually these "narratives" are the offspring of stories acted out in my head during periods of sensory deprivation.

My "awakened dreams" are about shifts. Thought shifts, reality shifts, gender shifts: one person metamorphoses into another in a world where people fly through the air, heal from mortal wounds. I am playing with my Self, I am playing with the world's soul, I am the dialogue between my Self and *el espíritu del mundo*. I change myself, I change the world.

Sometimes I put the imagination to a more rare use. I choose words, images, and body sensations and animate them to impress them on my consciousness, thereby making changes in my belief system and reprogramming my consciousness. This involves looking my inner demons in the face, then deciding which I want in my psyche. Those I don't want, I starve; I feed them no words, no images, no feelings. I spend no time with them, share not my home with them. Neglected, they leave. This is harder to do than to merely generate "stories." I can only sustain this activity for a few minutes.

I write the myths in me, the myths I am, the myths I want to become. The word, the image and the feeling have a palpable energy, a kind of power. *Con imágenes domo mi miedo, cruzo los abismos que tengo por dentro. Con palabras me hago piedra, pájaro, puente de serpientes arrastrando a ras del suelo todo lo que soy, todo lo que algún día seré.*

> *Los que están mirando (leyendo),*
> *los que cuentan (o refieren lo que leen).*
> *Los que vuelven ruidosamente las hojas de los códices.*
> *Los que tienen en su poder*
> *la tinta negra y roja (la sabiduría)*
> *y lo pintado,*
> *ellos nos llevan, nos guían,*
> *nos dicen el camino.*[6]

Writing Is A Sensuous Act

Tallo mi cuerpo como si estuviera lavando un trapo. Toco las saltadas venas de mis manos, mis chichis adormecidas como pájaras al anochecer. Estoy encorvada sobre la cama. Las imágenes aletean alrededor de mi cama como murciélagos, la sábana como que tuviese alas. El ruido de los trenes subterráneos en mi sentido como conchas. Parece que las paredes del cuarto se me arriman cada vez más cerquita.

Picking out images from my soul's eye, fishing for the right words to recreate the images. Words are blades of grass pushing past the obstacles, sprouting on the page; the spirit of the words moving in the body is as concrete as flesh and as palpable; the hunger to create is as substantial as fingers and hand.

I look at my fingers, see plumes growing there. From the fingers, my feathers, black and red ink drips across the page. *Escribo con la tinta de mi sangre.* I write in red. Ink. Intimately knowing the smooth touch of paper, its speechlessness before I spill myself on the insides of trees. Daily, I battle the silence and the red. Daily, I take my throat in my hands and squeeze until the cries pour out, my larynx and soul sore from the constant struggle.

Something To Do With the Dark

> *Quien canta, sus males espanta.*
> —*un dicho*

The toad comes out of its hiding place inside the lobes of my brain. It's going to happen again. The ghost of the toad that betrayed me—I hold it in my hand. The toad is sipping the strength from my veins, it is sucking my pale heart. I am a dried serpent skin, wind scuttling me across the hard ground, pieces of me scattered over the countryside. And there in the dark I meet the crippled spider crawling in the gutter, the day-old newspaper fluttering in the dirty rain water.

> *Musa bruja, venga. Cúbrese con una sábana y espante mis demonios que a rempujones y a cachetadas me roban la pluma me rompen el sueño. Musa, ¡misericordia!*
>
> *Óigame, musa bruja. ¿Por qué huye uste' en mi cara? Su grito me desarrolla de mi caracola, me sacude el alma. Vieja, quítese de aquí con sus alas de navaja. Ya no me despedaze mi cara. Vaya con sus pinche uñas que me desgarran de los ojos hasta los talones. Váyese a la tiznada. Que no me coman, le digo, Que no me coman sus nueve dedos caníbales.*
>
> *Hija negra de la noche, carnala, ¿Por qué me sacas las tripas, por qué cardas mis entrañas? Este hilvanando palabras con tripas me está matando. Jija de la noche ¡vete a la chingada!*

Writing produces anxiety. Looking inside myself and my experience, looking at my conflicts, engenders anxiety in me. Being a writer feels very much like being a Chicana, or being queer—a lot of squirming, coming up against all sorts of walls. Or its opposite: nothing defined or definite, a boundless, floating state of limbo where I kick my heels, brood, percolate, hibernate and wait for something to happen.

Living in a state of psychic unrest, in a Borderland, is what makes poets write and artists create. It is like a cactus needle embedded in the flesh. It worries itself deeper and deeper, and I keep aggravating it by poking at it. When it begins to fester I have to do something to put an end to the aggravation and to figure out why I have it. I get deep down into the place where it's rooted in my skin and pluck away at it, playing it like a musical instrument—the fingers pressing, making the pain worse before it can get better. Then out it comes. No more discomfort, no more ambivalence. Until another needle pierces the skin. That's what writing is for me, an endless cycle of making it worse, making it better, but always making meaning out of the experience, whatever it may be.

> My flowers shall not cease to live;
> my songs shall never end:
> I, a singer, intone them;
> they become scattered, they are spread about.
> —*Cantares mexicanos*

To write, to be a writer, I have to trust and believe in myself as a speaker, as a voice for the images. I have to believe that I can communicate with images and words and that I can do it well. A lack of belief in my creative self is a lack of belief in my total self and vice versa—I cannot separate my writing from any part of my life. It is all one.

When I write it feels like I'm carving bone. It feels like I'm creating my own face, my own heart—a Nahuatl concept. My soul makes itself through the creative act. It is constantly remaking and giving birth to itself through my body. It is this learning to live with *la Coatlicue* that transforms living in the Borderlands from a nightmare into a numinous experience. It is always a path/state to something else.

In *Xóchilt* in *Cuícatl* [7]

She writes while other people, sleep. Something is trying to come out. She fights the words, pushes them down, down, a woman with morning sickness in the middle of the night. How much easier it would be to carry a baby for nine months and then expel it permanently. These continuous multiple pregnancies are going to kill her. She is the battlefield for the pitched fight between the inner image and the words trying to recreate it. *La musa bruja* has no manners. Doesn't she know, nights are for sleeping?

She is getting too close to the mouth of the abyss. She is teetering on the edge, trying to balance while she makes up her mind whether to jump in or to find a safer way down. That's why she makes herself sick—to postpone having to jump blindfolded into the abyss of her own being and there in the depths confront her face, the face underneath the mask.

To be a mouth—the cost is too high—her whole life enslaved to that devouring mouth. *Todo pasaba por esa boca, el viento, el fuego, los mares y la Tierra.* Her body, a crossroads, a fragile bridge, cannot support the tons of cargo passing through it. She wants to install "stop" and "go" signal lights, instigate a curfew, police Poetry. But something wants to come out.

Blocks (*Coatlicue* states) are related to my cultural identity. The painful periods of confusion that I suffer from are symptomatic of a larger creative process: cultural shifts. The stress of living with cultural ambiguity both compels me to write and blocks me. It isn't until I'm almost at the end of the blocked state that I remember and recognize it for what it is. As soon as this happens, the piercing light of awareness melts the block and I accept the deep and the darkness and I hear one of my voices saying, "I am tired of fighting. I surrender. I give up, let go, let the walls fall. On this night of the hearing of faults, *Tlazolteotl, diosa de la cara negra,* let fall the cockroaches that live in my hair, the rats that nestle in my skull. Gouge out my lame eyes, rout my demon from its nocturnal cave. Set torch to the tiger that stalks me. Loosen the dead faces gnawing my cheekbones. I am tired of resisting. I surrender. I give up, let go, let the walls fall."

And in descending to the depths I realize that down is up, and I rise up from and into the deep. And once again I recognize that the internal tension of oppositions can propel (if it doesn't tear apart) the *mestiza* writer out of the *metate* where she is being ground with corn and water, eject her out as *nahual,* an agent of transformation, able to modify and shape primordial energy and therefore able to change herself and others into turkey, coyote, tree, or human.

I sit here before my computer, *Amiguita,* my altar on top of the monitor with the *Virgen de Coatlalopeuh* candle and copal incense burning. My companion, a wooden serpent staff with feathers, is to my right while I ponder the ways metaphor and symbol concretize the spirit and etherealize the body. The Writing is my whole life, it is my obsession. This vampire which is my talent does not suffer other suitors.[8] Daily I court it, offer my neck to its teeth. This is the sacrifice that the act of creation requires, a blood sacrifice. For only through the body, through the pulling of flesh, can the human soul be transformed. And for images, words, stories to have this transformative power, they must arise from the human body—flesh and bone—and from the Earth's body—stone, sky, liquid, soil. This work, these images, piercing tongue or ear lobes with cactus needle, are my offerings, are my Aztecan blood sacrifices.

7

La conciencia de la mestiza

Towards a New Consciousness

> *Por la mujer de mi raza*
> *hablará el espíritu.*[1]

José Vasconcelos, Mexican philosopher, envisaged *una raza mestiza, una mezcla de razas afines, una raza de color—la primera raza síntesis del globo.* He called it a cosmic race, *la raza cósmica,* a fifth race embracing the four major races of the world.[2] Opposite to the theory of the pure Aryan, and to the policy of racial purity that white America practices, his theory is one of inclusivity. At the confluence of two or more genetic streams, with chromosomes constantly "crossing over," this mixture of races, rather than resulting in an inferior being, provides hybrid progeny, a mutable, more malleable species with a rich gene pool. From this racial, ideological, cultural and biological cross-pollinization, an "alien" consciousness is presently in the making—a new *mestiza* consciousness, *una conciencia de mujer.* It is a consciousness of the Borderlands.

Una lucha de fronteras / A Struggle of Borders

> Because I, a *mestiza,*
> continually walk out of one culture
> and into another,
> because I am in all cultures at the same time,
> *alma entre dos mundos, tres, cuatro,*
> *me zumba la cabeza con lo contradictorio.*
> *Estoy norteada por todas las voces que me hablan*
> *simultáneamente.*

The ambivalence from the clash of voices results in mental and emotional states of perplexity. Internal strife results in insecurity and indecisiveness. The *mestiza*'s dual or multiple personality is plagued by psychic restlessness.

In a constant state of mental nepantilism, an Aztec word meaning torn between ways, *la mestiza* is a product of the transfer of the cultural and spiritual values of one group to another. Being tricultural, monolingual, bilingual, or multilingual, speaking a patois, and in a state of perpetual transition, the *mestiza* faces the dilemma of the mixed breed: which collectivity does the daughter of a darkskinned mother listen to?

El choque de un alma atrapado entre el mundo del espíritu y el mundo de la técnica a veces la deja entullada. Cradled in one culture, sandwiched between two cultures, straddling all three cultures and their value systems, *la mestiza* undergoes a struggle of flesh, a struggle of borders, an inner war. Like all people, we perceive the version of reality that our culture communicates. Like others having or living in more than one culture, we get multiple, often opposing messages. The coming together of two self-consistent but habitually incompatible frames of reference[3] causes *un choque,* a cultural collision.

Within us and within *la cultura chicana,* commonly held beliefs of the white culture attack commonly held beliefs of the Mexican culture, and both attack commonly held beliefs of the indigenous culture. Subconsciously, we see an attack on ourselves and our beliefs as a threat and we attempt to block with a counterstance.

But it is not enough to stand on the opposite river bank, shouting questions, challenging patriarchal, white conventions. A counterstance locks one into a duel of oppressor and oppressed; locked in mortal combat, like the cop and the criminal, both are reduced to a common denominator of violence. The counterstance refutes the dominant culture's views and beliefs, and, for this, it is proudly defiant. All reaction is limited by, and dependent on, what it is reacting against. Because the counterstance stems from a problem with authority—outer as well as inner—it's a step towards liberation from cultural domination. But it is not a way of life. At some point, on our way to a new consciousness, we will have to leave the opposite bank, the split between the two mortal combatants somehow healed so that we are on both shores at once and, at once, see through serpent and eagle eyes. Or perhaps we will decide to disengage from the dominant culture, write it off altogether as a lost cause, and cross the border into a wholly new and separate territory. Or we might go another route. The possibilities are numerous once we decide to act and not react.

A Tolerance For Ambiguity

These numerous possibilities leave *la mestiza* floundering in uncharted seas. In perceiving conflicting information and points of view, she is subjected to a swamping of her psychological borders. She has discovered that she can't hold concepts or ideas in rigid boundaries. The borders and walls that are supposed to keep the undesirable ideas out are entrenched habits and patterns of behavior; these habits and patterns are the enemy within. Rigidity means death. Only by remaining flexible is she able to stretch the psyche horizontally and vertically. *La mestiza* constantly has to shift out of habitual formations; from convergent thinking, analytical reasoning that tends to use rationality to move toward a single goal (a Western mode), to divergent thinking,[4] characterized by movement away from set patterns and goals and toward a more whole perspective, one that includes rather than excludes.

The new *mestiza* copes by developing a tolerance for contradictions, a tolerance for ambiguity. She learns to be an Indian in Mexican culture, to be Mexican from an Anglo point of view. She learns to juggle cultures. She has a plural personality, she operates in a pluralistic mode—nothing is thrust out, the good the bad and the ugly, nothing rejected, nothing abandoned. Not only does she sustain contradictions, she turns the ambivalence into something else.

She can be jarred out of ambivalence by an intense, and often painful, emotional event which inverts or resolves the ambivalence. I'm not sure exactly how. The work takes place underground—subconsciously. It is work that the soul performs. That focal point or fulcrum, that juncture where the *mestiza* stands, is where phenomena tend to collide. It is where the possibility of uniting all that is separate occurs. This assembly is not one where severed or separated pieces merely come together. Nor is it a balancing of opposing powers. In attempting to work out a synthesis, the self has added a third element which is greater than the sum of its severed parts. That third element is a new consciousness—a *mestiza* consciousness—and though it is a source of intense pain, its energy comes from continual creative motion that keeps breaking down the unitary aspect of each new paradigm.

En unas pocas centurias, the future will belong to the *mestiza.* Because the future depends on the breaking down of paradigms, it depends on the straddling of two or more cultures. By creating a new mythos—that is, a change in the way we perceive reality, the way we see ourselves, and the ways we behave—*la mestiza* creates a new consciousness.

The work of *mestiza* consciousness is to break down the subject-object duality that keeps her a prisoner and to show in the flesh and through the images in her work how duality is transcended. The answer to the problem between the white race and the colored, between males and females, lies in healing the split that originates in the very foundation of our lives, our culture, our languages, our thoughts. A massive uprooting of dualistic thinking in the individual and collective consciousness is the beginning of a long struggle, but one that could, in our best hopes, bring us to the end of rape, of violence, of war.

La encrucijada / The Crossroads

> A chicken is being sacrificed
>> at a crossroads, a simple mound of earth
> a mud shrine for *Eshu,*
>> *Yoruba* god of indeterminacy,
> who blesses her choice of path.
>> She begins her journey.

Su cuerpo es una bocacalle. La mestiza has gone from being the sacrificial goat to becoming the officiating priestess at the crossroads.

As a *mestiza* I have no country, my homeland cast me out; yet all countries are mine because I am every woman's sister or potential lover. (As a lesbian I have no race, my own people disclaim me; but I am all races because there is the queer of me in all races.) I am cultureless because, as a feminist, I challenge the collective cultural/religious male-derived beliefs of Indo-

Hispanics and Anglos; yet I am cultured because I am participating in the creation of yet another culture, a new story to explain the world and our participation in it, a new value system with images and symbols that connect us to each other and to the planet. *Soy un amasamiento,* I am an act of kneading, of uniting and joining that not only has produced both a creature of darkness and a creature of light, but also a creature that questions the definitions of light and dark and gives them new meanings.

We are the people who leap in the dark, we are the people on the knees of the gods. In our very flesh, (r)evolution works out the clash of cultures. It makes us crazy constantly, but if the center holds, we've made some kind of evolutionary step forward. *Nuestra alma el trabajo,* the opus, the great alchemical work; spiritual *mestizaje,* a "morphogenesis,"[5] an inevitable unfolding. We have become the quickening serpent movement.

Indigenous like corn, like corn, the *mestiza* is a product of crossbreeding, designed for preservation under a variety of conditions. Like an ear of corn—a female seed-bearing organ—the *mestiza* is tenacious, tightly wrapped in the husks of her culture. Like kernels she clings to the cob; with thick stalks and strong brace roots, she holds tight to the earth—she will survive the crossroads.

Lavando y remojando el maíz en agua de cal, despojando el pellejo. Moliendo, mixteando, amasando, haciendo tortillas de masa.[6] She steeps the corn in lime, it swells, softens. With stone roller on *metate,* she grinds the corn, then grinds again. She kneads and moulds the dough, pats the round balls into *tortillas.*

> We are the porous rock in the stone *metate*
> squatting on the ground.
> We are the rolling pin, *el maíz y agua,*
> *la masa harina. Somos el amasijo.*
> *Somos lo molido en el metate.*
> We are the *comal* sizzling hot,
> the hot *tortilla,* the hungry mouth.
> We are the coarse rock.
> We are the grinding motion,
> the mixed potion, *somos el molcajete.*
> We are the pestle, the *comino, ajo, pimienta,*

> We are the *chile colorado,*
> the green shoot that cracks the rock.
> We will abide.

El camino de la mestiza / The Mestiza Way

Caught between the sudden contraction, the breath sucked in and the endless space, the brown woman stands still, looks at the sky. She decides to go down, digging her way along the roots of trees. Sifting through the bones, she shakes them to see if there is any marrow in them. Then, touching the dirt to her forehead, to her tongue, she takes a few bones, leaves the rest in their burial place.

She goes through her backpack, keeps her journal and address book, throws away the muni-bart metromaps. The coins are heavy and they go next, then the greenbacks flutter through the air. She keeps her knife, can opener and eyebrow pencil. She puts bones, pieces of bark, *hierbas,* eagle feather, snakeskin, tape recorder, the rattle and drum in her pack and she sets out to become the complete *tolteca.*

Her first step is to take inventory. *Despojando, desgranando, quitando paja.* Just what did she inherit from her ancestors? This weight on her back—which is the baggage from the Indian mother, which the baggage from the Spanish father, which the baggage from the Anglo?

Pero es difícil differentiating between *lo heredado, lo adquirido, lo impuesto.* She puts history through a sieve, winnows out the lies, looks at the forces that we as a race, as women, have been a part of. *Luego bota lo que no vale, los desmientos, los desencuentos, el embrutecimiento. Aguarda el juicio, hondo y enraízado, de la gente antigua.* This step is a conscious rupture with all oppressive traditions of all cultures and religions. She communicates that rupture, documents the struggle. She reinterprets history and, using new symbols, she shapes new myths. She adopts new perspectives toward the darkskinned, women and queers. She strengthens her tolerance (and intolerance) for ambiguity. She is willing to share, to make herself vulnerable to foreign ways of seeing and thinking. She surrenders all notions of safety, of the familiar. Deconstruct, construct. She becomes a *nahual,* able to transform herself into a tree, a coyote, into another person. She learns to transform the small "I" into the total Self. *Se hace moldeadora de su alma. Según la concepción que tiene de sí misma, así será.*

Que no se nos olviden los hombres

> *"Tú no sirves pa' nada—*
> you're good for nothing.
> *Eres pura vieja."*

"You're nothing but a woman" means you are defective. Its opposite is to be *un macho*. The modern meaning of the word "machismo," as well as the concept, is actually an Anglo invention. For men like my father, being "macho" meant being strong enough to protect and support my mother and us, yet being able to show love. Today's macho has doubts about his ability to feed and protect his family. His "machismo" is an adaptation to oppression and poverty and low self-esteem. It is the result of hierarchical male dominance. The Anglo, feeling inadequate and inferior and powerless, displaces or transfers these feelings to the Chicano by shaming him. In the Gringo world, the Chicano suffers from excessive humility and self-effacement, shame of self and self-deprecation. Around Latinos he suffers from a sense of language inadequacy and its accompanying discomfort; with Native Americans he suffers from a racial amnesia which ignores our common blood, and from guilt because the Spanish part of him took their land and oppressed them. He has an excessive compensatory hubris when around Mexicans from the other side. It overlays a deep sense of racial shame.

The loss of a sense of dignity and respect in the macho breeds a false machismo which leads him to put down women and even to brutalize them. Coexisting with his sexist behavior is a love for the mother which takes precedence over that of all others. Devoted son, macho pig. To wash down the shame of his acts, of his very being, and to handle the brute in the mirror, he takes to the bottle, the snort, the needle, and the fist.

Though we "understand" the root causes of male hatred and fear, and the subsequent wounding of women, we do not excuse, we do not condone, and we will no longer put up with it. From the men of our race, we demand the admission/acknowledgment/disclosure/testimony that they wound us, violate us, are afraid of us and of our power. We need them to say they will begin to eliminate their hurtful put-down ways. But more than the words, we demand acts. We say to them: We will develop equal power with you and those who have shamed us.

It is imperative that *mestizas* support each other in changing the sexist elements in the Mexican-Indian culture. As long as woman is put down, the Indian and the Black in all of us is put down. The struggle of the *mestiza* is above all a feminist one. As long as *los hombres* think they have to *chingar mujeres* and each other to be men, as long as men are taught that they are superior and therefore culturally favored over *la mujer,* as long as to be a *vieja* is a thing of derision, there can be no real healing of our psyches. We're halfway there—we have such love of the Mother, the good mother. The first step is to unlearn the *puta/virgen* dichotomy and to see *Coatlalopeuh-Coatlicue* in the Mother, *Guadalupe.*

Tenderness, a sign of vulnerability, is so feared that it is showered on women with verbal abuse and blows. Men, even more than women, are fettered to gender roles. Women at least have had the guts to break out of bondage. Only gay men have had the courage to expose themselves to the woman inside them and to challenge the current masculinity. I've encountered a few scattered and isolated gentle straight men, the beginnings of a new breed, but they are confused, and entangled with sexist behaviors that they have not been able to eradicate. We need a new masculinity and the new man needs a movement.

Lumping the males who deviate from the general norm with man, the oppressor, is a gross injustice. *Asombra pensar que nos hemos quedado en ese pozo oscuro donde el mundo encierra a las lesbianas. Asombra pensar que hemos, como femenistas y lesbianas, cerrado nuestros corazónes a los hombres, a nuestros hermanos los jotos, desheredados y marginales como nosotros.* Being the supreme crossers of cultures, homosexuals have strong bonds with the queer white, Black, Asian, Native American, Latino, and with the queer in Italy, Australia and the rest of the planet. We come from all colors, all classes, all races, all time periods. Our role is to link people with each other—the Blacks with Jews with Indians with Asians with whites with extraterrestrials. It is to transfer ideas and information from one culture to another. Colored homosexuals have more knowledge of other cultures; have always been at the forefront (although sometimes in the closet) of all liberation struggles in this country; have suffered more injustices and have survived them despite all odds. Chicanos need to acknowledge the political and artistic contributions of their queer. People, listen to what your *jotería* is saying.

The *mestizo* and the queer exist at this time and point on the evolutionary continuum for a purpose. We are a blending that proves that all blood is intricately woven together, and that we are spawned out of similar souls.

Somos una gente

> *Hay tantísimas fronteras*
> *que dividen a la gente,*
> *pero por cada frontera*
> *existe también un puente.*
> —Gina Valdés[7]

Divided Loyalties. Many women and men of color do not want to have any dealings with white people. It takes too much time and energy to explain to the downwardly mobile, white middle-class women that it's okay for us to want to own "possessions," never having had any nice furniture on our dirt floors or "luxuries" like washing machines. Many feel that whites should help their own people rid themselves of race hatred and fear first. I, for one, choose to use some of my energy to serve as mediator. I think we need to allow whites to be our allies. Through our literature, art, *corridos,* and folktales we must share our history with them so when they set up committees to help Big Mountain Navajos or the Chicano farmworkers or *los Nicaragüenses* they won't turn people away because of their racial fears and ignorances. They will come to see that they are not helping us but following our lead.

Individually, but also as a racial entity, we need to voice our needs. We need to say to white society: We need you to accept the fact that Chicanos are different, to acknowledge your rejection and negation of us. We need you to own the fact that you looked upon us as less than human, that you stole our lands, our personhood, our self-respect. We need you to make public restitution: to say that, to compensate for your own sense of defectiveness, you strive for power over us, you erase our history and our experience because it makes you feel guilty—you'd rather forget your brutish acts. To say you've split yourself from minority groups, that you disown us, that your dual consciousness splits off parts of yourself, transferring the "negative" parts onto us. (Where there is persecution of minorities, there is shadow projection. Where there is violence and war, there is repression of shadow.) To say that you are afraid of us, that to put distance between us, you wear the mask of contempt. Admit that Mexico is your double, that she exists in the shadow of this country, that we are irrevocably tied to her. Gringo, accept the doppelganger in your psyche. By taking back your collective shadow the intracultural split will heal. And finally, tell us what you need from us.

By Your True Faces We Will Know You

I am visible—see this Indian face—yet I am invisible. I both blind them with my beak nose and am their blind spot. But I exist, we exist. They'd like to think I have melted in the pot. But I haven't, we haven't.

The dominant white culture is killing us slowly with its ignorance. By taking away our self-determination, it has made us weak and empty. As a people we have resisted and we have taken expedient positions, but we have never been allowed to develop unencumbered—we have never been allowed to be fully ourselves. The whites in power want us people of color to barricade ourselves behind our separate tribal walls so they can pick us off one at a time with their hidden weapons; so they can whitewash and distort history. Ignorance splits people, creates prejudices. A misinformed people is a subjugated people.

Before the Chicano and the undocumented worker and the Mexican from the other side can come together, before the Chicano can have unity with Native Americans and other groups, we need to know the history of their struggle and they need to know ours. Our mothers, our sisters and brothers, the guys who hang out on street corners, the children in the playgrounds, each of us must know our Indian lineage, our afro-*mestizaje,* our history of resistance.

To the immigrant *mexicano* and the recent arrivals we must teach our history. The 80 million *mexicanos* and the Latinos from Central and South America must know of our struggles. Each one of us must know basic facts about Nicaragua, Chile and the rest of Latin America. The Latinoist movement (Chicanos, Puerto Ricans, Cubans and other Spanish-speaking people working together to combat racial discrimination in the marketplace) is good but it is not enough. Other than a common culture we will have nothing to hold us together. We need to meet on a broader communal ground.

The struggle is inner: Chicano, *indio*, American Indian, *mojado*, *mexicano*, immigrant Latino, Anglo in power, working class Anglo, Black, Asian—our psyches resemble the bordertowns and are populated by the same people. The struggle has always been inner, and is played out in the outer terrains. Awareness of our situation must come before inner changes, which in turn come before changes in society. Nothing happens in the "real" world unless it first happens in the images in our heads.

El día de la Chicana

> I will not be shamed again
> Nor will I shame myself.

I am possessed by a vision: that we Chicanas and Chicanos have taken back or uncovered our true faces, our dignity and self-respect. It's a validation vision.

Seeing the Chicana anew in light of her history. I seek an exoneration, a seeing through the fictions of white supremacy, a seeing of ourselves in our true guises and not as the false racial personality that has been given to us and that we have given to ourselves. I seek our woman's face, our true features, the positive and the negative seen clearly, free of the tainted biases of male dominance. I seek new images of identity, new beliefs about ourselves, our humanity and worth no longer in question.

Estamos viviendo en la noche de la Raza, un tiempo cuando el trabajo se hace a lo quieto, en lo oscuro. El día cuando aceptamos tal y como somos y para donde vamos y porque—ese día será el día de la Raza. Yo tengo el conpromiso de expresar mi visión, mi sensibilidad, mi percepción de la revalidación de la gente mexicana, su mérito, estimación, honra, aprecio, y validez.

On December 2nd when my sun goes into my first house, I celebrate *el día de la Chicana y el Chicano.* On that day I clean my altars, light my *Coatlalopeuh* candle, burn sage and copal, take *el baño para espantar basura,* sweep my house. On that day I bare my soul, make myself vulnerable to friends and family by expressing my feelings. On that day I affirm who we are.

On that day I look inside our conflicts and our basic introverted racial temperament. I identify our needs, voice them. I acknowledge that the self and the race have been wounded. I recognize the need to take care of our personhood, of our racial self. On that day I gather the splintered and disowned parts of *la gente mexicana* and hold them in my arms. *Todas las partes de nosotros valen.*

On that day I say, "Yes, all you people wound us when you reject us. Rejection strips us of self-worth; our vulnerability exposes us to shame. It is our innate identity you find wanting. We are ashamed that we need your good opinion, that we need your acceptance. We can no longer camouflage our needs, can no longer let defenses and fences sprout around us. We can no longer withdraw. To rage and look upon you with contempt is to rage and be contemptuous of ourselves. We can no longer blame you, nor disown the white parts, the male parts, the pathological parts, the queer parts, the vulnerable parts. Here we are weaponless with open arms, with only our magic. Let's try it our way, the *mestiza* way, the Chicana way, the woman way."

On that day, I search for our essential dignity as a people, a people with a sense of purpose—to belong and contribute to something greater than our *pueblo.* On that day I seek to recover and reshape my spiritual identity. *¡Anímate! Raza, a celebrar el día de la Chicana.*

El retorno

> All movements are accomplished in six stages,
> and the seventh brings return.
> —I Ching[8]

> *Tanto tiempo sin verte casa mía,*
> *mi cuna, mi hondo nido de la huerta.*
> — *"Soledad"*[9]

I stand at the river, watch the curving, twisting serpent, a serpent nailed to the fence where the mouth of the Rio Grande empties into the Gulf.

I have come back. *Tanto dolor me costó el alejamiento.* I shade my eyes and look up. The bone beak of a hawk slowly circling over me, checking me out as potential carrion. In its wake a little bird flickering its wings, swimming sporadically like a fish. In the distance the expressway and the slough of traffic like an irritated sow. The sudden pull in my gut, *la tierra, los aguaceros.* My land, *el viento soplando la arena, el lagartijo debajo de un nopalito. Me acuerdo como era antes. Una región desértica de vasta llanuras, costeras de baja altura, de escasa lluvia, de chaparrales formados por mesquites y huizaches.* If I look real hard I can almost see the Spanish fathers who were called "the cavalry of Christ" enter this valley riding their *burros,* see the clash of cultures commence.

Tierra natal. This is home, the small towns in the Valley, *los pueblitos* with chicken pens and goats picketed to mesquite shrubs. *En las colonias* on the other side of the tracks, junk cars line the front yards of hot pink and lavender-trimmed houses— Chicano architecture we call it, self-consciously. I have missed the TV shows where hosts speak in half and half, and where awards are given in the category of Tex-Mex music. I have missed the Mexican cemeteries blooming with artificial flowers, the fields of aloe vera and red pepper, rows of sugar cane, of corn hanging on the stalks, the cloud of *polvareda* in the dirt roads behind a speeding pickup truck, *el sabor de tamales de rez y venado.* I have missed *la yegua colorada* gnawing the wooden gate of her stall, the smell of horse flesh from Carito's corrals. *Hecho menos las noches calientes sin aire, noches de linternas y lechuzas* making holes in the night.

I still feel the old despair when I look at the unpainted, dilapidated, scrap lumber houses consisting mostly of corrugated aluminum. Some of the poorest people in the U.S. live in the Lower Rio Grande Valley, an arid and semi-arid land of irrigated farming, intense sunlight and heat, citrus groves next to chaparral and cactus. I walk through the elementary school I attended so long ago, that remained segregated until recently. I remember how the white teachers used to punish us for being Mexican.

How I love this tragic valley of South Texas, as Ricardo Sánchez calls it; this borderland between the Nueces and the Rio Grande. This land has survived possession and ill-use by five countries: Spain, Mexico, the Republic of Texas, the U.S., the Confederacy, and the U.S. again. It has survived Anglo-Mexican blood feuds, lynchings, burnings, rapes, pillage.

Today I see the Valley still struggling to survive. Whether it does or not, it will never be as I remember it. The borderlands depression that was set off by the 1982 peso devaluation in Mexico resulted in the closure of hundreds of Valley businesses. Many people lost their homes, cars, land. Prior to 1982, U.S. store owners thrived on retail sales to Mexicans who came across the border for groceries and clothes and appliances. While goods on the U.S. side have become 10, 100, 1000 times more expensive for Mexican buyers, goods on the Mexican side have become 10, 100, 1000 times cheaper for Americans. Because the Valley is heavily dependent on agriculture and Mexican retail trade, it has the highest unemployment rates along the entire border region; it is the Valley that has been hardest hit.[10]

"It's been a bad year for corn," my brother, Nune, says. As he talks, I remember my father scanning the sky for a rain that would end the drought, looking up into the sky, day after day, while the corn withered on its stalk. My father has been dead for 29 years, having worked himself to death. The life span of a Mexican farm laborer is 56—he lived to be 38. It shocks me that I am older than he. I, too, search the sky for rain. Like the ancients, I worship the rain god and the maize goddess, but unlike my father I have recovered their names. Now for rain (irrigation) one offers not a sacrifice of blood, but of money.

"Farming is in a bad way," my brother says. "Two to three thousand small and big farmers went bankrupt in this country last year. Six years ago the price of corn was $8.00 per hundred pounds," he goes on. "This year it is $3.90 per hundred pounds." And, I think to myself, after taking inflation into account, not planting anything puts you ahead.

I walk out to the back yard, stare at *los rosales de mamá.* She wants me to help her prune the rose bushes, dig out the carpet grass that is choking them. *Mamagrande Ramona también tenía rosales.* Here every Mexican grows flowers. If they don't have a piece of dirt, they use car tires, jars, cans, shoe boxes. Roses are the Mexican's favorite flower. I think, how symbolic— thorns and all.

Yes, the Chicano and Chicana have always taken care of growing things and the land. Again I see the four of us kids getting off the school bus, changing into our work clothes, walking into the field with Papi and Mami, all six of us bending to the ground. Below our feet, under the earth lie the watermelon seeds. We cover them with paper plates, putting *terremotes* on top of the plates to keep them from being blown away by the wind. The paper plates keep the freeze away. Next day or the next, we remove the plates, bare the tiny green shoots to the elements. They survive and grow, give fruit hundreds of times the size of the seed. We water them and hoe them. We harvest them. The vines dry, rot, are plowed under. Growth, death, decay, birth. The soil prepared again and again, impregnated, worked on. A constant changing of forms, *renacimientos de la tierra madre.*

> This land was Mexican once
> was Indian always
> and is.
> And will be again.

Notes

The Homeland, Aztlán / *El otro México*

1. Los Tigres del Norte is a *conjunto* band.

2. Jack D. Forbes, <u>*Aztecas del Norte:* The Chicanos of Aztlán</u>. (Greenwich, CT: Fawcett Publications, Premier Books, 1973), 13, 183; Eric R. Wolf, <u>Sons of Shaking Earth</u> (Chicago, IL: University of Chicago Press, Phoenix Books, 1959), 32.

3. John R. Chávez, <u>The Lost Land: The Chicano Images of the Southwest</u> (Albuquerque, NM: University of New Mexico Press, 1984), 9.

4. Chávez, 9. Besides the Aztecs, the Ute, Gabrillino of California, Pima of Arizona, some Pueblo of New Mexico, Comanche of Texas, Opata of Sonora, Tarahumara of Sinaloa and Durango, and the Huichol of Jalisco speak Uto-Aztecan languages and are descended from the Cochise people.

5. Reay Tannahill, <u>Sex In History</u> (Briarcliff Manor, NY: Stein and Day/Publishers/Scarborough House, 1980), 308.

6. Chávez, 21.

7. Isabel Parra, <u>*El Libro Mayor de Violeta Parra*</u> (Madrid, España: Ediciones Michay, S.A., 1985), 156-7.

8. From the Mexican *corrido, "Del peligro de la Intervención"* Vicente T. Mendoza, <u>*El Corrido Mexicano*</u> (México. D.F.: Fondo De Cultura Económica, 1954), 42.

9. Arnoldo De León, <u>They Called Them Greasers: Anglo Attitudes Toward Mexicans in Texas, *1821-1900*</u> (Austin, TX: University of Texas Press, 1983), 2-3.

10. The Plan of San Diego, Texas, drawn up on January 6, 1915, called for the independence and segregation of the states bordering Mexico: Texas, New Mexico, Arizona, Colorado, and California. Indians would get their land back, Blacks would get six states from the south and form their own independent republic. Chávez, 79.

11. Jesús Mena, "Violence in the Rio Grande Valley," <u>*Nuestro*</u> (Jan/Feb. 1983), 41-42.

12. *Nosotros los pobres* was the first Mexican film that was truly Mexican and not an imitation European film. It stressed the devotion and love that children should have for their mother and how its lack would lead to the dissipation of their character. This film spawned a generation of mother-devotion/ungrateful-sons films.

13. From the Navajo "Protection Song" (to be sung upon going into battle). George W. Gronyn, ed., <u>American Indian Poetry: The Standard Anthology of Songs and Chants</u> (New York, NY: Liveright, 1934), 97.

14. Grace Halsell, _Los ilegales_, trans. Mayo Antonio Sánchez (Editorial Diana Mexica, 1979).

15. Margarita B. Melville, "Mexican Women Adapt to Migration," <u>International Migration Review</u>, 1978.

Movimientos de rebeldía y las culturas que traicionan

1. Francisco Guerra, <u>The Pre-Columbian Mind: A study into the aberrant nature of sexual drives, drugs affecting behaviour, and the attitude towards life and death, with a survey of psychotherapy in pre-Columbian America</u> (New York, NY: Seminar Press, 1971).

Entering Into the Serpent

1. From the song "_Sueño Con Serpientes_" by Silvio Rodrígues, from the album _Días y flores._ Translated by Barbara Dane with the collaboration of Rina Benmauor and Juan Flores.

2. _Nalgas:_ vagina, buttocks.

3. _Dicen que las culebras_ like to suck _chiches:_ they say snakes like to suck women's teats.

4. _Ella tiene su tono:_ she has supernatural power from her animal soul, the _tono._

5. _Quelite:_ weed.

6. _Azadón:_ hoe.

7. _Veneno:_ venom, poison.

8. _Culebra de cascabel:_ rattlesnake.

9. In some Nahuatl dialects _Tonantsi_ is called _Tonantzin,_ literally "Our Holy Mother." "_Tonan_ was a name given in Nahuatl to several mountains, these being the congelations of the Earth Mother at spots convenient for her worship." The Mexica considered the mountain mass southwest of Chapultepec to be their mother. Burr Cartwright Brundage, <u>The Fifth Sun: Aztec Gods, Aztec World</u> (Austin, TX: University of Texas Press,1979), 154, 242.

10. Ena Campbell, "The Virgin of Guadalupe and the Female Self -Image: A Mexican Case History," <u>Mother Worship: Themes and Variations,</u> James J. Preston, ed. (Chapel Hill, NC: University of North Carolina Press, 1982), 22.

11. Alan R. Sandstrom, "The Tonantsi Cult of the Eastern Nahuas," Mother Worship: Themes and Variations, James J. Preston, ed.

12. *Una tela tejida con ásperas fibras de agave.* It is an oblong cloth that hangs over the back and ties together across the shoulders.

13. Andres Gonzales Guerrero, Jr., The Significance of *Nuestra Señora de Guadalupe* and *La Raza Cósmica* in the Development of a Chicano Theology of Liberation (Ann Arbor, MI: University Microfilms International, 1984), 122.

14. *Algunos dicen que Guadalupe es una palabra derivida del lenguaje árabe que significa "Río Oculto."* Tomie de Paola, The Lady of Guadalupe (New York, NY: Holiday House, 1980), 44.

15. *"Desde el cielo una hermosa mañana,"* from *Propios de la misa de Nuestra Señora de Guadalupe*, Guerrero, 124.

16. From *"La Virgen Ranchera,"* Guerrero, 127.

17. *La Virgen María* is often equated with the Aztec *Teleoinam,* the Maya *Ixchel,* the Inca *Mamacocha* and the Yoruba *Yemayá.*

18. Geoffrey Parrinder, ed., World Religions: From Ancient History to the Present (NewYork, NY: Facts on File Publications, 1971), 72.

19. Levi-Strauss' paradigm which opposes nature to culture and female to male has no such validity in the early history of our Indian forebears. June Nash, "The Aztecs and the Ideology of Male Dominance," Signs (Winter, 1978), 349.

20. Parrinder, 72.

21. Parrinder, 77.

22. Nash, 352.

23. Nash, 350, 355.

24. Parrinder, 355.

25. Jacques Soustelle, The Daily Life of the Aztecs on the Eve of the Spanish Conquest (New York, NY: Macmillan Publishing Company, 1962). Soustelle and most other historians got their information from the Franciscan father, Bernardino de Sahagún, chief chronicler of Indian religious life.

26. Nash, 252-253.

27. Nash, 358.

28. Nash, 361-362.

29. Karl W. Luckert, <u>Olmec Religion: A Key to Middle America and Beyond</u> (Norman, OK: University of Oklahoma Press, 1976), 68, 69, 87, 109.

30. Bernardino de Sahagún, <u>General History of the Things of New Spain</u> (Florentine Codex), Vol.1 Revised, trans. Arthur Anderson and Charles Dibble (Santa Fe, NM: School of American Research, 1950), 11.

31. The Aztecs muted Snake Woman's patronage of childbirth and vegetation by placing a sacrificial knife in the empty cradle she carried on her back (signifying a child who died in childbirth), thereby making her a devourer of sacrificial victims. Snake Woman had the ability to change herself into a serpent or into a lovely young woman to entice young men who withered away and died after intercourse with her. She was known as a witch and a shape-shifter. Bundage, 168-171.

32. Anthropologist Lucien Levy-Bruhl coined the word *participation mystique*. According to Jung, "It denotes a peculiar kind of psychological connection . . . [in which] the subject cannot clearly distinguish himself from the object but is bound to it by a direct relationship which amounts to partial identity." Carl Jung, "Definitions," in <u>Psychological Types, The Collected Works of C.G. Jung</u>, Vol. 6 (Princeton, NJ: Princeton University Press, 1953), par. 781.

33. I have lost the source of this quote. If anyone knows what it is, please let the publisher know.

34. Some *mexicanos* and Chicanos distinguish between *aire*, air, and *mal aigre*, the evil spirits which reside in the air.

La herencia de Coatlicue / The *Coatlicue* State

1. Marius Schneider, <u>*El origen musical de los animales-símbolos en la mitología y la escultura antiguas*</u> (Barcelona, 1946).

2. C.A. Burland and Werner Forman, <u>Feathered Serpent and Smoking Mirror: The Gods and Cultures of Ancient Mexico</u> (New York, NY: G.P. Putnam & Sons, 1975), 55.

3. Gershen Kaufman, <u>Shame: The Power of Caring</u> (Cambridge, MA: Schenkman Books, Inc. 1980), viii. This book was instrumental in my understanding of shame.

4. Alfonsina Storni, <u>*Antología Poética, Séptima Edición*</u> (Buenos Aires, Argentina: Editorial Losada, S.A., 1956), 42.

5. The suffix "*cue*" means skirt and is a word to describe a lady. "*Coatl*" not only means serpent, it also means twin.

6. According to Jung and James Hillman, "archetypes" are the presences of gods and goddesses in the psyche. Hillman's book, Re-Visioning Psychology (New York, NY: Harper Colophon Books, 1975), has been instrumental in the development of my thought.

7. *Yemayá* is also known as the wind, *Oyá* as the whirlwind. According to Luisah Teish, I am the daughter of *Yemayá*, with *Oyá* being the mother who raised me.

8. Another form of the goddess *Coatlicue* is *Chimalma*, Shield Hand, a naked cave goddess of the Huitznahua who was present at Aztlán when the Aztecs left from that point of origin. Burland, 166-167.

9. A sculpture, described as the most horrifying and monstrous in the world, was excavated from beneath the Zocalo, the cathedral square in Mexico City, in 1824, where it had lain since the destruction of the Aztec capital of Tenochtitlán. Every year since the Conquest, people had come during an autumn festival with gifts of fruit and flowers which they laid on the pavement of the central square. The Indians maintained that there was somebody very holy and powerful underneath. Burland, 39-40.

10. Juan Eduardo Cirlot, A Dictionary of Symbols, translated from the Spanish by Jack Sage (New York, NY: Philosophical Library, 1962), 76.

How to Tame a Wild Tongue

1. Ray Gwyn Smith, Moorland is Cold Country, unpublished book.

2. Irena Klepfisz, "*Di rayze aheym*/The Journey Home," in The Tribe of Dina: A Jewish Women's Anthology, Melanie Kaye/Kantrowitz and Irena Klepfisz, eds. (Montpelier, VT: Sinister Wisdom Books, 1986), 49.

3. R.C. Ortega, *Dialectología Del Barrio*, trans. Hortencia S. Alwan (Los Angeles, CA: R.C. Ortega Publisher & Bookseller, 1977), 132.

4. Eduardo Hernandéz-Chávez, Andrew D. Cohen, and Anthony F. Beltramo, *El Lenguaje de los Chicanos:* Regional and Social Characteristics of Language Used By Mexican Americans (Arlington, VA: Center for Applied Linguistics, 1975), 39.

5. Hernandéz-Chávez, xvii.

6. Irena Klepfisz, "Secular Jewish Identity: Yidishkayt in America," in The Tribe of Dina Kaye/Kantrowitz and Klepfisz, eds., 43.

7. Melanie Kaye/Kantrowitz, "Sign," in We Speak In Code: Poems and Other Writings (Pittsburgh, PA: Motheroot Publications, Inc., 1980), 85.

8. Rodolfo Gonzales, I Am Joaquín / *Yo Soy Joaquín* (New York, NY: Bantam Books, 1972). It was first published in 1967.

9. Kaufman, 68.

10. Chávez, 88-90.

11. "Hispanic" is derived from *Hispanis* (*España*, a name given to the Iberian Peninsula in ancient times when it was a part of the Roman Empire) and is a term designated by the U.S. government to make it easier to handle us on paper.

12. The Treaty of Guadalupe Hidalgo created the Mexican-American in 1848.

13. Anglos, in order to alleviate their guilt for dispossessing the Chicano, stressed the Spanish part of us and perpetrated the myth of the Spanish Southwest. We have accepted the fiction that we are Hispanic, that is Spanish, in order to accommodate ourselves to the dominant culture and its abhorrence of Indians. Chávez, 88-91.

Tlilli, Tlapalli / The Path of the Red and Black Ink

1. R. Gordon Wasson, The Wondrous Mushroom: Mycolatry in Mesoamerica (New York, NY: McGraw-Hill Book Company, 1980), 59, 103.

2. Robert Plant Armstrong, The Powers of Presence: Consciousness, Myth, and Affecting Presence (Philadelphia, PA: University of Pennsylvania Press, 1981), 11, 20.

3. Armstrong, 10.

4. Armstrong, 4.

5. Miguel Leon-Portilla, *Los Antiguos Mexicanos:A través de sus cróni- cas y cantares* (México, D.F.: Fondo de Cultura Económica, 1961), 19, 22.

6. Leon-Portilla, 125.

7. In *Xóchitl* in *Cuícatl* is Nahuatl for flower and song, *flor y canto.*

8. Nietzsche, in The Will to Power, says that the artist lives under a curse of being vampirized by his talent.

La conciencia de la mestiza / Towards a New Consciousness

1. This is my own "take off" on José Vasconcelos' idea. José Vasconcelos, *La Raza Cósmica: Misión de la Raza Ibero-Americana* (México: Aguilar S.A. de Ediciones, 1961).

2. Vasconcelos.

3. Arthur Koestler termed this "bisociation." Albert Rothenberg, The Creative Process in Art, Science, and Other Fields (Chicago, IL: University of Chicago Press, 1979), 12.

4. In part, I derive my definitions for "convergent" and "divergent" thinking from Rothenberg, 12-13.

5. To borrow chemist Ilya Prigogine's theory of "dissipative structures." Prigogine discovered that substances interact not in predictable ways as it was taught in science, but in different and fluctuating ways to produce new and more complex structures, a kind of birth he called "morphogenesis," which created unpredictable innovations. Harold Gilliam, "Searching for a New World View," This World (January, 1981), 23.

6. *Tortillas de masa harina:* corn tortillas are of two types, the smooth uniform ones made in a tortilla press and usually bought at a tortilla factory or supermarket, and *gorditas,* made by mixing *masa* with lard or shortening or butter (my mother sometimes puts in bits of bacon or *chicharrones*).

7. Gina Valdés, *Puentes y Fronteras: Coplas Chicanas* (Los Angeles, CA: Castle Lithograph, 1982), 2.

8. Richard Wilhelm, The I Ching or Book of Changes, trans. Cary F. Baynes (Princeton, NJ: Princeton University Press, 1950), 98.

9. *"Soledad"* is sung by the group *Haciendo Punto en Otro Son.*

10. Out of the twenty-two border counties in the four border states, Hidalgo County (named for Father Hidalgo who was shot in 1810 after instigating Mexico's revolt against Spanish rule under the banner of *la Virgen de Guadalupe*) is the most poverty-stricken county in the nation as well as the largest home base (along with Imperial in California) for migrant farmworkers. It was here that I was born and raised. I am amazed that both it and I have survived.

Un Agitado Viento

Ehécatl, The Wind

I

Más antes en los ranchos

Dicen que no tengo duelo, Llorona,
porque no me ven llorar.
Hay muertos que no hacen ruido, Llorona
y es más grande su penar.
Ay de mí, Llorona.
    —*"La Llorona,"* a Mexican song

White-wing Season

The whitemen with their guns
        have come again
        to fill the silence and the sky
with buckshot.

        She shakes out the wrinkles
        snapping the sheets,
        they crack like thunder
            lean on the wind.

The *gringos* pull their caps
        down to their eyes
        hand her the bills,
the green flutter in her hand
will reshingle her roof.

        Once her tender arms raised up
        her brother's rifle
        pointed at the cooing sounds
        sprigs and two feathers floated down
            near her feet twitching plumage
            translucent eyelid blinking
            across its eye
            the small opened bill
            blood from its mouth

She pours blueing into the washtub
plunges her arms in
        puncturing the sky.
        She wrings the *sábanas*
        they sail and snap in the wind.
        Startled, plump bodies rise
        from the wooded areas and desert brush.
            The beating of feathers
            white patches on wings and tail.

The shots
feathers fall over the fields
cover her roof.

On their way back
to the midwest
the hunters drop two birds
on her washboard.

Her eyes shiny pellets
watching the wind
trying to lift their wings.
Tinges of pink
small twisted necks
line the furrows.

She dunks the doves in the boiling pot
plucks out the feathers

in her belly a rumble
the sky reddens then blackens
a flurry of night rain
gentle as feathers.

Cervicide

La venadita. The small fawn. They had to kill their pet, the fawn. The game warden was on the way with his hounds. The penalty for being caught in possession of a deer was $250 or jail. The game warden would put *su papi en la cárcel.*

How could they get rid of the fawn? Hide it? No, *la guardia*'s hounds would sniff Venadita out. Let Venadita loose in the *monte*? They had tried that before. The fawn would leap away and seconds later return. Should they kill Venadita? The mother and Prieta looked toward *las carabinas* propped against the wall behind the kitchen door—the shiny barrel of the.22, the heavy metal steel of the 40-40. No, if *they* could hear his pickup a mile and a half down the road, he would hear the shot.

Quick, they had to do something. Cut Venadita's throat? Club her to death? The mother couldn't do it. She, Prieta, would have to be the one. The game warden and his *perros* were a mile down the road. Prieta loved her *papi.*

In the shed behind the corral, where they'd hidden the fawn, Prieta found the hammer. She had to grasp it with both hands. She swung it up. The weight folded her body backwards. A thud reverberated on Venadita's skull, a wave undulated down her back. Again, a blow behind the ear. Though Venadita's long lashes quivered, her eyes never left Prieta's face. Another thud, another tremor. *La guardia* and his hounds were driving up the front yard. The *venadita* looked up at her, the hammer rose and fell. Neither made a sound. The tawny, spotted fur was the most beautiful thing Prieta had ever seen. She remembered when they had found the fawn. She had been a few hours old. A hunter had shot her mother. The fawn had been shaking so hard, her long thin legs were on the edge of buckling. Prieta and her sister and brothers had bottle-fed Venadita, with a damp cloth had wiped her skin, had watched her tiny, perfectly formed hooves harden and grow.

Prieta dug a hole in the shed, a makeshift hole. She could hear the warden talking to her mother. Her mother's English had suddenly gotten bad—she was trying to stall *la guardia*. Prieta rolled the fawn into the hole, threw in the empty bottle. With her fingers raked in the dirt. Dust caked on her arms and face where tears had fallen. She patted the ground flat with her hands and swept it with a dead branch. The game warden was strutting toward her. His hounds sniffing, sniffing, sniffing the ground in the shed. The hounds pawing, pawing the ground. The game warden, straining on the leashes, *les dio un tirón, sacó los perros.* He inspected the corrals, the edge of the woods, then drove away in his pickup.

Cervicide—the killing of a deer. In archetypal symbology the Self appears as a deer for women.

su papi en la cárcel—her father in jail

monte—the woods

Prieta—literally one who is dark-skinned, a nick-name

les dio un tirón, sacó los perros—jerked the dogs out

horse
(*para la gente de* Hargill, Texas)

Great horse running in the fields
come thundering toward
the outstretched hands
nostrils flaring at the corn
only it was knives in the hidden hands
can a horse smell tempered steel?

Anoche some kids cut up a horse
it was night and the *pueblo* slept
the Mexicans mutter among themselves:
they hobbled the two front legs
the two hind legs, kids aged sixteen
but they're *gringos*
and the sheriff won't do a thing
he'd just say boys will be boys
just following their instincts.

But it's the mind that kills
the animal the *mexicanos* murmur
killing it would have been a mercy
black horse running in the dark
came thundering toward
the outstretched hands
nostrils flaring at the smell
only it was knives in the hidden hands
did it pray all night for morning?

It was the owner came running
30-30 in his hand
put the *caballo* out of its pain
the Chicanos shake their heads
turn away some rich father
fished out his wallet
held out the folds of green
as if green could staunch red

pools dripping from the ribbons
on the horse's flanks
could cast up testicles
grow back the ears on the horse's head
no ears of corn but sheaths
hiding blades of steel
[earth drinking blood sun rusting it]
in that small Texas town
the *mexicanos* shuffle their feet
shut their faces stare at the ground.

Dead horse neighing in the night
come thundering toward the open faces
hooves iron-shod hurling lightning

only it is red red in the moonlight
in their sleep the *gringos* cry out
the *mexicanos* mumble if you're Mexican
you are born old.

Immaculate, Inviolate: *Como Ella*

She never lived with us
we had no bed for her
but she always came to visit.
A gift for *m'ijita*
two folded dollar bills secretly put in my hand.

I'd sit at her side
away from the bucket of *brasas*
enveloped *en el olor de vieja*
watch her roll her Buglar
yellowed talons plucking tobacco
knotted fingers rolling it thin, thinner,
tongue gumming edge of paper
sealing it pinching the ends
stroking it before striking match on thumbnail
watch smoke escape between chapped lips
curl through her white hair and pink skull.
They said at sixteen it had turned white overnight.

My grandmother could not tolerate heat.
She kept well away from fires.
A long time ago she burned herself.
She'd bent over the belly
of her woodburning stove
had seen no glimmer of a spark
had heaved up a can of kerosene

propping the edge on her hip
and cradling it to her chest
she'd let a few drops fall
on the charred sticks.
An invisible spark ignited
shot up the spout into her windpipe,
boom.
It took my uncle a long time
to carry the buckets of water from the well
soak the blankets
wrap them around her.

Mamá, usted ya no puede quedarse aquí sóla
They made her give up the ranchhouse
photographs, books, letters, yellowing
Armarios, pantry closets looted
rot growing under the covers

She'd stay two weeks with one, two with another
back and forth in her black dress
and with her thick *velices*
white sweat streaks across her round back
under arms
She never stopped wearing *luto*
first for my *papagrande*
who died before I was born
then for her brother
and, until she died eleven years ago
she wore black for my father
I didn't go to her funeral
[that too must have made her suffer]

Platícame del rancho Jesús María
de los Vergeles, Mamagrande
where I was reared
Tell me about the years of drought
the cattle with hoof 'n mouth
the rabid coyotes
And as she talked I saw her breathing in the fire
coughing up sooty spittle
skin blistering, becoming pus
nerve endings exposed
sweating, skin pallid, clammy
the nausea, the dizziness
swelling to twice her size

I watched the charred scars
on her throat and breasts
turn into parchment splotches
they catch the sheen of the coals
glow pink and lavender over the blue skin
She'd felt numb, she told me

her voice hoarse from the fire
or the constant cigarette in her mouth
as though frostbitten

Once I looked into her blue eyes
asked, Have you ever had an orgasm?
She kept quiet for a long time
Finally she looked into my brown eyes
told me how Papagrande would flip the skirt
of her nightgown over her head
and in the dark take out his *palo,* his stick
and do *lo que hacen todos los hombres*
while she laid back and prayed
he would finish quickly

She didn't like to talk about such things
Mujeres no hablan de cosas cochinas.
Her daughters, my *tías,* never liked to talk about it
their father's other women, their half-brothers

Sometimes when I get too close to the fire
and my face and chest catch the heat
I can almost see Mamagrande's face
watching him leave
taking her two eldest
to play with his other children
watching her sons *y los de la otra*
grow up together

I can almost see that look
settle on her face
then hide behind parchment skin
and clouds of smoke
Pobre doña Locha, so much dignity
everyone said she had
and pride

---

como ella—like her
m'ijita—an endearment; my dear daughter

brasas—live coals
usted ya no puede—You can't live here by yourself any longer.
armarios—cupboards
velices—suitcases
luto—mourning clothes
platícame del rancho—Tell me about the ranch.
lo que hacen todos los hombres—what all men do
mujeres no hablan—women don't talk about such filth
tías—aunts
y los de la otra—and those of his other woman

Nopalitos

It's that time of day
when the musty smell of dust hangs in the air
mingling with the scent of orange blossoms.
Dogs sprawl in the heat
tongues loll, drip saliva,
flanks ripple off flies.
The wind shifts.
I smell mesquite burning.

Next door in her back yard
la señora stirs a huge *olla* of *menudo*.
On the steps of the back porch
hunched over a bucket
I carefully pull out a sprig of mesquite
cushioning the top layer of cactus,

pluck out a tiny *nopalito*.
At the base of the stump I lay
the sharp blade
under the tender curl
sheathing each thorn.
A tangy green smell
seeps through the afternoon.

I throw the bleeding *nopal*
into a pan, pull out another.
It takes hours to defang cactus.
The thought of them: tender,
cooked in *chile colorado*
keeps me stooped over the *cubeta*
ignoring the tiny slivers
piercing my thumb.

Under the sighing leaves
and the lengthening shadows of the *palo blanco*
a *gallo* stretches his wings,
darts headlong toward a hen   pounces
beak seizing crest he pumps her.

Squawking she shakes him off,
fluffing her feathers

raining gold dust in the sunlight.
Overhead, the immense blue.
Across the road Tío Nasario unwinds his hose,
water mists dusk, jasmine, and rose.
The women gather on porches
in twos and threes, murmur
and rock, chairs lapping
the edges.
Their laughter swells over the garden,
laves me,
then evaporates in the still air.
Though I'm part of their *camaradería*
am one of them

I left and have been gone a long time.
I keep leaving and when I am home
they remember no one but me had ever left.
I listen to the *grillos* more intently
than I do their *regaños.*
I have more languages than they,
am aware of every root of my *pueblo;*
they, my people, are not.
They are the living, sleeping roots.

I sweep up mesquite leaves,
thorns embedded in my flesh,
stings behind my eyes.

Nopalitos—tender cactus leaves of the *nopal*
olla of *menudo*—black pot of a soup made of stomach, *chile colorado,*
  and hominy
cubeta—pail
palo blanco—a tree
gallo—rooster
grillos—cicadas
regaños—scoldings

·

II

La Pérdida

¡Qué lejos estoy del suelo donde he nacido!
intensa nostalgia invade mi pensamiento;
y al verme tan solo y triste cual hoja al viento,
quisiera llorar, quisiera morir de sentimiento.
   — *"Canción Mixteca,"* a Mexican *corrido*

sus plumas el viento
(for my mother, Amalia)

Swollen feet
tripping on vines in the heat,
palms thick and green-knuckled,
sweat drying on top of old sweat.
She flicks her tongue over upper lip
where the salt stings her cracked mouth.
Stupid Pepita and her jokes and the men licking
her heels,
but only the field boss,
un bolillo, of course, having any.

    Ayer entre las matas de maíz
    she had stumbled upon them:
    Pepita on her back
    grimacing to the sky,
    the anglo buzzing around her like a mosquito,
    landing on her, digging in, sucking.
    When Pepita came out of the irrigation ditch
    some of the men spit on the ground.

    She listens to Chula singing *corridos*
    making up *los versos* as she
    plants down the rows
    hoes down the rows
    picks down the rows
    the chorus resounding for acres and acres
    Everyone adding a line
    the day crawls a little faster.

She pulls ahead
kicking *terremotes,*
el viento sur secándole el sudor
un ruido de alas humming songs in her head.
Que le de sus plumas el viento.
The sound of hummingbird wings
in her ears, *pico de chuparrosas.*

She looks up into the sun's glare,
las chuparrosas de los jardines
¿en dónde están de su mamagrande?
but all she sees is the obsidian wind
cut tassels of blood
from the hummingbird's throat.

She husks corn, hefts watermelons.
Bends all the way, digs out strawberries
half buried in the dirt.
Twelve hours later
roped knots cord her back.

Sudor de sobacos chorriando,
limpia de hierba la siembra
Claws clutching hoe, she tells the
two lead spatulas stirring the sand,
jump into it, *patas,* wallow *en el charco de mierda,*
breathe it in through the soles of your feet.
There was nothing else but surrender.
If she hadn't read all those books
she'd be singing up and down the rows
like the rest.

She stares at her hands
Manos hinchadas, quebradas,
thick and calloused like a man's,
the tracks on her left palm
different from those on the right.
Saca la lima y raspa el azadón
se va a mochar sus manos,
she wants to chop off her hands
cut off her feet
only Indians and *mayates*
have flat feet.

Burlap sack wet around her waist,
stained green from leaves and the smears of worms.
White heat no water no place to pee
the men staring at her ass.

Como una mula,
she shifts 150 pounds of cotton onto her back.
It's either *las labores*
or feet soaking in cold puddles *en bodegas*

cutting   washing   weighing   packaging
broccoli spears carrots cabbages in 12 hours   15
double shift the roar of machines inside her head.
She can always clean shit
out of white folks toilets—the Mexican maid.
You're respected if you can use your head
instead of your back, the women said.
Ay m'ijos, ojalá que hallen trabajo
in air-conditioned offices.

The hoe, she wants to cut off . . .
She folds wounded birds, her hands
into the nest, her armpits
looks up at the Texas sky.
Si el viento le diera sus plumas.

She vows to get out
of the numbing chill, the 110 degree heat.
If the wind would give her feathers for fingers
she would string words and images together.
Pero el viento sur le tiró su saliva
pa' 'trás en la cara.

She sees the obsidian wind
cut tassels of blood
from the hummingbird's throat.
As it falls
the hummingbird shadow
becomes the navel of the Earth.

---

bolillo—a derogatory term for Anglos meaning hard crust of loaf of white
    bread.
entre las matas de maíz—between the corn stalks
terremotes—sods

El viento sur secándole el sudor—The south wind drying her sweat
un ruido de alas—a sound of wings
¿En dónde están las chuparrosas de los jardines de su mamagrande?—
Where are the hummingbirds from her grandmother's gardens?
Sudor de sobacos chorriando limpia de hierba la siembra—The sweat
dripping from her armpits, she weeds the plants.
manos hinchadas, quebradas—swollen, broken hands
mayates—a derogatory term for Blacks
como una mula—like a mule
Ay m'ijos, ojalá que hallen trabajo—Oh my children, I hope you find work
Si el viento le diera sus plumas—if the wind would give her its feathers
Pero el viento le tiró su saliva pa' 'trás en la cara—But the wind threw her
spit back in her face

Cultures

vete
go out take the pick axe
take the shovel
my mother would tell me

hard brown earth with the axe
I'd pick at its dark veins
disinter a rotting tin can
unmould a shell from a lost ocean
bones of an unknown animal

with my eyes I'd measure out a rectangle
I'd swing and shove and lift
my sweat dripping on the swelling mounds

into the hole I'd rake up and pitch
rubber-nippled baby bottles
cans of Spam with twisted umbilicals
I'd overturn the cultures
spawning in Coke bottles
murky and motleyed

my brothers never helped
woman's work and beneath them
under the clothesline
three times a year, two feet apart

I'd dig and sweat and grunt
above me clothes flapping like banners
wire taut between the crossed posts
crucifixes over earlier graves

when it rots
trash replenishes the soil
my mother would say
but nothing would grow in
my small plots except
thistle sage and nettle.

sobre piedras con lagartijos

(para todos los mojaditos que han cruzado para este lado)

Pst!
ese ruido rumbo al Norte, muchachos,
párense, aquí nos separamos.

Tengo que descanzar,
Ay que tierra tan dura como piedra.
Desde que me acuerdo
así ha sido mi cama,
mi vida. Maldito fue el día
que me atreví a cruzar.
Nada más quiero hacer unos cuantos centavos
y regresar a mi tierra.
Dicen que unos norteamericanos son puros jijos
Bueno, pues, yo puedo trabajar como un burro.
Lo único que me falta es el huír
porque hasta sus dientes tengo.
Uno tiene que hacer la lucha
¿Cómo la estará pasando mi vieja?

Ayá la dejé con los seis chiquíos.
Tuve que dejarlos,
dejar ese pinche pedazo de tierra
El maíz no levantaba cabeza
ni llegaba hasta mi rodilla.
Por mis hijos estoy aquí echado como animal
en el regazo de la madre tierra.
Ojalá que la Santisima virgen me tenga en sus manos.

¡Qué sol tan miserable!
y el nopal por todos rumbos.
Ni un árbol ni nada, ay madrecita,
los lagartijos y yo—tenemos el mismo cuero
pero yo ya no soy ligero.
Los trozos de leña que cargaba al mercado
los costales de maíz, empinado desde niño
tratando de sacarle algo verde
al caliche que era mi parcela.

La vida me ha jorobado,
ando como anciano
ladiando de un lado al otro.
Ya casi ni veo.

La niña le estará preguntando
¿Cuándo viene mi papi?
y los chiquillos chillando
sus manitas estirándole la falda
bocas chupando sus chiches secas
pobre vieja. Al menos no tengo que ver
esa mirada en sus ojos
que me hace un nudo en mi pecho.

Que se que les pasó a los otros.
Cuando oímos el ruido
de la camioneta
corrimos por todos rumbos.
Yo me hice bola y me metí
debajo de un cholla
allí estuve atorado en una cuevita
que algún animalito había hecho.
No pude aguantar los piquetes—madrotas.
Todavía las siento remolineándose debajo de mi piel
y ahorita que desperté
vi que una víbora me estaba velando.
Pues, allí estuve echo bola
en la panza de ese cacto dos o tres días
la sed me quita la memoria,
mi boca seca de hechar maldiciones, de miedo

Dicen que si llego a Ogaquinahua
ayá me encontraré con unos paisanos
que me ayudarán a hallar chamba, a sacar papeles.
Pronto volveré a mi tierra
a recojer mi señora y mis hijos.

Mira como los lagartijos se alejan
aventando piedritas por todos lados
Oy, ¿Qué es ese ruido

*que arrebata a mi corazón, que me para el aliento y
seca más mi boca?
¿De quién son esas botas
lujísimas que andan
hacia mi cara?*

El sonavabitche
(for Aishe Berger)

Car flowing down a lava of highway
just happened to glance out the window
in time to see brown faces bent backs
like prehistoric boulders in a field
so common a sight no one
notices
blood rushes to my face
twelve years I'd sat on the memory
the anger scorching me
my throat so tight I can
barely get the words out.

I got to the farm
in time to hear the shots
ricochet off barn,
spit into the sand,
in time to see tall men in uniforms
thumping fists on doors
metallic voices yelling Halt!
their hawk eyes constantly shifting.

When I hear the words, *"Corran muchachos"*
I run back to the car, ducking,
see the glistening faces, arms outflung,
of the *mexicanos* running headlong
through the fields
kicking up clouds of dirt

see them reach the tree line
foliage opening, swishing closed behind them.
I hear the tussling of bodies, grunts, panting
squeak of leather squawk of walkie-talkies
sun reflecting off gunbarrels
the world a blinding light
a great buzzing in my ears
my knees like aspens in the wind.

I see that wide cavernous look of the hunted
the look of hares
thick limp blue-black hair
The bare heads humbly bent
of those who do not speak
the ember in their eyes extinguished.

I lean on the shanty wall of that migrant camp
north of Muncie, Indiana.
Wets, a voice says.
I turn to see a Chicano pushing
the head of his *muchachita*
back into the *naguas* of the mother
a tin plate face down on the floor
tortillas scattered around them.
His other hand signals me over.
He too is from *el valle de Tejas*
I had been his kid's teacher.
I'd come to get the grower
to fill up the sewage ditch near the huts
saying it wouldn't do for the children
to play in it.
    Smoke from a cooking fire and
    shirtless *niños* gather around us.

    Mojados, he says again,
leaning on his chipped Chevy station wagon
Been here two weeks
about a dozen of them.
The *sonavabitche* works them
from sunup to dark—15 hours sometimes.
Como mulas los trabaja
no saben como hacer la perra.
Last Sunday they asked for a day off
wanted to pray and rest,
write letters to their *familias.*
¿Y sabes lo que hizo el sonavabitche?
He turns away and spits.
Says he has to hold back half their wages
that they'd eaten the other half:

sack of beans, sack of rice, sack of flour.
Frijoleros sí lo son but no way
could they have eaten that many *frijoles*.
I nod.

Como le dije, son doce—started out 13
five days packed in the back of a pickup
boarded up tight
fast cross-country run no stops
except to change drivers, to gas up
no food they pissed into their shoes—
those that had *guaraches*
slept slumped against each other
sabe Dios where they shit.
One smothered to death on the way here

Miss, you should've seen them when they
stumbled out.
First thing the *sonavabitche* did was clamp
a handkerchief over his nose
then ordered them stripped
hosed them down himself
in front of everybody.
They hobbled about
learning to walk all over again.
Flacos con caras de viejos
aunque la mita' eran jóvenes.

Como le estaba diciendo,
today was payday.
You saw them, *la migra* came busting in
waving their *pinche pistolas.*
Said someone made a call,
what you call it? Anonymous.
Guess who? That *sonavabitche,* who else?
Done this three times since we've been coming here
Sepa Dios how many times in between.
Wets, free labor, *esclavos.*
Pobres jijos de la Chingada.
This the last time we work for him

no matter how *fregados* we are
he said, shaking his head,
spitting at the ground.
Vámonos, mujer, empaca el mugrero.

He hands me a cup of coffee,
half of it sugar, half of it milk
my throat so dry I even down the dregs.
It has to be done.
Steeling myself
I take that walk to the big house.

Finally the big man lets me in.
How about a drink? I shake my head.
He looks me over, opens his eyes wide
and smiles, says how sorry he is immigration
is getting so tough
a poor Mexican can't make a living
and they sure do need the work.
My throat so thick the words stick.
He studies me, then says,
Well, what can I do you for?
I want two weeks wages
including two Saturdays and Sundays,
minimum wage, 15 hours a day.
I'm more startled than he.
Whoa there, sinorita,
wets work for whatever you give them
the season hasn't been good.
Besides most are halfway to Mexico by now.
Two weeks wages, I say,
the words swelling in my throat.

Miss uh what did you say your name was?
I fumble for my card.
You can't do this,
I haven't broken no law,
his lidded eyes darken, I step back.
I'm leaving in two minutes and I want cash
the whole amount right here in my purse

when I walk out.
No hoarseness, no trembling.
It startled both of us.

You want me telling every single one
of your neighbors what you've been doing
all these years? The mayor, too?
Maybe make a call to Washington?
Slitted eyes studied the card again.
They had no cards, no papers.
I'd seen it over and over.
Work them, then turn them in before paying them.

Well, now, he was saying,
I know we can work something out,
a sweet young thang like yourself.
Cash, I said. I didn't know anyone in D.C.
now I didn't have to.
You want to keep it for yourself?
That it? His eyes were pin pricks.
Sweat money, Mister, blood money,
not my sweat, but same blood.
Yeah, but who's to say you won't abscond with it?
If I ever hear that you got illegals on your land
even a single one, I'm going to come here
in broad daylight and have you
hung by your balls.
He walks slowly to his desk.
Knees shaking, I count every bill
taking my time.

Corran muchachos—Run boys.

muchachita—little girl

naguas—skirt

el valle de Tejas—Rio Grande Valley in Texas

mojados—wetbacks, undocumented workers, illegal immigrants from Mexico and parts south

Como mulas los trabaja.—He works them like mules.

no saben como hacer la perra.—They don't know how to make the work easier for themselves.

¿Y sabes lo que hizo?—And you know what he did?

Frijoleros sí lo son.—Bean eaters they are.

Como le dije, son doce.—Like I told you, they're 12.

guarache—sandal

sabe Dios—God knows

Flacos con caras viejos—skinny with old faces

aunque la mita' eran jóvenes—though half were youths

Como le estaba diciendo—as I was telling you

la migra—slang for immigration officials

pistolas—guns

esclavos—slaves

Pobres jijos de la Chingada—poor sons of the fucked one

fregados—poor, beaten, downtrodden, in need

Vámanos, mujer, empaca el mugrero.—Let's go, woman, pack our junk.

Mar de repollos
(para la gente que siempre ha trabajado en las labores)

Hincado, manos hinchadas
sudor floreciendo en su cara
su mirada en altas veredas
sus pensamientos torciendo cuerdas
para pescar esa paloma de las alturas.
Siglo tras siglo nadando

brazos artríticos dando vueltas
y vueltas y vueltas recorriendo surcos
un gusano en un mar verde.
una vida estremecida por el viento
meciéndose en una goma de esperanza
atrapada en las redes con la paloma.

A mediodía en la orilla
de las verdes colmenas
en la labor de un ranchito en Tejas
saca sus tortillas con chile
toma agua hecha caldo por el sol.
A veces maldice

su suerte, la tierra, el sol.
Sus ojos: inquietos pájaros volando
sobre veredas altas en busca
de esa paloma blanca
y su nido.

Hombre en verde mar.
Su herencia: manos gordas manchadas
hechando raíces en la tierra.

Aunque empinado, vivía cara arriba,
en sus ojos telarañas
pescaban las plumas blancas.
Sus manos rompen repollos de sus nidos
rompen venudas hojas cubriendo hojas tiernitas
cubriendo hojas más pálidas, el corazón.

Siglo tras siglo revatando
deshojándose en un mar de repollos.
Mareado
cuerpo sosteniendo el azote del sol
En sus manos los repollos se contuercen como peces.
Espesa lengua tragando

la amarga escoria.
El sol, pesada piedra sobre su espalda
quebrándose.
La tierra se estremece y le pega en la cara
espuma brota en sus labios, se derrama
ojos abiertos, cara arriba, buscando, buscando.

Los blancos de sus ojos se congelan.
Oye el viento barriendo los pedazos quebrados
y luego el ruido de plumas dulce en su garganta.
No escapa de su trampa—
su fe: paloma hecha carne.

A Sea of Cabbages
(for those who have worked in the fields)

On his knees, hands swollen
sweat flowering on his face
his gaze on the high paths
the words in his head twinning cords
tossing them up to catch that bird of the heights.
Century after century swimming

with arthritic arms, back and forth
circling, going around and around
a worm in a green sea
life shaken by the wind
swinging in a mucilage of hope
caught in the net along with *la paloma.*

At noon on the edge
of the hives of cabbage
in the fields of a *ranchito* in *Tejas*
he takes out his chile wrapped in tortillas
drinks water made hot soup by the sun.
Sometimes he curses

his luck, the land, the sun.
His eyes: unquiet birds
flying over the high paths
searching for that white dove
and her nest.

Man in a green sea.
His inheritance: thick stained hand
rooting in the earth.

His hands tore cabbages from their nests,
ripping the ribbed leaves covering tenderer leaves
encasing leaves yet more pale.
Though bent over, he lived face up,
the veins in his eyes
catching the white plumes in the sky.

Century after century flailing,
unleafing himself in a sea of cabbages.
Dizzied
body sustained by the lash of the sun.
In his hands the cabbages contort like fish.
Thickened tongue swallowing

the stench.

The sun, a heavy rock on his back,
cracks,
the earth shudders, slams his face
spume froths from his mouth spilling over
eyes opened, face up, searching searching.

The whites of his eyes congeal.
He hears the wind sweeping the broken shards
then the sound of feathers surging up his throat.
He cannot escape his own snare—
faith: dove made flesh.

—translated from the Spanish by the author

We Call Them Greasers

I found them here when I came.
They were growing corn in their small *ranchos*
raising cattle, horses
smelling of woodsmoke and sweat.
They knew their betters:
took off their hats
placed them over their hearts,
lowered their eyes in my presence.

Weren't interested in bettering themselves,
why they didn't even own the land but shared it.
Wasn't hard to drive them off,
cowards, they were, no backbone.
I showed 'em a piece of paper with some writing
tole 'em they owed taxes
had to pay right away or be gone by *mañana*.
By the time me and my men had waved
that same piece of paper to all the families
it was all frayed at the ends.

Some loaded their chickens children wives and pigs
into rickety wagons, pans and tools dangling
clanging from all sides.
Couldn't take their cattle—
during the night my boys had frightened them off.
Oh, there were a few troublemakers
who claimed we were the intruders.
Some even had land grants
and appealed to the courts.
It was a laughing stock
them not even knowing English.
Still some refused to budge,
even after we burned them out.
And the women—well I remember one in particular.

She lay under me whimpering.
I plowed into her hard
kept thrusting and thrusting

felt him watching from the mesquite tree
heard him keening like a wild animal
in that instant I felt such contempt for her
round face and beady black eyes like an Indian's.
Afterwards I sat on her face until
her arms stopped flailing,
didn't want to waste a bullet on her.
The boys wouldn't look me in the eyes.
I walked up to where I had tied her man to the tree
and spat in his face. Lynch him, I told the boys.

Matriz sin tumba o
"el baño de la basura ajena"

Tendida estoy en una cama angosta,
calzones empapados de sangre.
Se que yo callada no soy nada.
Desdichada,
muy lejana con boca hinchada,
vomitando algo amarillo,
revolviendo y repitiendo palabras sin sentido.
Siento algo reventándose
en un lugar interno.
Estoy parada en la orilla
de una noche oscura.

Una espina gruesa le pica la nalga,
su cuerpo se estremece.
Se entrega a un sabor de hierro
y al éter.
Sueña con una mujer que orina pus
y que come su propio excremento.

Revuelvo y repito palabras sin sentido.
Algo se rompe en un lugar interno.
Como basura un agitado viento me empuja.
Me siento muy lejana, juzgada
por ese buitre en la panza.
La bestia noche entra armada con navajas,
se me arrima muy cerquita,
me manotea, me agujera dos veces, tres veces.
Miro que me saca las entrañas,
que avienta la matriz en la basura—
matriz sin tumba.

Sueña que toma "el baño de la basura ajena"
en honor de Tlazolteotl
Detrás de ella mira una figura

tragándose el sol.
Con obsidiana le punza cuatro veces, cinco.
¿Estoy muerta? le pregunto.
Por favor entierren mi matriz conmigo.

Un relámpago perforando el cielo
dispersa la noche.
Me sangran, me sangran.
Tengo señas de la muerte:
un color de humo en medio de los ojos
que relucen poco;
cara que se enegrece.
Alguien me empuja entre la lumbre,
aspiro humo de cabellos chamuscados.
Esta pequeña muerte,
una comezón que no me deja a gusto.
Un dedo sale del cielo, y descende,
se insinúa entre mis rajadas cavidades.
Chispas salen del agujero
me preparo a despedirme de la vida asesina.
Revuelvo y repito palabras sin sentido.
En un lugar interno alguien se queja.

Sueña de una cara tiznada,
de una boca escupiendo sangre
y luego comiendo atole de miel y chile.
Hacia el oriente una larga cicatriz
raja el cielo.
Le punza dos veces, tres, siete.

Padezco de un mal: la vida,
una enfermedad recurrente
que me purga de la muerte.
Me sangra, me sangra.
Derramando un aguacero,
vierte la muerte por mi boca.
Volteo la cara,

revuelvo y repito palabras sin sentido:
la vida enena, matriz sin tumba.
En un lugar interno algo se revienta
y un agitado viento empuja los pedazos.

III

Crossers

y otros atravesados

Al otro lado está el río
y no lo puedo cruzar,
al otro lado está el mar
no lo puedo atravesar.
  —Isabel Parra, *"En La Frontera"*

On the other side is the river
and I cannot cross it
on the other side is the sea
I cannot bridge it.
  —Isabel Parra, "At The Border"

Poets have strange eating habits
(for Irenita Klepfisz)

Dark windowless   no moon glides
across the nightsky
                I coax and whip the balking mare
                        to the edge
                        peel the scabs from her wounds
                Her body caves into itself
                through the hole
                my mouth

In the border between dusk and dawn
I listen to frozen thumpings, my soul
                Should I jump   face tumbling
                down   the steps of the temple
                heart offered up to the midnightsun

She takes that plunge
        off the high cliff
                hooves tumbling in the vagrant air
                        head tucked between her legs
                                a cold wind tugging at her back
cutting tears from my eyes
the obsidian knife, air
the nightsky   alone   alone

        She spreads out her legs
        to catch the wind
                rushes to fill *el abismo*
                the nightride has ripped open
                its hunger rimmed with teeth
        I feed it my throat   my hands
        let it glut itself on me
        till it's pregnant with me.
                Wounding is a deeper healing.

        Suspended in fluid sky
        I, eagle fetus, live serpent
                feathers growing out of my skin

the buffeting wind
the rock walls rearing up
the Earth.

I bend my knees, break the fall
no arm snapping
a stunned animal
I burrow deep into myself
pull the emptiness in
its hollows chisel my face
growing thin thinner
eyesockets empty
tunneling here tunneling there
the slither of snakes
their fangs pierce my flesh

falling

into faceless air
Taking the plunge an act as
routine as cleaning my teeth.

The Earth parts
I hit the bottom of the chasm
peer over the edge
coax and whip the balking mare
take that plunge again
jumping off cliffs an addiction
flailing   pummeling
flesh into images
sticking feathers
in my arms
slithering into holes
with rattlesnakes

dark windowless no moon glides
across the nightsky
the maw opens wide   I slip inside
Taking deep breaths   eyes closed
*me la tragó todita**

---

me la tragó   *todita—*I swallow it   whole

Yo no fui, fue Teté
(para Mando Gaítan y Ronnie Burks)

a lo macho, simón que sí
estaba anocheciendo
salí a la calle del dormido pueblo a putear
y allí me estaban esperando
los chingones, batos grifos.
orale, ¿pos qué train conmigo?
¿qué pedo es éste?

me llevaron al yonke
zs, me dieron mis crismas
jijo 'ela chingada we struggled man, *piel a piel*
me escupieron en la cara
"lambiscón, culero, pinche puto"
me arrinconaron, me dieron una paliza
me partieron la madre
conocí la cara del odio, del miedo
sentí la navaja
esas miradas enloquecidas
y tienen los huevos de llamarnos "locas"
que verguenza, mi misma raza
jijo 'ela chingada
me ensucié en los pantalones
allí en el pavimento
allí me quedé jodido
aullando por la noche como huérfano
allí me dejaron
de volada me pelé pa' la casa

The Cannibal's *Canción*

It is our custom
    to consume
    the person we love.
    Taboo flesh: swollen
    genitalia nipples
    the scrotum the vulva
    the soles of the feet
    the palms of the hand
    heart and liver taste best.
    Cannibalism is blessed.

    I'll wear your jawbone
    round my neck
    listen to your vertebrae
    bone rapping bone in my wrists.
    I'll string your fingers round my waist—
    what a rigorous embrace.
    Over my heart I'll wear
    a brooch with a lock of your hair.
    Nights I'll sleep cradling
    your skull sharpening
    my teeth on your toothless grin.

    Sundays there's Mass and communion
    and I'll put your relics to rest.

En mi corazón se incuba
(*para* Sonia Alvarez)

Todo comienza a partir de este día,
Una tristeza me invade y
Algo extraño se oculta en mi vientre—
Un golpe de soledad que me consume.
En mi corazón se incuba una espina.

La luz de las luciérnagas se retira y
De los árboles me llaman las lechuzas.
Inmersa en un abandono, tragando miedos,
Me siento muy lejos
De la huella del amor.

En tumbas huérfanas gasto largas noches,
Los minutos pasan como agujas por mi piel.
Soy una sombra pálida en una noche opaca.
Hondo escondo mi pena, hondo.
Hondo se enraíza un sueño noconfesado.

En este oscuro monte de nopal
Algo secretamente amado
Se oculta en mi vientre
Y en mi corazón se incuba
Un amor que no es de este mundo.

Corner of 50th St. and Fifth Av.

Taking my usual walk
I run into sirens flashing red, turning
and a small crowd
watching the dark-haired man
with the thin mustache,
PR about 30,
maricón, a voice in the crowd shouts.

Two uniforms have his head
wedged down in the gap
between the bucket seats,
red sirens turning turning
just over his head.

Another pulls down his pants
holds him tight around the waist
the fourth pummels
the pale orbs over and over
till the PR's face is flushed
the cop's fist red
the sirens turning turning.
The first two look bored
eyes drifting slowly
over the crowd
not meeting our eyes.
He just thud got out thud of jail
I hear a Rican say
thud, the cop's arms like baseball bats.
Finally the thuds end.
They pull his head
out of the crack,
pull pants over livid cheeks,
manacled hands going down
to cover his buttocks

the sirens turning turning
I wade through the thick air thinking
that's as close as they let themselves get
to fucking a man, being men.

Compañera, cuando amábamos
(for Juanita Ramos and other spik dykes)

¿Volverán, compañera, esas tardes sordas
Cuando nos amábamos tiradas en las sombras bajo otoño?
Mis ojos clavados en tu mirada
Tu mirada que siempre retiraba al mundo
Esas tardes cuando nos acostábamos en las nubes

Mano en mano nos paseábamos por las calles
Entre niños jugando handball
Vendedores y sus sabores de carne chamuzcada.
La gente mirando nuestras manos
Nos pescaban los ojos y se sonreían
Cómplices en esto asunto del aire suave.
En un café u otro nos sentábamos bien cerquita.
Nos gustaba todo: las bodegas tiznadas
La música de Silvio, el ruido de los trenes
Y habichuelas. Compañera,
¿Volverán esas tardes sordas cuando nos amábamos?

¿Te acuerdas cuando te decía ¡tócame!?
¿Cuándo ilesa carne buscaba carne y dientes labios
En los laberintos de tus bocas?
Esas tardes, islas no descubiertas
Cuando caminábamos hasta la orilla.
Mis dedos lentos andaban las lomas de tus pechos,
Recorriendo la llanura de tu espalda
Tus moras hinchándose en mi boca
La cueva mojada y racima.
Tu corazón en mi lengua hasta en mis sueños.
Dos pescadoras nadando en los mares
Buscando esa perla.
¿No te acuerdas como nos amábamos, compañera?

¿Volverán esas tardes cuando vacilábamos
Pasos largos, manos entrelazadas en la playa?
Las gaviotas y las brizas
Dos manfloras vagas en una isla de mutua melodía.
Tus tiernas palmas y los planetas que se caían.

Esas tardes tiñadas de mojo
Cuando nos entregábamos a las olas

Cuando nos tirábamos
En el zacate del parque
Dos cuerpos de mujer bajo los árboles
Mirando los barcos cruzando el río
Tus pestañas barriendo mi cara
Dormitando, oliendo tu piel de amapola.
Dos extranjeras al borde del abismo
Yo caía descabellada encima de tu cuerpo
Sobre las lunas llenas de tus pechos
Esas tardes cuando se mecía el mundo con mi resuello
Dos mujeres que hacían una sola sombra bailarina
Esas tardes andábamos hasta que las lámparas
Se prendían en las avenidas.

¿Volverán,
Compañera, esas tardes   cuando nos amábamos?

Interface
(for Frances Doughty)

She'd always been there
        occupying the same room.
It was only when I looked
        at the edges of things
my eyes going wide watering,
        objects blurring.
Where before there'd only been empty space
        I sensed layers and layers,
felt the air in the room thicken.
        Behind my eyelids a white flash
a thin noise.
        That's when I could see her.

        Once I accidentally ran my arm
through her body
        felt heat on one side of my face.
        She wasn't solid.
The shock pushed me against the wall.
A torrent of days swept past me
        before I tried to "see" her again.
She had never wanted to be flesh she told me
        until she met me.
At first it was hard to stay
        on the border between
the physical world
        and hers.
It was only there at the interface
        that we could see each other.
See? We wanted to touch.
        I wished I could become
pulsing color, pure sound, bodiless as she.
        It was impossible, she said
        for humans to become noumenal.

What does it feel like, she asked
        to inhabit flesh,
wear blood like threads

constantly running?
I would lie on the bed talking
she would hover over me.
Did I say talk?
We did not use words.
I pushed my thoughts toward her.
Her "voice" was a breath of air
stirring my hair
filling my head.
Once Lupe my roommate
walked right through her
dangling the car keys.
I felt Leyla shiver.
I named her Leyla,
a pure sound.

I don't know when I noticed
that she'd begun to glow,
to look more substantial
than the blurred furniture.
It was then I felt a slight touch,
her hand—a tendril of fog—
on the sheets where she'd lain
a slight crease, a dampness,
a smell between candles and skin.
You're changing, I told her.
A yearning deluged me—
her yearning.
That's when I knew
she wanted to be flesh.
She stayed insubstantial day after day
so I tried to blur
my borders, to float, become pure sound.
But my body seemed heavier,
more inert.

I remember when she changed.
I could hear the far away slough of traffic
on the Brooklyn-Queens Expressway,
the people downstairs were playing salsa.

We lay enclosed by margins, hems,
where only we existed.
　　　She was stroking stroking my arms
my legs, marveling at their solidity,
　　　the warmth of my flesh, its smell.
Then I touched her.
　　　Fog, she felt like dense fog,
the color of smoke.
　　　She glowed, my hands paled then gleamed
as I moved them over her.
　　　Smoke-fog pressing against my eyelids
my mouth, ears, nostrils, navel.
　　　A cool tendril pressing between my legs
entering.
Her finger, I thought
but it went on and on.
　　　At the same time
an iciness touched my anus,
　　　and she was in
and in and in
　　　my mouth opening
I wasn't scared just astonished
　　　rain drummed against my spine
　　　turned to steam as it rushed through my veins
light flickered over me from toe to crown.
　　　Looking down my body I saw
　　　her forearm, elbow and hand
sticking out of my stomach
　　　saw her hand slide in.
I wanted no food no water nothing
　　　just her—pure light sound inside me.
My roommate thought I was
　　　having an affair.
I was "radiant," she said.
　　　Leyla had begun to swell
I started hurting a little.
　　　When I started cramping
she pushed out
　　　her fingers, forearm, shoulder.
Then she stood before me,

fragile skin, sinews tender as baby birds
and as transparent.
She who had never eaten
began to hunger.
I held a cup of milk to her mouth,
put her hand on my throat
made swallowing motions.
I spooned mashed banana into her bird mouth,
hid the baby food under the bed.
One day my roommate asked
who was staying in my room,
she'd heard movements.
A friend recovering from a contagious
skin disease, I said.
She ran out saying, I'm going to the Cape
indefinitely. See you.
We had the house to ourselves.
I taught her how to clean herself,
to flush.
She would stand before the mirror
watching her ears, long and diaphanous,
begin to get smaller, thicker.
She spent a lot of time at the window.
Once I caught her imitating
the shuffle of the baglady.
No, like this, I told her.
Head up, shoulders back.
I brought in the TV.
This is how humans love, hate, I said.
Once we sat on the stoop
watching a neighbor sweep the sidewalk.
Hello, he yelled, hello, I yelled back,
eh-oh, she whispered.
Watch my lips, Ley-la.
Say it, Ley-la.
Good. I love you.
Ah uff oo, she said.
Soon Leyla could pass,
go for milk at the bodega, count change.
But no matter how passionately we made

love
            it was never like before
she'd taken on skin and bone.

            Do you ever want to go back, I asked her.
No, it's slower here and I like that.
            I hate summers in NYC, I told her,
wish it was winter already.
            The temperature dropped 10 degrees 20
and when a chill wind began to blow in Brooklyn
            I told her to stop
messing with the cycles that affected others.
            I watched what I said
and let Leyla run the place.
            She had snow in the livingroom
and a tree in the bathtub.
            Nights I lit the illegal fireplace.
Once when reaching toward a high shelf,
            I wished I was taller.
When my head touched the ceiling
            I had to yell at her to stop,
            reverse.
How do you do it, I asked her.
            You do it, too, she said,
my species just does it faster,
            instantly, merely by thinking it.

The first time she rode the subway
            I had to drag her out.
I suppose it was the noise,
            the colors flashing by, the odd people
that held her open-mouthed gaze.
            I had to do a gig in L.A.,
speak at a conference, was short on cash,
            but she wanted to come.
She walked past the flight attendants
            didn't even have to hide in the lavatory.
She laughed at my amazement, said
            humans only saw what they were told to see.
Last Christmas I took her home to Texas.
            Mom liked her.
Is she a lez, my brothers asked.
            I said, No, just an alien.
Leyla laughed.

IV

Cihuatlyotl, Woman Alone

Yo llamo a mujer,
canto por mujer.
Cubierta con serpientes vengo yo,
al lugar del encuentro me acerco,
repito conjuros para provocar amor.
Clamo por mujer.
Ya llego, llamo.
        —Gloria Anzaldúa

Holy Relics
(for Judy Grahn & V. Sackville-West)

> We are the holy relics,
> the scattered bones of a saint,
> the best loved bones of Spain.
> We seek each other.

City of Ávila,
88 crenellated towers crowning a low hill.
A silent landscape rises toward indigo mountains,
empty save for clumps of broom and tormented ilex.
Here and there strange stones
like prehistoric ruins.
A granite city in a dour land,
with a cathedral for a fortress.
A land where no mists soften the rocks,
where light is relentless.

When she* died, flesh of our bones,
they buried her at the Alba de Tormes
50 miles west of Ávila.
They finally buried her
in her patched and shabby habit.
Buried her in her threadworn veil.
Bricked her in a wall of grey stone.

Nine months she lay in the grey stone.
Nine months she lay quietly.
Her daughters, the nuns of Alba, came to her daily—

came to that bricked-up place in the wall.
From that place issued a scent
to which they could give no name.
From within that tomb
issued a sound to which they could give no name.

Day by day they waited.
They waited for the good father Gracian,

---

* Teresa de Cepeda Dávila y Ahumada

Teresa's beloved confessor,
waited to tell him of that scent and of that sound.

Entombed nine months.
Four days it took them.
Four days in silence, in secret.
The nuns held the torches
while Father and friar shoveled.
The nuns held the torches,
then cleared away the rubble.
At last the hallowed moment,
the coffin pulled from the cavern.
The moment when the lid is broken,
when the coffin is opened.
They gazed at last at their beloved:
spider webs netted black hair to eyebrows,
earth clotted her arched nostrils.
They gazed and gazed at their beloved.
The nuns of Alba removed her mouldy habit,
with knives scraped away the earth clinging to her skin,
looked their fill,
then wrapped her in clean linen.
The good Father drew near,
lifted her left hand as if to kiss it,
placed a knife under her wrist
and from her rigid arm he severed it.
The father Teresa had loved stood smiling,
hugging her hand to his body.

We are the holy relics,
the scattered bones of a saint,
the best loved bones of Spain.
We seek each other.

Two years she lay in her tomb.
Pero para los santos no hay descanso,
for saints there is no rest.
Another priest fell upon her tomb
to claim her holy body for Ávila.
At midnight he sent the nuns

to the upper choir to sing Matins.
Then quietly removed the bricked-up stones,
quietly reopened the tomb.
The mysterious scent and her unspoiled face
(a little more dried than before) greeted him.
And bright red as if freshly soaked
was the cloak of white bunting
that had staunched the flow from her mouth at her deathbed.

It stained whatever piece of cloth touched it.
The scent drifted to the upper choir
drawing the nuns down to the tomb like flies to honey
in time to see Father Gregorio de Naciancene
insert his knife under the truncated arm,
in time to see the blade pass through flesh
as if through cheese.
And flinging the arm at the nuns of Alba
as one would a bone to a dog
he detained them long enough
to mount the shroud on horseback
and gallop away.

> We are the holy relics,
> the scattered bones of a saint,
> the best loved bones of Spain.
> We seek each other.

Through the bitter winds of Ávila
Teresa raced from the grave.
She traveled at night,
and briefly during the run she stopped
to resuscitate a dying child
with the edge of her bloodstained rag,
paused to heal the fiery eyes of a shepherd.
Toward the 88 towers and their indented embrasures
they galloped.
Through streets of Ávila,
past highwalled houses where black eyes behind lattices
stared down at the shroud riding on horseback.
Into San José convent he took her

and placed her upon a bright carpet.
A small group gathered around,
each held a flaming torch.
All were crying.

Later, one witness described the corpse:
"The body is erect, though bent a little forward,
as with old people.
It can be made to stand upright,
if propped with a hand between the shoulders,
and this is the position they hold it
when it is to be dressed or undressed,
as though it were alive.
The colour of the body
is of the colour of dates; the face darker,
because the veil became stuck to it,
and it was maltreated more than the rest;
nevertheless, it is intact.
And even the nose is undamaged.
The head has retained all its hair.
The eyes, having lost their vital moisture,
are dried up, but the eyelids are perfectly preserved.
The moles on her face retain their little hairs.
The mouth is tightly shut and cannot be opened.
The shoulder from which the arm was severed
exudes a moisture that clings to the touch
and exhales the same scent as the body."

News of her disinterment spread.
It reached the ears of the Duke of Alba.
He petitioned the pope for the immediate return of the body.

Once more Teresa traveled,
traveled at night
away from the 88 towers.
Through the bitter winds of Ávila
she galloped toward her grave.
Abbots on well-fed mules turned and gaped.
Peasants stopped thrashing their corn.
They followed the mysterious smell

and saw it cure a monk's malaria.
Through the gates of Alba
the priest rode.
He laid the shroud before the nuns.
Raising his torch high,
he uncovered the body.
"If these be the remains of your Foundress
acknowledge them before God."

Again she lay quietly
in her granite grave.
The third time she was exhumed,
a crowd gathered round,
eyes coveting her body.
Over-ardent fingers—
fingers that once had loved her—
pinched off pieces of her flesh.
A priest raised her one remaining hand,
gave a sharp twist snapping off two fingers.
Another grasped her right foot
and blessing her
severed it from her ankle.
A third fell upon her breast
and from her side
plucked three ribs.
Scraps of her bones they sold
to the aristocracy for money.
They auctioned tiny pieces of her fingernails
and one small white tooth.

Again they laid her in her grey stone grave.
And priests fell upon her body.
Her dried carnal husk
could still be torn into morsels.
They cut off her head,
laid it on a cushion of crimson satin
embroidered with silver and gold.
Like a crippled bird it lay,
left eye gouged out,
right eye protruding through full lashes,
its black lone gaze frozen.

A fifth time they dug her up years later.
A gaping hole where her heart had been ripped out
to be placed in a reliquary.
Three centuries later physicians would examine it,
would find a wound an inch and a half in length,
the edges of the wound charred
as though by a burning iron.
Above the high altar at Alba,
the fifth and final resting place,
lie the remains of a woman.

    We are the holy relics,
    the scattered bones of a saint,
    the best loved bones of Spain.
    We seek each other.

En el nombre de todas las madres
que han perdido sus hijos en la guerra

Le cubro su cabecita,
mi criatura con sus piecesitos fríos.
Aquí lo tendré acurrucado en mis brazos
hasta que me muera.
Parece años desde que estoy sentada aquí
en este charco de sangre.
Esto pasó esta mañana.

Cuando oí ese tiroteo
se me paró la sangre.
Con el niño dormido en mis brazos
corrí pa' fuera.
Trozos de tierra se levantaban,
volaban por todos rumbos.
Pedazos de ramas caían como lluvia,
una lluvia mohosa.
Vi a mis vecinos caer heridos,
la sangre chirispitiando en mis brazos,
cayendo en su carita.

Unos soldados pecho a tierra
disparaban sus rifles
y más ayá vi unos hombres armados con ametralladoras,
disparaban a la gente, a los jacales.
Cerca de mis pies la balacera rompía la tierra.
Detrás de mí sentí mi jacal echar fuego,
un calor fuerte me aventó adelante.
Tres golpes en el pecho sentí, uno tras otro,
vi los agujeros en su camisita.

Sentí que el niño apretó su manita,
la que tenía alrededor de mi dedo gordo.
Sangre saltó como agua aventada de una cubeta.
Cayó pintando las piedras
y las uñas de mis patas.
¿Quién hubiera creído
que un chiquitillo cargara tanta sangre?

Todo mundo olía a sangre.
Madre dios, ¿quién habrá cometido este mal?

Con un pedazo de mi falda,
le limpio su carita
salpicada de sangre.
Ay, Madre dios, un ojito le cuelga
y el otro no parpadea.
Ay mijito, no pude atajarte la muerte.
Un duelo me sube como una fiebre.
¿Quién curará a mi hijo?

Mojo su cuerpecito.
Entre su pavico meto su intestino.
Aplico a sus ojos agua fría.
Pongo su ojito izquierdo en su cuenca,
se le sale y se resbala por su mejilla.
Limpio la sangre en sas párpados.
Soplo sobre su cabecita,
soplo sobre sas cuevas.
Nueve veces soplo.
Sane, mi hijo, sane.

¿Qué voy hacer, Madre dios?
No siente alivio mi enfermito.
De aquí no me muevo,
en este rincón de mi tierra me quedo,
aquí que me abandone mi destino.
Aquí me quedo
hasta que mi hijo se haga polvo.
Aquí sentada,
viendo mis gruesos callos
en las plantas de los pies,
aquí viendo mis sandalias de hule
hinchadas con su sangre.
Aquí espantando las moscas,
viendo las sombras cuajadas de sangre.
Aquí me quedo hasta que me pudra.
Toda la noche lo arrullo en mis brazos.
Saco la chiche,

se la arrimo a su boquita quebrada.
El nunca ha de beber.
El día amanece,
vivo a ver otro amanecer,
que extraño.

Tiendo al niño boca abajo
en mis piernas.
Le tapo su cara,
cubro sus huesitos rotos.
Me fijo hacia el cielo.
Busco su alma.
Alma de mijo, venga aquí a mis piernas.
Plumita ensangrada,
devuelva de los cinco destinos.
Mi inocente criatura
que no temía a nada,
que nunca lloraba,
ni cuando se le acercó la muerte.
Quiero saber si ha perdido el alma.
Aquí en mis naguas su cuerpecito,
cada hora más frío.

Te invoco Madre dios,
mujer de nuestro sustento.
¿Qué querías que hiciera, Madre mía?
Soy una pobre india.
A mi hijo no le tocaba,
no todavía no.
Estos agujeros en su pecho,
esto no es su destino.
Aquí me tiro en la tierra
soy sólo un quejido.
Le pido que alivie a mi hijo,
que le devuelva su alma.
¿Qué culpa tiene una criatura?
Sí, Madre dios,
yo traté de proteger a mis hijos.
Al mayor lo mataron en el llano.
Al segundo lo mataron en el cerro.

Y el mes pasado mataron a mi hija en el monte.
Ayá se les acabó su destino.
Ya nada más me quedaba el chiquillo,
éste que está aquí cubierto con mi falda.
Sí, este de los piecesitos fríos.

Madre dios, quiero matar
a todo hombre que hace guerra,
que quebra, que acaba con la vida.
Esta guerra me ha quitado todo.
¿Que han hecho con nuestra tierra?
¿Pa' qué hacemos niños?
¿Pa' qué les damos vida?
¿Para qué sean masacrados?
¿Para qué los güeros
se burlen de la gente?
En sus ojos nosotros los indios
somos peores que los animales.

Mire como se me esta enfriándo mi hijo.
Hijito, ¿por qué te quitaron la vida
antes de que aprendieras a andar?
Esta pestilencia, la guerra,
me ha quitado todo.
Esta enfermedad colorada
convierte todo a gusano.
De lugares remotos viene
este ataque contra el pueblo.

Me quieto morir, Madre dios,
que vengan más balas.
Aquí tirenme al corazón.
El resto de mi ya está muerto.
Madre dios, le suplico
en el nombre de todas las madres
que han perdido hijos en la guerra.
Madre dios, le pido que vaya
tras de su alma,
búsquelo, recójelo.

Letting Go

It's not enough
deciding to open.

You must plunge your fingers
into your navel, with your two hands
split open,
spill out the lizards and horned toads
the orchids and the sunflowers,
turn the maze inside out.
Shake it.

Yet, you don't quite empty.
Maybe a green phlegm
hides in your cough.
You may not even know
that it's there until a knot
grows in your throat
and turns into a frog.

It tickles a secret smile
on your palate
full of tiny orgasms.

But sooner or later
it reveals itself.
The green frog indiscreetly croaks.
Everyone looks up.

It's not enough
opening once.
Again you must plunge your fingers
into your navel, with your two hands
rip open,
drop out dead rats and cockroaches
spring rain, young ears of corn.
Turn the maze inside out.
Shake it.

This time you must let go.
Meet the dragon's open face
and let the terror swallow you.
—You dissolve in its saliva
—no one recognizes you as a puddle
—no one misses you
—you aren't even remembered
and the maze isn't even
of your own making.

You've crossed over.
And all around you space.
Alone. With nothingness.

Nobody's going to save you.
No one's going to cut you down,
cut the thorns thick around you.
No one's going to storm
the castle walls nor
kiss awake your birth,
climb down your hair,
nor mount you
on the white steed.

There is no one who
will feed the yearning.
Face it. You will have
to do, do it yourself.
And all around you a vast terrain.
Alone. With night.
Darkness you must befriend if
you want to sleep nights.

It's not enough
letting go twice, three times,
a hundred. Soon everything is
dull, unsatisfactory.
Night's open face
interests you no longer.
And soon, again, you return

to your element and
like a fish to the air
you come to the open
only between breathings.
But already gills
grow on your breasts.

I Had To Go Down

I hardly ever set foot on the floors below.
   Creaking wood expanding   contracting,
  erratic ticking of the furnace
      wild animal kicking at its iron cage
     frighten   me.

I don't know what impelled me to go down.
I should have waited till morning.
The stairs were dark
dust devils eddied in the corners
and the fringes of unraveling carpet
nagged at one like an abandoned child
left too long in soiled diapers
dust streaking down my nightgown.

I lingered on the second floor
shivering in the cold
gripping my broom dustpan mop and pail.
I flicked on every light,
pulled down curtains thickened by time,
scraped the caked tears from the windows,
stripped the bed of its stiff sheets
carried my bundle down to the first floor.

I had to make a seam on the wall
pry the door open
with the claw end of the hammer.
I heard footsteps in the basement,
an intruder breaking in.
But it was only a flurry of rain drops
hitting the windowpane
or the wind knocking the candle out of my hand.

I stood among the winter trees
grey and leafless in the sunken yard
the sky vast and eternal.
I gathered the rotting wood.
It took me a time to light the fire.

The house filled with smoke
before I could flush out the leaves
and the hollow furry animal in the stove pipes
before I could plug up the tubing.

I couldn't put it off any longer.
I had to go down.
Did I keep the washer and dryer in the basement?
I swung the kerosene lamp before me.
The steps down had disappeared.
I saw them lying off to one side.
I would have to lower myself
and then drop,
hope not to break anything.

The dirt floor cushioned my fall.
A rank earth smell thickened the air
in the cavernous room
flanked by four smaller rooms
with arched openings.
I stepped on a clothes hanger
that my fright had turned soft
like a hose or a snake.
Spiderwebs shrouded the narrow windows.
I brushed them off with a broomstick.
A bit of moonlight came in.

A half fallen wall
stood in a pool of bricks,
bedsprings and headboards leaning against it.
And over a broken chair stretched a dress
fading slowly from crimson into mouse.
The lace around neck and sleeves lay limp
but when I touched it it was stiff.

I could find no machines
but I found a twin cement sink
squatting on four thick legs.
In place of spouts and handles
I saw a mouth and eyes.

A dark shape rose near the center.
It was a square cast-iron boiler
perched on a wooden platform.

I scraped the grime off the gauge
H.E. Smith, Massachusetts.
Pipes thick as my hips reared up from it,
smaller ones hung in rows across the ceiling.
It wasn't until I'd filled
the glass gauge with water
that I tripped over something
sticking out of the floor.

A gnarled root had broken through
into the belly of the house
and somehow a shoot
had sprung in the darkness
and now a young tree was growing
nourished by a nightsun.
Then I heard the footsteps again
making scuffing sounds
on the packed dirt floor.

It was my feet making them.
It had been my footsteps I'd heard.

Cagado abismo, quiero saber

*por qué en los hielos de noviembre
arrastro mi bruto cuerpo hacia tu hocico
por qué en enero tiritando de frío espero abril.
Quiero saber, pinche abismo
por qué estoy rodeada de paredes
prisionera frente de una hambre
que no tiene nombre
por qué fui pendeja, por qué joy desgraciada.
Te digo,* you fucker, *nunca quise
que tú lamieras mi boca con la tuya.*

*Aquí me tienes tronándome los dedos
encadenando el futuro con las barajas
enredándome más honda en tus barbas
haciéndole preguntas a Urano.
Quiero saber por qué el alma indomado
contintúa rastreando
mi bruta carne sobre espinas de nopal.
Sin flautas y sin flores este viaje
de murciélago ciego va hacia tu rumbo.
Nunca quise que tú mordieras mi boca.*

*Cagado abismo, quiero saber
por qué paso la vida aguantando
noches sin ti.
Quiero saber si pasaré mis días sola
haciéndome más piedra cada día.*

*Quiero saber por qué mi ser desnudo
pasa mudo de rodillas
tragándose el polvo de tus caminos.
Quiero saber por qué las sombras
se hinchan más cada día,
por qué yo vivo cuando tú me quieres muerta.
Ya me di cuenta después de tantos años
que ser mujer no es cosa tan dichosa.
Querido abismo, nomás esto he querido:
que tú me quieras, que tú me devoraras.
¿Por qué no me arrebatas de una vez?*

that dark shining thing
(for Sandra Rounds, Bessie Jo Faris, & Denise Brugman)

You've shut the door again
to escape the darkness
only it's pitch black in that closet.

Some buried part of you prevailed
elected me to pry open a crack
hear the unvoiced plea
see the animal behind the bars
of your eyelashes.

This is not new.
Colored, poor white, latent queer
passing for white
seething with hatred, anger
unaware of its source
crazed with not knowing
who they are
choose me to pick at the masks.

I am the only round face,
Indian-beaked, off-colored
in the faculty lineup, the workshop, the panel
and reckless enough to take you on.
I am the flesh you dig your fingernails into
mine the hand you chop off while still clinging to it
the face spewed with your vomit
I risk your sanity
and mine.

I want to turn my back on you
wash my hands of you
but my hands remember each seam
each nail embedded in that wall
my feet know each rock you tread on
as you stumble I falter too
and I remember
he/me/they who shouted

push Gloria breathe Gloria
feel their hands holding me up, prompting me
until I'm facing that pulsing bloodied blackness
trying to scream
from between your legs
feel again the talons raking my belly.
I remember hating him/me/they who pushed me
as I'm pushing you
remember the casing breaking
flooding the walls
remember opening my eyes one day
sensing that something was missing.

Missing was the pain, gone the fear
that all my life had walked beside me.
It was then I saw the numinous thing
it was black and it had my name
it spoke to me and I spoke to it.

Here we are four women stinking with guilt
you for not speaking your names
me for not holding out my hand sooner.
I don't know how long I can keep naming
that dark animal
coaxing it out of you, out of me
keep calling it good or woman-god
while everyone says no no no.

I know I am that Beast that circles your house
peers in the window
and that you see yourself my prey.

> But I know you are the Beast
> its prey is you
> you the midwife
> you that dark shining thing
> I know it's come down to this:
> *vida o muerte,* life or death.

Cihuatlyotl, Woman Alone

Many years   I have fought off your hands, *Raza*
father mother   church   your rage at my desire to be
with myself,   alone.   I have learned
to erect barricades   arch my back against
you   thrust back fingers, sticks   to
shriek no   to kick and claw   my way out of
your heart   And as I grew   you hacked away
at the pieces   of me   that   were   different
attached your tentacles   to my face and breasts
put a lock between my legs.   I had to do it,
Raza,   turn my back on your crookening finger
beckoning beckoning   your   soft brown
landscape, tender *nopalitos.*   Oh,   it was hard,
Raza   to cleave flesh from flesh   I risked
us both   bleeding to death.   It took   a long
time   but   I learned   to let
your values   roll off   my body   like water
those I swallow to stay alive   become tumors
in my belly.   I refuse   to be taken over   by
things   people   who fear that hollow
aloneness   beckoning   beckoning.   No self,
only race *vecindad familia.*   My soul   has always
been yours   one spark   in the roar of your fire.
We Mexicans are collective animals.   This I
accept   but my life's work   requires autonomy
like oxygen.   This lifelong battle has ended,
Raza.   I don't need to flail against you.
Raza india mexicana norteamericana,   there's nothing more you can chop off   or graft on me that
will change my soul.   I remain who I am, multiple
and one   of the herd, yet not of it.   I walk
on the ground of my own being   browned and
hardened by the ages.   I am fully formed   carved
by the hands of the ancients,   drenched with
the stench of today's headlines.   But my own
hands whittle   the final work   me.

V

Animas

Por una mujer ladina
perdí la tranquilidad
ella me clavó una espina
que no la puedo arrancar.
  —"Por una mujer ladina," a Mexican *corrido*

La curandera

I'll tell you how I became a healer.
I was sick, my leg had turned white.
Sobrino went to Juan Dávila
asked if Juan Dávila knew
anyone who could cure me.
Yes, Juan Dávila told him,
there is a healer in Mexico.

Juan Dávila crossed the border
to bring the healer.
When Juan Dávila didn't come back,
Sobrino followed him and found the healer dead.
Sobrino's leg became white
Juan Dávila prayed and prayed
Sobrino died.
Juan Dávila thought,
"It doesn't matter if one is sick or not
what matters is that one thinks so."
In his mind Sobrino wanted to die
In his mind he thought he was dying
so he died.

The Border Patrol came
found *el sobrino* dead.
We'll take the body back to the other side, they said.
No, said Juan Dávila, I'll bury him here.
Under the ground it doesn't matter
which side of the border you're in.
When they were out of sight
Juan Dávila opened his eyes.

Juan Dávila went back across the border
The Border Patrol said no way.
She's dying, he told them, meaning me.
The Border Patrol let him through.
Juan Dávila found me in pain,
the maggots in my body ate my flesh,
my dress, my hair, my teeth.

When Juan Dávila went to bury me
the ground where my body had lain was empty.
There was nothing to bury.

Juan Dávila saw pain crawling toward him.
He backed away.
Still it followed him,
until he was pressed into the wall.
He watched the pain climb up his feet, legs.
When it reached his heart,
it began to eat him.
"My thoughts cause this," he cried out.
In his head he made a picture of the pain backing off,
of the pain sliding down his leg,
of the pain crawling toward the door.

Then Juan Dávila saw the pain turn around
and come back.
"If I must die, then I'll die," he said
looking at his leg turning white.
Juan Dávila kneeled to pray.
Juan Dávila saw the pain
crawling to where my body had lain.
He saw my clothes appear,
saw my dress begin to move,
saw me sit up and open my eyes.
"You're not dead," he said.
"You prayed for me to be well," I told him.
"No, I prayed for myself," he said.
"You are every one, when you prayed for yourself,
you prayed for all of us."

Juan Dávila looked into my eyes,
saw the longing.
"You want to die, don't you," he said.
"No, I want to be with her, *la virgen santísima.*
"But you are with her," he said,
eyes clear like a child's.
"She is everywhere."
And I heard the wind begin to blow.

As I breathed the air in and out,
I breathed her in and out.
I walked into my *jacal* to lie down
and there on the floor by my bed,
lay Juan Dávila asleep.

Get up, Juan Dávila, get in the bed.
I lay in the bed and slept.
When I woke up I saw
squirming serpents on the floor
shiny serpents on the walls
serpents moving on the windows.
A small fear appeared and entered me.
I heard a big black snake say,
"We are your healing spirit guides."
The serpents slithered off the walls
I couldn't see them any more,
but I felt them all around me.
"What do I do now," I asked them.
"We will teach you," they said,
"but first you must gather the herbs."

Juan Dávila and I went into the fields.
"No, this way," Juan Dávila told me.
I smiled and followed him.
We found nothing but weeds.
"*Curandera*, you knew
there were no *yerbitas* here."
"Oh, there's a few," I said.
"Look behind that big weed."
Juan Dávila bent down,
saw a tiny *romero* plant.
When he reached out to pick it
I said, "No leave it, it's too small."

"The weeds are choking it," he said,
"and it's got no leaves."
"Help it," I told him.
"I'll go get the hoe," he said.
"No, there's no time, the plant will die.

She needs room," I said.
The weeds began to move back.
The *romero* began to grow.
The weeds moved further back.
"No, *pendejos,* let's kill her," said a big ugly *quelite.*
"No, she's so pretty," the others said
holding him back.

The tiny *romero* grew and grew,
told them, "You're pretty too."
The weeds became long graceful grasses,
they bowed down to the *romero.*
Herbs of all kinds
poked their heads out of the earth
covered the fields.
I've been a *curandera*
since that day
and Juan Dávila has been my apprentice.

mujer cacto

La mujer del desierto
tiene espinas
las espinas son sus ojos
si tú te le arrimas te arraña.
La mujer del desierto
tiene largas y afiladas garras.

La mujer del desierto mira la avispa
clavar su aguijón
y chingar a una tarántula
mira que la arrastra a un agujero
pone un huevo sobre ella
el huevo se abre
el bebé sale y se come la tarántula
No es fácil vivir en esta tierra.

La mujer del desierto
se entierra en la arena con los lagartos
se esconde como rata
pasa el día bajo tierra
tiene el cuero duro
no se reseca en el sol
vive sin agua.

La mujer del desierto
mete la cabeza adentro como la tortuga
desentierra raíces con su hocico
junta con las javalinas
caza conejos con los coyotes.

Como un flor la mujer del desierto
no dura mucho tiempo
pero cuando vive llena el desierto
con flores de nopal o de árbol paloverde.

La mujer del desierto
enroscada es serpiente cascabel
descansa durante el día

por la noche cúando hace fresco
bulle con la lechuza,
con las culebras alcanza un nido de pájaros
y se come los huevos y los pichoncitos.

Cuando se noja la mujer del desierto
escupe sangre de los ojos como el lagarto cornudo
cuando oye una seña de peligro
salta y corre como liebre
se vuelve arena
> *La mujer del desierto, como el viento*
> *sopla, hace dunas, lomas.*

Cuyamaca
(for Beth Brant and Chrystos)

"This tribe is the most numerous
and the most restless, stubborn,
haughty, warlike and hostile
toward us . . . . "
—Don Pedro Fages, 1787

Driving down the canyon
on a road gouged out of the side of the mountain
red red earth and exposed roots
sticking out like amputated fingers.
145 acres for sale
the Indians safely locked up in reservations
or urban ghettos.

Driving around the mountain
inside the car
fighting for silence.
Houses stick out like pimples
on the face of the mountain.

At this skirt of the mountain ranges
I met a woman from a nearly extinct tribe,
the Kumeyaay.
Her name was Til'pu,
meaning Roadrunner.
By a stream amidst the gushing water
under the olive woolly head of the mountain
I met her.

Under the encina tree I sat.
She emerged out of the smooth amber flesh
of the manzanita,
in sandals of woven yucca,
skin polished bronze by the sun
she appeared
with a tattoo on her arm

pricked by cactus thorns
ground charcoal rubbed on the wound.

There's a forest fire in the Cuyamaca Peaks,
a sign: 4 Parcels For Sale,
the Indians locked up in reservations
and Til'pu behind glass in the museum.

My Black *Angelos*

In the night I hear her soft whimper
wild masses of hair
rustling in the silence.
Una mujer vaga en la noche
anda errante con las almas de los muertos.

Aiiii aiiiii aiiiiii
She is crying for the dead child
the lover gone, the lover not yet come:
Her *grito* splinters the night
fear drenches me.
I stink of carrion,
she turns upwind tracking me.
Her teeth reflect the fire
from her rouged eyes
my black *Angelos*,
la bruja con las uñas largas,
I hear her at the door.

Taloned hand on my shoulder
behind me putting words, worlds in my head
turning, her hot breath
she picks the meat stuck between my teeth
with her snake tongue
sucks the smoked lint from my lungs
with her long black nails
plucks lice from my hair.

aiiiii aiiiii aiiiiii
She crawls into my spine
her eyes opening and closing,
shining under my skin in the dark
whirling my bones twirling
till they're hollow reeds.

aiiiiii aiiiiiaaaaaaaa
Una mujer vaga en la noche

anda errante con las almas de los muertos.
We sweep through the streets
con el viento corremos
we roam with the souls of the dead.

Creature of Darkness

Three weeks I've wallowed
in this deep place
        this underplace
        this grieving place
getting heavier and heavier
sleeping by day creeping out at night

Nothing I can do
nothing I want to do
but stay small and still in the dark
no thought   I want not to think
        that stirs up the pain
        opens the wound
        starts the healing

I don't want it to stop
I want to sit here and pick at the scabs
           watch the blood flow
           lick the salt from my face
while all the time
a part of me cries Stop Stop

Behind that voice
shadows snicker
        No, we like it here in the dark
        we like sitting here with our grief
            and our longing

This is where we live
Home, they whisper
We're a creature of darkness.

A lump of me says
What are you hiding
     under that black log
        that grey fog
           a pink salamander
           a mole without eyes

              things that slide into holes
Oh creature of darkness
   creature of night
   creature afraid of the light.

I let my friends think
I'm doing a gig
somewhere on the other coast
They would come around
      coax me out of the deep
      no one must find me here in the dark

So I feed that hole to stifle the loss
          to muffle the loss
          to smother the loss
      but its mouth grows and grows
        and I grow fat
        and I grow numb
   sole inhabitant of this dark underplace
        this grieving place
no one must find me suspended in darkness
        soft furry body
        loose hanging skin
swinging upside down
to the yierp yierp of bats

Three weeks I rocked with that wide open maw
        refusing to move
        barely daring to breathe
    sinking deeper
   growing great with mouth
      a creature afraid of the dark
      a creature at home in the dark.

Antigua, mi diosa

Descalza, gateando a ciegas voy
sigo tus huellas ligeras y tu linaje viejo.
Con astillas en las rodillas voy.
Furtiva, con paso de tortuga
camino bajo la noche desaforada.
Antigua, mi diosa, por ti sacrifiqué
las plantas de mis pies.
Acantilada por tus ojos vulnerada voy,
testiga de este largo invierno.
      En medio de un chillido de trenes
veniste a las ruinas de Brooklyn
con tu sonido de cascabeles.
Tu voz un millón de alas.
Como un chubasco veniste
oliendo a almendras quemadas y copal.
      Me diste tu golpe de hacha
caí como un árbol despetalando mis ojos.
Te tendiste a mi lado, tus dedos cantando como espadas
haciendo dibujos en mi cara.
Me entraste por todas las rendijas
con tu luz llenaste el hueco de mi cuerpo.
      Me consumaste enterita,
sí, mi antigua diosa,
sembraste tus semillas de luz
en los surcos de mi cuerpo.
La cosecha: esta inquietud
que se madura en agonía.
Y ahora huyes en mis entrañas como un animal.
Toditito ha cambiado, nada me satisface.
Ancient, querida, parece que no tengo cura.
      Hace diez meses que me hago y me deshago—
que tarea inacabable tu me dejaste.
No te puedo darme no,
no me puedo entregar a tu regazo.
¿Cómo? si nunca me he dado a mí misma.
Antigua, mi madre, ya no soy dueña
ni de mis desengaños.
Tú acabaste con todo eso.

Deseos insepultos velan la noche
Mira como me has arruinado.
No tengo remedio.
      Este pobre cuerpo renacido
tres veces ha resurrecto.
La última vez me sentenciaste
con esta aflicción:
años y años de tu ausencia.
Que gran deshandaruda me pediste.
Y ahora por todas las tierras vulneradas te busco.
Antigua, tu hija errante no puede alcanzarte.
      Deme otra seña,
otra migaja de su luz.
Mi incendiada piel urge el saberte.
Antigua, mi diosa, quiero brotar otra vez
en tu negrísima piel.

VI

El Retorno

Arriba mi gente

(*para* Tirsa Quiñones who wrote the music
and Cherríe Moraga who sang it)

Chorus: *Arriba mi gente,*
toda gente arriba.
In spirit as one,
all people arising
Toda la gente junta
en busca del Mundo Zurdo
en busca del Mundo Zurdo

Un pueblo de almas afines
encenderemos los campos
con una llamarada morada—
la lumbre del Mundo Zurdo.

Chorus

Ya no, sin fe, mi gente
camino entre ilusiones   repeat
de muebles, perro, cielo
sin libro, letra. Herida.
Y con mi gente
andando mi vida   repeat
voy dando mi mensaje.

Mi gente, despierta,
limpia la Madre Tierra.   repeat
Y entre la llama púrpura
allí renaceremos
allí renaceremos.   repeat

Chorus

Hijas de la Chingada,
born of the violated *india,*
guerrilleras divinas—
mujeres de fuego ardiente
que dan luz a la noche oscura
dan lumbre al Mundo Zurdo

Chorus

¡Volveremos!
Prenderemos la guerra de bien adentro
con esa luz del alma.
En esta noche Zurda |
renacerá el Espíritu | repeat
de nuestra Tierra.

Retornará nuestra antigua fe
y levantará el campo.
Arriba, despierten, mi gente |
a liberar los pueblos. | repeat

In spirit as one
all people arising.

En esta noche Zurda, mi vida,
mirar, nuestras trescientas luces
y ver la llamarada morada |
la lumbre del Mundo Zurdo. | repeat

Chorus

Levantémonos, Raza
mujeres de séptimo rayo
que ya llegamos y aquí estamos.
Arriba, despierta mi gente
a liberar los pueblos |
Arriba mi gente, despierta. | repeat

To live in the Borderlands means you

are neither *hispana india negra española*
ni gabacha, eres mestiza, mulata, half-breed
caught in the crossfire between camps
while carrying all five races on your back
not knowing which side to turn to, run from;

To live in the Borderlands means knowing
that the *india* in you, betrayed for 500 years,
is no longer speaking to you,
that *mexicanas* call you *rajetas,*
that denying the Anglo inside you
is as bad as having denied the Indian or Black;

Cuando vives en la frontera
people walk through you, the wind steals your voice,
you're a *burra, buey,* scapegoat,
forerunner of a new race,
half and half—both woman and man, neither—
a new gender;

To live in the Borderlands means to
put *chile* in the borscht,
eat whole wheat *tortillas,*
speak Tex-Mex with a Brooklyn accent;
be stopped by *la migra* at the border checkpoints;

Living in the Borderlands means you fight hard to
resist the gold elixir beckoning from the bottle,
the pull of the gun barrel,
the rope crushing the hollow of your throat;

In the Borderlands
you are the battleground
where enemies are kin to each other;
you are at home, a stranger,
the border disputes have been settled
the volley of shots have shattered the truce
you are wounded, lost in action
dead, fighting back;

To live in the Borderlands means
>the mill with the razor white teeth wants to shred off
>your olive-red skin, crush out the kernel, your heart
>pound you pinch you roll you out
>smelling like white bread but dead;

To survive the Borderlands
>you must live *sin fronteras*
>be a crossroads.

---

gabacha—a Chicano term for a white woman
rajetas—literally, "split," that is, having betrayed your word
burra—donkey
buey—oxen
sin fronteras—without borders

Canción de la diosa de la noche
(for Randy Conner)

I am a vine
creeping down the moon.
I have no keeper.

I fall into this world.
The Mother, catching me in her net,
entangles me in human flesh.

I wander on a path
come to the patio of a ruined temple.
Flutes lure me to a fire.
A litany fondles my hip
horns pin me to the ground.
To cast out the brute,
I shake earth, air, fire, and water
in the lunar sistrum.
I devour the roses of Isis.

I pass
through the gate,
come to the path on the left,
past the wellspring
beside the gnarled cypress.

At the crossroads
where her spirit shocks
she comes sweeping
through the night,
spirits and hounds
baying behind her.
Her wings keep me warm.
Three jackals
watch with me.

I am the gate
demons and vanquished gods invade
then pass into this world to get to you.

I do not want to keep to myself,
but none see the brand on my forehead
save you and the few who can look me in the face.
I pass unseen, my shawl wrapped around me.
Choosing to walk alone, I return to myself.

Daily, the present menaces,
Splinters fly from my eyes,
pricking liars and fools.
Thorns and thistles grow in my hair
drawing the blood
of you who embrace me.

I am mad
but I choose this madness.
The godhead is unstrung.
He has a grudge against me and all flesh.
He rejects the dark within the flame.
As for me, I renounce my kinship
with the whole and all its parts,
renounce my fealty to nature.

A black cock crows three times.
Casting no shadow,
I wake from drunkenness
holding my own hand.
Cloaked in panther skin,
I sound the maddening cymbals.

I slip my knots and garments,
utter the first no.
It begins where it ends.

Memory
ignites like kindling
the time when I filled the sky.
Parting brought death.
Now, I drum on the carcass of the world
creating crises to recall my name.
The filth you relegate to Satan,

I absorb. I convert.
When I dance it burgeons out
                as song.

              I seek *la diosa*
            darkly awesome.
          In love with my own kind,
        I know you and inspirit you.
    All others flee from me.

                I buff the old scratches from bone.
              With flint knife, cut in our marks.
          I keep the moon from bleeding
        and the sun from turning black.
                But water drains from the earth.

              Terror seizes me.
              Death's warm hand on me.
              Night, unfurl your wings
              and your long hair over me.
              Bring your breast
              to my mouth and never wean me.

              With chant I break the spell,
              disperse the watchers from the gates.
              Wake the sleepers.
              With my fist I rive
              a hole in the wall:

            the winds rush in,
            I am the gate no longer.
            You are the gate.

The deep below, the deep above.
The waters overflow.

It begins where it ends,
I descend into black earth,
dark primordial slime,
no longer repellent to me,

nor confining.
The four winds
fire welds splinter with splinter.
I find my kindred spirits.

The moon eclipses the sun.
    La diosa lifts us.
        We don the feathered mantle
          and charge our fate.

No se raje, chicanita
(*para* Missy Anzaldúa)

No se raje mi prietita,
apriétese la faja aguántese.
Su linaje es antiguísimo,
sus raíces como las de los mesquites,
bien plantadas, horadando bajo tierra
a esa corriente, el alma de tierra madre—
tu origen.

Sí m'ijita, su gente se creó en los ranchos
aquí en el Valle cerquita del río Grande
en la mera frontera.
en el tiempo antes de los gabachos
cuando Tejas era México
De los primeros vaqueros descendiste
allá en los Vergeles, en Jesús María—tierra Dávila
Mujeres fuertísimas te crearon:
tu mamá, mi hermana, mi madre, y yo.

Y sí, nos han quitado las tierras.
Ya no nos queda ni el camposanto
donde enterraron a Don Urbano, tu vis-visabuelo.
Tiempos duros como pastura los cargamos
derechitas caminamos.

Pero nunca nos quitarán ese orgullo
de ser mexicana-Chicana-tejana
ni el espíritu indio.
Y cuando los gringos se acaban—
mira como se matan unos a los otros—
aquí vamos a parecer
con los horned toads *y los lagartijos*
survivors *del* First Fire Age, *el Quinto Sol.*

Quizá muriéndonos de hambre como siempre
pero una nueva especie
piel entre negra y bronce

segunda pestaña bajo la primera
con el poder de mirar al sol ojos desnudos.
Y vivas, m'ijita, retevivas.

Sí, se me hace que en unos cuantos años o siglos
la Raza se levantará, lengua intacta
cargando lo mejor de todas las culturas.
Esa víbora dormida, la rebeldía, saltará.
Como cuero viejo caerá la esclavitud
de obedecer, de callar, de aceptar.
Como víbora relampagueando nos moveremos, mujercita.
¡Ya verás!

Don't Give In, *Chicanita*
(*para* Missy Anzaldúa)

Don't give in *mi prietita*
tighten your belt, endure.
Your lineage is ancient,
your roots like those of the mesquite
firmly planted, digging underground
toward that current, the soul of *tierra madre*—
your origin.

Yes, *m'ijita,* your people were raised *en los ranchos*
here in the Valley near the Rio Grande
you descended from the first cowboy, the *vaquero,*
right smack in the border
in the age before the Gringo when Texas was Mexico
over *en los ranches los Vergeles y Jesús María*—
Dávila land.
Strong women reared you:
my sister, your mom, my mother and I.

And yes, they've taken our lands.
Not even the cemetery is ours now
where they buried Don Urbano
your great-great-grandfather.
Hard times like fodder we carry
with curved backs we walk.

But they will never take that pride
of being *mexicana*-Chicana-*tejana*
nor our Indian woman's spirit.
And when the Gringos are gone—
see how they kill one another—
here we'll still be like the horned toad and the lizard
relics of an earlier age
survivors of the First Fire Age—*el Quinto Sol.*

Perhaps we'll be dying of hunger as usual
but we'll be members of a new species
skin tone between black and bronze

second eyelid under the first
with the power to look at the sun through naked eyes.
And alive *m'ijita,* very much alive.

Yes, in a few years or centuries
la Raza will rise up, tongue intact
carrying the best of all the cultures.
That sleeping serpent,
rebellion-(r)evolution, will spring up.
Like old skin will fall the slave ways of
obedience, acceptance, silence.
Like serpent lightning we'll move, little woman.
You'll see.

—translated from the Spanish by the author

Appendix

Introductions to
Previous Editions

Gloria Anzaldúa ¡Presente!
An Introduction in Ten Voices

It has been twenty years since the birth of *Borderlands/La Frontera*, and it has been three years since Gloria Anzaldúa's unexpected death. Aunt Lute felt it would be fitting to use the occasion of this 20th year to celebrate the importance of Gloria's work, now her legacy. However, we wanted to enact that celebration in a manner consistent with the spirit of that work: hybrid, inclusive, many-voiced. To that end, we asked a number of her contemporaries to reflect on the significance of Gloria's work out in the world. We have gathered those responses here. Individually, each contributor illuminates the significance of Gloria's contribution as an artist, as an activist, and as a political and social theorist. Together, these pieces constitute a powerful testament to the emotional and intellectual reach of Gloria's work.

Encuentros en la Encrucijada / *Norma Alarcón*

In the Spring of 2004, several weeks after Gloria Anzaldúa died, I had a dream about her. I was going round and round a twelve-foot stone wall which in fact was round itself. Its structure was circular. I was looking for an entrance and couldn't find it. On the third go-around, I directed myself to keep driving and stop trying to find an entrance. As I was coming to a fork in the road, I was startled by the figure of Gloria Anzaldúa with a flower in her hair, smiling and waving at me. She seemed to be expecting me. She was standing at a door in the circular wall. I parked at the juncture of the fork in order to go visit with her. Was this the only entrance? As I approached her, I was able to get a glimpse beyond the door's opening and caught sight of a cemetery. I had been circling a cemetery! That was the end of the dream. I was beckoned and I stopped to greet and talk, but it didn't happen in the dream.

In September of 2004, Cherríe Moraga organized a memorial for Gloria in San Francisco's public library and invited me to participate. I had five minutes, which was okay because I am given to stage fright. I told the audience of the dream. It was a well-lighted film strip when I dreamed it, and still is. However, after all had spoken remembrances of Gloria, a woman I knew, Louisah Teish, came up to me in what seemed to me a very concerned way. She had something urgent to tell me. She was saying to me that Gloria's spirit had not passed yet and that I should go to the cemetery, any cemetery, and talk to Gloria. Tell her that you are not ready to leave yet. Was there anything special I had to do? No. Just go talk with her and tell her you are not ready to leave.

Towards December of that year, I began to imagine going to a cemetery. Where were the cemeteries in Oakland? I finally remembered the high-toned cemetery in Piedmont; surely there must be a gorgeous view of the sunset somewhere in that hill cemetery. I had not asked Louisah Teish if my visit to the cemetery was meant to be a ritual, but I treated it as a ritual anyway. As such, I decided to go to the cemetery on December 12th, and syncretize Tonantzin, Guadalupe and Gloria. Since the hill faces west towards Australia and other places, I imagined that in this ritual Gloria and I would watch the sunset and the sunset on empire-makers. We would be witness to their demise. Through this ritual, it would of course be so. In that spirit I went to the cemetery looking for Gloria one hour before sunset on December 12th.

I had no idea what to say. What do you say to a spirit that is restless and floating about the environment? What do you say to someone you assume will hear you because you assume that the spirit is there? I didn't know. I decided to tell her stories about her work and my admiration, the influence her work has wrought, her legacy to all of us, and to me specifically. To daydream with her spirit about our shared desire for a different world where one is no longer an "atravesada" and empire-making forever disappears from the face of the earth.

Whenever we talked on the phone, as we hung up, she said "adiosita." And on that day—December 12, 2004—we said "adiosita" for the last time. May her spirit-breath dance to the rhythms of the cosmos.

Gloria Anzaldúa, *que en paz descanse* / *Julia Alvarez*

As one in that first generation of Latinas who came of age in those pre-multicultural, pre-women's movement days, I floundered as to what it meant to be a hyphenated, bicultural, bilingual American. The old model of immigration I was presented with was an assimil-ationist, melting-pot model: you became an American by cutting off your ties to that "old world," including its language, its culture, its ways of making meaning, and you blended in with the mainstream American culture.

This might have been a viable model when immigration was among Caucasian-Europeans, and mobility was circumscribed, so there was no chance you would ever return to that little village in Germany or Ireland or Poland, or Russia. But for this new wave of immigrants—and in some cases, long-term Mexican-American natives of the South-west, this model did not apply. Racially different, we could not blend in, even if we tried. Mobility allowed us to maintain our connection to our native cultures and countries and language, so our old homelands were still a part of our new selves. But by being here, that homeland had also undergone a change within us. We could not go back. We did not fit in there; we did not fit in here. We were caught between worlds, a no man's land, no place for troubled mujeres. . .

Many of us got very lost. I began to write out of necessity, a way to integrate the many selves, to understand the confusion, string for the labyrinth. But my writing was a private matter, a lonely way to make sense of the divisions. To drown out, momentarily, what the larger culture was telling me—something was wrong with me for not being able to assimilate and be grateful for the opportunities I had received.

It was a lifesaver to discover other Latinas undergoing similar journeys. It turned out that many of us who came of age in the 60s and early 70s felt a kind of cultural schizophrenia, torn and divided by pulls in so many directions. Feminism not only sharpened the divisions inside us but also gave us a sense of agency and urgency as to how we were going to integrate our many selves and integrate ourselves within our communities. The Civil Rights movement gave us hope. And Gloria Anzaldúa, along with other Latina writers who began to publish in the early 80s, helped us to understand what was happening to us.

In 1981 *This Bridge Called My Back*, edited by Anzaldúa and Cherríe Moraga, was published by Persephone Press. Two years later, Moraga published *Loving in the War Years*. In 1984 came *Cuentos: Stories by Latinas* (Kitchen Table Press) and *The House on Mango Street* by Sandra Cisneros. And there were other stories, essays, poems, novels, plays—voices were emerging, a conversation had begun among ourselves and with the rest of America, north and south. But it wasn't until 1987 when Gloria Anzaldúa published *Borderlands/La Frontera: The New Mestiza* that a map was charted—the old divisive no man's land became a borderland, a place where a new kind of self was being created.

When I read *Borderlands* in 1988 in preparation for teaching the first course on Latino literature at Middlebury College, my heart was in my throat. Anzaldúa was giving voice to what it meant to be a hybrid, a mixture, a mestiza: "Alienated from her mother culture, 'alien' in the dominant culture, the woman of color [is] caught between los intersticios, the spaces between the different worlds she inhabits." This book not only provided a way to understand the literature we would be reading, it also confirmed personally the painful sense of marginality many of us had been feeling.

But what I was most grateful for was that Anzaldúa refused to stay stuck in that divided place, battered by opposing forces. This is what makes her 1987 memoir seem prophetic and more timely than ever. Anzaldúa believed in the evolution of a new Latina consciousness based on a tolerance for the contradictions we have inherited. That painful borderland world can also be the place "where the possibility of uniting all that is separate occurs."

Gloria Anzaldúa was one of the first to crystallize and celebrate the potential of a borderland state of mind. A state of being betwixt and between, "of belonging to at least two identities at the same time, and not being confused or hurt by it," to quote Ed Morales in *Living in Spanglish.* John Keats called it the quality of negative capability, ideal for the "poetical Character...the camelion Poet": that ability to entertain dualities and "to be in uncertainties, Mysteries, doubts without any irritable reaching after fact & reason." Mike Davis in *Magical Urban-ism* notes that because of this deep understanding of borderlands and hybridity, Latino/as could well be the ones who teach America how to be—of all things!—American:

> To be Latino in the U.S. is rather to participate
> in a unique process of cultural syncretism that
> may become a transformative template for the
> whole society.

Why not? Statisticians predict that by the year 2050 one out of every four Americans will be of Hispanic origin. More and more of us borderland people! But immigration into a new culture or into a mainstream is no longer an experience exclusive to Latinos. Globalization brings the "immigration experience" beyond our borders and makes the collision of cultures a reality everywhere. And so when we wonder about how to deal with these confusions and contradictions, we are really addressing how to evolve a new kind of world consciousness that is transformative and synthesizing. Anzaldúa was right. The question is no less than how to be a new kind of human being!

Circulations: Thinking with Gloria Anzaldúa in Paris / *Paola Bacchetta*

I read *Borderlands/La Frontera* in 1989, two years after it was first published. At the time I was engaged in movements in Paris against racism, lesbophobia and sexism, and for immigrants' rights. I had recently become documented. I was also a student. I had access to Gloria's book thanks to a U.S. friend who sent it. Otherwise, U.S. feminist and queer of color writing, work that addresses gender, sexuality, racialization, class and colonialism inseparably, including Gloria's, was unavailable in France. Today, only a handful of such U.S. articles, and no books, exist in French. Among them, there is not yet *one* by any Chicana feminist or queer. I have been able to share Gloria's ideas in *Borderlands/La*

Frontera with friends in France throughout these years, but certainly such circulations remain quite limited.

In this context, Gloria's entrance into my life was intensely intimate and political. In *Borderlands/La Frontera* I encountered a Gloria expansive enough to include within herself the many worlds that comprised both her present and her genealogy. Her spaces were quite different from my own. Yet, I felt at home with her words. She knew about inhabiting the body of a brown postcolonial queer in the U.S.; the indio parts of herself remained alive to her; she was also a queer mestiza in her postcolonial Chicano enclaves in Texas. The spaces I had inhabited in my brown queer body outside the U.S. were France and India. Gloria moved me to reflect on the positionalities I am assigned from one site to another, and their consequences. In the U.S.: Latina, Indian, Carribean. In France: Algerian. In India: Kashmiri, Punjabi, Hindu, Muslim, Syrian Christian. I would make claims to nothing except plurality.

Gloria invited me to reflect upon the effects of being repeatedly obliged to address misidentifications ("I am not"…). About intrusive misrecognitions, projections, demands for clarification. About multiple interpellations ("hey you…do this, be that"). About how the dominant keeps us preoccupied with his/her concerns and quest to know ("okay, let me try harder to explain myself to you"). They keep us exhausted (no conduct or explanation is ever adequate). They keep us in check (we are not to imagine a becoming for ourselves). They oblige us to respond within a dominant grid of intelligibility (that erases and silences us) thereby reinforcing that grid (and our erasure and silence). If inter-subjectivity requires two subjects in dialogue, then in these situations where I cannot exist even in my telling of myself, there is no inter-subjectivity. In France, a major struggle, individually and collectively, has been to arrive at an "I exist" and "we exist." One of the first collective public declarations of lesbians targeted by racism in France would become simply "we exist."

In Gloria's own struggle for "I exist" and "we exist" in *Border-lands/La Frontera* there are moments of intense, meaningful, even respectful, silence. There is also forced silence. There is the nearly audible silence, the internal "oh no" that certain words and conduct acutely evoke. And then there is the silence that shock produces. In *Borderlands/La Frontera* I came upon several sites of blankness, an indescribable accumulation of too-much, an everythingness-at-once. The last straw of violence accrued from forever, in the present. For example, this happens in Gloria's poem-story "horse" (128) wherein a horse is slowly tortured, battered with knives, its flesh cut into pieces, by young gringo men. What kind of dominant subject does the enactment of brutality produce? What kind of Other? What did the horse feel other than the dominant's quest for pleasure in the context of relations of power, that flow, that crystallize here and there, that flow.

Gloria opens a path for rethinking existence beyond the present forced silence of racialized, sexual violence of all sorts, through cognitive decolonization. In Francophone contexts, decolonization procedures have been developed in the work of Fanon, Memmi, Cesaire, and others; as useful as these might be, however, they do not specifically consider subalternly gendered, sexed subjects. Gloria does. She tells us that one has to "take inventory," then "differentiate between *lo heredado, lo adquirido, lo impuesto*" (104). Then, "rupture with all oppressive traditions of all cultures and religions," "reinterpret history," and "using new symbols" "shape new myths" (104).

One strand (among many) of Gloria's decolonization procedures that I found particularly compelling for us in France is her playful analytics of space and time. In "The Homeland, Aztlán/El Otro México," Gloria unravels and displaces the official archives of her history. She seeks what is submerged under official narratives. She constructs a different understanding of herself, mentally and emotionally elsewhere. She evokes a specific genealogy: Chicanas through Indias in Aztlán; Cochises, mestizas. She re-envisions official temporal categories (as in the linearity of past-present-future to date Chicana history beginning in 35000 BC), but also elaborates otherwise erased temporalities, such as repetition, cyclical time, or time that meanders like the body of the snake. There is a deliberate precision in her account. With these spatialities and these temporalities, she generates submerged voices, acts, symbolics, and ways of understanding. She reclaims her own becoming.

In France, the possibilities for subalternly gendered, sexed subjects are severely limited but not impossible. The French state moves between the forced imposition of its own dominant narrative about French colonialism and calculated colonial amnesia. This imposition-erasure dance is integral to the French procedures of assimilating postcolonial immigrants. One "becomes" French by becoming first a blank slate that can then be cultured like a plant to take shape as a French nationalized sub-citizen subject. Producing such subjects is one of the express aims of the French public school system.

Several groups of lesbians targeted by racism have worked directly against the grain of this assimilation project. At least one group, Les 'L' en Couleur, also attempts to create a new postcolonial, postslavery lesbian analytics, an elsewhere, where an unshackled, new subject-in-process can come into existence. In this, Gloria's own playful circulations in time and space, her critical and creative weavings, her silences and articulations, her expansive spirit, are exquisite, vital gifts.

Gloria's Legacy / *Rusty Barcelo*

It was 1981 when I was first introduced to the work of Gloria Anzaldúa through her co-edited book, *This Bridge Called My Back*. I was a young educator at the University of Iowa, struggling with how to work and live in a world that did not recognize or value me as a Chicana lesbian. Gloria's words, along with those of other contributors in the book, provided me with needed solace. Realizing I was not alone gave me strength to move forward in new ways; to take risks. Most importantly, Gloria inspired me to think about how my work could be built around the important parts of my own identity, how I could encourage other Chicanas to also take risks and move beyond barriers.

A few years later the staff at Aunt Lute Books talked to those of us who were on the Aunt Lute Board about a new work from Gloria that they would be publishing. When I heard the nature of the content, I realized that this could be a major body of work and that it needed to be out in the world in a way that was accessible to *all* Chicanas. So, when, a year later, I received the finished book, *Borderlands/La Frontera,* I put all my other work aside and sat down to read. From the very first page of the preface I knew it was a special text, exceeding my earlier hopes. I read it eagerly, hanging on to key messages that captured my imagination and heart and gave new meaning to Chicana identity. I re-read it many times, and each time it was like reading it for the first time because there was always something new to be learned and to ponder.

Later, when I'd become the Associate Vice President for Multicultural and Academic Affairs at the University of Minnesota, I taught a course entitled La Chicana. *Borderlands* was a required text. Chicanas represented only a handful out of fifty students, and what I remember most was how Gloria's work invigorated and challenged the class to rethink their own notions and beliefs about Chicanas. The non-Chicanas, who were mostly Women's Studies or Spanish majors, were often at odds with the text because it contradicted what they knew as budding scholars. Some women of color and Chicanas felt threatened by issues of sexuality. Because the text and discussions could make the students feel uncomfortable, they would often raise questions about its authenticity. However, more often than not, Chicanas and other women of color would resonate with understanding and personal identification—much like I did in 1981—because they felt validated. Gloria's words, to my surprise and joy, made it possible for the Chicanas and women of color in the class to change the class dynamic by re-positioning themselves at the center. This was the first time in my teaching career that I had witnessed this powerful shift.

Through Gloria's writing I have come to understand that having a strong sense of self, not only as an educational administrator and teacher but as a cultural being, has provided me with the understanding and confidence to move in and out of multiple worlds, allowing me to navigate the borders of the academy, which remain contested terrain for Chicanas and other marginalized groups.

It was very painful when I learned of Gloria's passing and felt the loss of her important voice. It is clear that her work has had a major impact, not only on the lives of Chicanas but in the academic disciplines, like Women's Studies, Chicano Studies, Cultural Studies, and on society in general. Her death made me consider how we might continue to expand on Gloria's work and her legacy. How we could continue to create conversations that could help to transform our world. How we could create the kind of spaces where voices like Gloria's can emerge and thrive, so they might challenge and inspire people in the way I was inspired. This is the legacy that Gloria and *Borderlands* has left me: to challenge myself to continue a type of activism in education that guarantees the work Gloria began.

Doing Work that Matters: In memory of Gloria Anzaldúa, paisana y compañera / *Norma Elia Cantú*

Gloria and I shared many things, but coming from that contested land that is "the wound that will not heal" was perhaps the most significant. She chose to leave and I to stay in that land; neither choice was easy. When we were with each other, we often spoke of these choices. I felt at home talking to her, for we could lapse into the familiar Tex-Mex that we both relished; I felt as at home as when platicando con mi hermana. Perhaps it was due to her voice, her mannerisms, so familiar, tan conocidos. But probably it was because of an affinity that came from having a similar background in a similar terrain. Over the course of 25 years, mas o menos, we met at conferences—in New Mexico, Maryland, and, of course, California—and on university campuses dispersed all over the country; there was even a memorable visit to the National Zoo when I was living in DC. But the space that I feel we shared most deeply was not a physical one; it was one of the mind and of the spirit. Gloria taught me to be fearless in the face of those who would silence our voices in all their complexities. The most obvious one is that of our border languages, but she also strengthened my resolve to speak in the languages of spiritualities and of feminisms that the mainstream academic or intellectual circles may not sanction. In that land where much of our common spiritual quest exists, there are few wounds, just bumps along the road. Just as when we were punished for speaking Spanish, we felt that we were treading dangerous ground when speaking about our power, our inner knowledge.

In December 2005, when I attended a panel at the Modern Languages Association Meeting on the work of Gloria Anzaldúa, I was moved beyond words as I sat in the room filled to capacity and listened to the scholarly papers presented. Although I was elated and overjoyed to see Gloria's legacy in action, I also wondered if this was the extent of her legacy, if we would continue to use her words and her thoughts to move our academic agendas forward, to contribute the new knowledge that the scholarly enterprise purports to find. What about the spiritual content? The negotiation of queerness? The contact with our community? I came away from the conference with the idea of organizing like-minded scholars and others to insure that her legacy would be honored and kept for subsequent generations of scholars, of community activists, of "atravesadas" and ultimately for generations of women. In the fall of 2006, I organized the Society for the Study of Gloria Anzaldúa and made it an affiliate of the Society for the Study of American Women Writers. Getting that organization off the ground was not easy or simple, but it was necessary and critical.

When I first read *Borderlands,* I was an assistant professor at Laredo State University in Laredo, Texas and in dire need of a voice that felt like my own, that spoke to the anxieties and contradictions inherent in working at a university on the border. I was working to start a literacy program, desperately working with Central American detainees in the detentions center through Amnesty International and facing the usual sexist and racist policies of a border institution. Gloria's words were exactly what I needed, and I told her so soon after that.

Her death came to me in Spain via an e-mail. Ana Castillo and I were sitting next to each other in front of computer monitors in an internet café in Granada when we got the news. Throughout the next two months during my travels in Spain I lit candles on altars laid out in Gloria's honor, knowing that her path was one of light and that she had reached a peace beyond my understanding. I was not at the service her family and loved ones prepared for her funeral, but I know they honored the Gloria they knew and loved—the daughter, sister, niece, tía and friend—the one who was my paisana and whose last homecoming to that land where she was born, where her ombligo was buried, sent ripples into the universe, into the fabric of our existence. I miss her terribly, and yet I know she is still here. I teach her work, and

I hear her voice and her quiet laugh. She continues doing work that matters as she urged us all to do in her last published piece "Let us Be the Healing of the Wound: The Coyolxauhqui Imperative—La sombra y el sueño" (2005), for as she says, "Vale la pena, it's worth the pain" (102).

As Relevant Today... / *Ana Castillo*

It has been exactly twenty years since I read *Borderlands/ La Frontera: The New Mestiza* by Gloria Anzaldúa. As both physical place and metaphor it reads as relevant today as it did then. It isn't surprising. Anzaldúa addressed a condition which mestizas had been experiencing—born of two cultures, destined to navigate through various worlds at once—since the Conquest of Mexico.

Recently, regarding the U.S./Mexican border (and at least since the early twenties with the installation of the U.S. Border Patrol), the issue of the Mexican as a foreigner on these lands remains as critical as ever. Anzaldúa's subject, the mestiza at the lower rungs of society, continues to be vital to running this economic system by virtue of her labor and low salary. Undocumented workers, in particular, while arguably necessary to sustaining our economy, also continue to be the objects of scorn and even blatant racism.

Anzaldúa extended her metaphor of the U.S./Mexican border as a bleeding wound to the body, psyche and life experience of the mestiza. To the tune of her day, like other radical feminists, she believed it was paramount to give voice to the lived reality of the Chicana who, until the late 60s to mid 70s, was kept at the margins of mainstream society. *"I see oposición e insurrección,"* she wrote, as a description of entering a kind of meditative state before writing, "And I am not afraid." Indeed, they were times that called for nothing short of fearlessness to speak our truth of centuries.

In order to make the point resound with urgency and validity, this generation could not afford to compromise lest it lose all ground. It was the courage of writers like Anzaldúa that brings us to where we are today, with U.S. Latina writers who consider it their right to address issues of sexuality and alternative lifestyles and to opine on politics without hesitation or apologies.

While we should all be grateful for the sacrifices made by writers, artists and thinkers on the fringe, capitalism once again, with all its tempting rewards and trappings, rears its ugly head and appropriates the underdog for its own. For better or for worse, perhaps as an idea whose time has come, the uncompromising positioning of such Chicana writers as Gloria Anzaldúa and María López (the playwright who wrote and later produced for film, *Real Women Have Curves*) finds its way into the mainstream and takes on new meaning. "Ugly Betty," a prime time sitcom produced by the Mexican actress Selma Hayek, and featuring the actress who played in the film *Real Women Have Curves,* comes immediately to mind. While it is based on a highly popular Spanish telenovela, it is germane to the Chicana politic which states that the mestiza, for her color, ethnicity, body type and humble background, is considered undesirable on all levels by gringo society. While *Vogue* has just featured a full figured, pudgy faced African American who has just rocketed to stardom, I am not all that sure that these were the goals radical feminists of color were aiming for as their definition of success. Nevertheless, at least in some respects we can no longer say such women are emphatically rejected on the basis of their physical appearance.

If the twenty-first century has proven anything, especially to the U.S. voter, it is that democracy is still a goal. For my part, I remain indebted to the peers and colleagues of my generation, such as Gloria Anzaldúa, who took up the collective banner to speak for and on behalf of the silenced and silent. In 2007, however, it is important for us as Chicanas to remember that the social and political struggles of our sisters in the labor force and those who cross over without documents are still critical. I only hope the prospects of potential fame and fortune or just obtaining a piece of the much-coveted piece of the American pie, don't claim all of our new and future writers. Otherwise, I suspect, it will have Gloria Anzaldúa rolling in her grave.

A Note to Gloria from the Bottom of the Sea / *Sandra Cisneros*

I wish I had a wonderful story to tell about Gloria Anzaldúa. I wish I could say she slept on my fold-out futon in my living room. Or that we once went shoe-shopping together at the Vogue in downtown San Antonio before they went out of business. Or that once, on a hot, sticky Texas afternoon, we stripped to our slips and shared beer and gossip on my back porch under the thwack of ceiling fans and painted our toes. But those stories belong to other friends.

I only met Gloria a handful of times in my life, usually with a whole bunch of people hanging around. Once we had dinner together alone at the Liberty Bar because I demanded it, but most of the time, our lives were so cluttered we never had the opportunity to meet each other as people, only as "Authors." And always as writers. By this I mean we knew each other most intimately on the page.

I think with writers like Gloria, you hate to impose on their time. I know I didn't want to be another *chupacabra* and take away from the quiet and energy she needed to write. It's that way with my closest friends who write. I don't want to take away the most valuable thing they have—the solitude necessary to hear the things inside your heart. So I can't tell you anything personal about Gloria since I didn't know her that way. And I don't have a funny anecdote either. I only know had I lived any closer and been a neighbor, perhaps I would've known her even less. Maybe I would have allowed for Gloria to disappear for long lapses of time without giving it a second thought. After all, I wouldn't want to be called *una fregona,* or worse, *una fisgona.*

Maybe I wouldn't have thought it strange, Gloria disappearing that week she died, closing herself up and just ducking into herself. That would've been perfectly natural for a writer. Both the retreat and the silence, I mean. It's why she moved away from Texas to California no doubt. It's why I moved away from Illinois to Texas. So that the relatives and family would allow me the liberty to disappear into myself. To reinvent myself if I had to. As Latinas, we have to.

Because writing is like putting your head underwater. It takes a great effort to go under, to push yourself to the sea bottom, a tremendous courage to withstand the pressure and pain and stay down there. Then the bobbing to the surface when a lifeline tugs you back. She was a fellow explorer. Someone I knew who was also studying the bottom of the sea. She drew up different flora and fauna, and her scientific efforts yielded discoveries beautiful and brilliant that encouraged me in my own solitary expeditions and made me feel less lonely. Recently there was a rumor going round in Buenos Aires that I had died. It took a while to realize I had been confused with Gloria Anzaldúa. But I think the rumor of Gloria Anzaldúa's death is also greatly exaggerated. I knew Gloria through her writing, and for me that writing is as alive and intimate as ever.

Tejana Writing, Scholarship, and Activism: Living in the Borderlands with—and without—Gloria Anzaldúa / *T. Jackie Cuevas*

La Gloria's work arrived in my life when I needed it most. I was twenty-four, living in Corpus Christi, Texas, struggling with who I wanted to be, in particular, trying to figure out my sexuality. And the Tejana music star Selena had just died. That year, the very week that Selena died, I stopped living in my own private borderlands, and I came out to myself and to my familia, "choosing" to live queer, as la Gloria has called it. I also decided to go back to graduate school. I tattooed a flaming red corazón onto my left shoulder, to remind myself not to forget my heart as I went into that other, headstrong world of the academy.

Besides my distant second step-cousin Irene, who I saw only between her periodic prison terms, Gloria Anzaldúa was the first model of a Chicana activist intellectual I encountered. Until then, my learning how to be a survivor in this topsy-turvy world came from my mother and the other creative women in my family. The daughter of a poor single Tejana mother gets two kinds of training: How to cook chicken hearts is one. The other is how to break your own heart before anyone else can get their hands on it. I frequently draw on both of these skills in order to survive as a radical queer Chicana in graduate school. Although I'm not as low on economic resources as I was in my childhood, I still eat chicken hearts to remind myself that I can survive. And la Gloria's work taught me to claim that, the painful struggle to nourish mind/body/spirit, as a shared personal/political struggle.

From la Gloria's legacy, I have also learned that I must write to you. Now. Someone has to talk around here before the mass inherited and learned silences grow so strong nobody will remember what we were trying to forget in the first place. Like Gloria, I'm scared to write my way into what those truth-myths might be. It's dangerous work. But Gloria showed many of us the way.

How do you turn a queer sense of being in the world into *la facultad,* into a skill you can harness and use to make meaning, make connection, make peace, make change? La Gloria gave me a map of hope. *Borderlands/La Frontera* and her other texts offer me narratives of how to not just survive the crucible of the borderlands, but also develop a fierceness of spirit. Reading and grappling with her work has taught me how a young, working-class Chicana can make meaning— even beauty—out of senseless subjugation. Through an Anzaldúan commitment to turn "ambivalence into something else," I seek to recode cultural "shame" into dignity.

In a time of hidden fascism practiced by the so-called superpower nations, in which those in power attempt to play deadly war games with our individual and collective lives, Anzaldúa's sense of activist-scholarship reminds the queer-minded, left-of-center that we must remember to hope—and to act—as we theorize. And that we must continue to make our own theories, not just believe the insidious lies that we are taught about ourselves and each other. Anzaldúa's work put the borderlands on the map of the U.S. consciousness—and conscience. This is no small feat. I'm grateful to la Gloria as I navigate living Chicana, living queer, living poet, living storyteller, living teacher, living activist-scholar, living borderlands every day.

Coatlicue-Poet, *Nepantlera* and *Curandera Cultural* / *Claire Joysmith*

Gloria, *la curandera* cultural, language *nagüal*, genre *coyote, alebrije* essayist-theorist, Coatlicue-poet, *patlache* feminist, *nepantlera*, barbed-wire-border-crosser, cross-cultural bridge-builder, Borderlands survivor, Coyolxauhqui visionary, *conocimiento*-seeker, spiritual *activista,* and, yes, wound-healer.

¡Cuánto regalo nos has dejado! ¿Cómo agradecerte? ¿Cómo devolverte sólo un cachito de corazón que tú, siempre generosa, entregaste?

How to say gracias, Gloria, for gifting wise insight into multiple *fronteras, coyote*-smuggling them back into *México* for those of us fortunate to be recipient-readers of your legacy, your *conocimiento* ways, your *lengua-bruja* miracles, your complex visionary re-creations, your simple straightforward sharing.

I first read *Borderlands/La Frontera* when Gloria generously gave me a signed copy at the time I interviewed her. She was in Mexico City at the UNAM (Universidad Nacional Autónoma de México) giving a series of talks. That was fifteen years ago. I had read other Chicana writers, Sandra Cisneros, Ana Castillo, Helena María Viramontes, but not Gloria's book. It was a revelation. It shook me to the roots of each *pelito.* Spoke obsidian-hard to my heart. *Me dolió. Me dolío. Me dolió.* I had to stop reading, had to keep on. As a Mexicana it scared me, it was so forceful, so intensely personal-political, so unabashed: *sin pelos en la lengua.*

Gloria and *Borderlands* have influenced what I do today, who I am today (chicana-literature *coyote,* inverse chicana, *me han llamado*) on this other side of *la frontera: una gringa*-alien-looking *mexicana* that has experienced the markings of gender, class and race for being *mujer,* for being *descolorida* in this tawny-colored land, *México de este lado.*

Curiously—or maybe not—*Borderlands/La Frontera* remains untranslated into Spanish after 20 years, making it linguistically inaccessible to many. How to translate it, of course, is a true challenge, as Gloria agreed years ago when we talked about it. Only a few sections and some poems from the book have been translated so far.[1] Even in the original version, though, she remains unavailable in bookstores in *México.*

Still nowadays, Gloria crosses into *México* with her *alebrije* texts as a transgressor, a fork-tongued alien—ironically regarded as more *gringa* than *mexicana*—because she writes mostly in English, even if in her writings Spanish is scattered like corn on fertile land.

Her *Borderlands/La Frontera* raises eyebrows because her Spanish is peopled by class-branded archaic oral-rooted Spanish: *ansina, chorriando, pa"trás.* In *México* she also straddles *dos mundos o más.*

And, of course, reading Gloria's work *es todo un reto,* multi-challenging. Not many are willing to cross those borders. Her forked tongue plays *la* scary bogey-Llorona to many readers on this side of the border, still wary (maybe a little less so nowadays) of her radical conceptions, her daring iconographic-mythic-linguistic hybridity, her *patlache* perspective.

Other linguistic-cultural straddlers do read her, however. On the *frontera* itself and in certain academic-literary circles her work has planted corn-seeds that now sprout and spread in unexpected places, although there are admittedly few spaces on this side of *la Frontera* (compared to the proliferation of colleges and universities in the U.S., for instance) where her work can be taught, read, discussed.

Perhaps one of the signs of a unique transborder book such as *Borderlands/La Frontera* is how its image-symbols cross book-bound boundaries, walk out on the streets, *cruzando tantas fronteras.* Perhaps one of the signs of a great transborder *bruja*-writer is the capacity to shift and flow free from realm to realm, beyond temporal *fronteras,* seemingly effortlessly, but with subtle precision, never losing a grip on those filaments of particular collective truths, of creative transformative challenges.

Gloria wrote twenty years ago in *Borderlands:* "The U.S.-Mexican border *es una herida abierta* where the Third World grates against the first and bleeds. And before a scab forms it hemorrhages again, the lifeblood of two worlds merging to form a third country—a border culture"(25). This is now a forked-tongue legacy and it has journeyed much. In March 2002, Gloria wrote a cyber-*testimonio* as part of a project that originated in Mexico in response to 9-11-01: "We are all wounded but we can connect through the wound that's alienated us from others. When the wound forms a cicatrize, the scar can become a bridge linking people split apart."[2] Wound-scar-bridge: "Let us be the healing of the wound." The conceptual legacy Gloria has left us, embodied in these startling metaphors, remain a kind of *bruja*-potion for our post-9-11-01 *nepantla* times.

So, yes, despite all, Gloria, you and your words have crossed borders, into other borderlands. Your essence remains alive in your work. Not even Mictecacíhuatl herself can steal that away. *No te hemos perdido.* We can find you *una vez y otra,* once and again, in each of your words. You inspire every one of us to focus, listen, speak, write, and carry on: "May we do work that matters" ("Let Us Be the Healing of the Wound" 102).

Notes

1 Exceptions are "How to Tame a Wild Tongue," translated by Liliana Valenzuela (Antología Vintage Español de literatura mexicana y chicana contemporánea, ed. Cristina García, Random House), a few poems I translated in *Cantar de Espejos/Singing Mirrors,* as well as various other translations, many of them unpublished, all of them scattered.

2 Gloria Anzaldúa,"Let Us Be the Healing of the Wound:The Coyolxauhqui Imperative—La Sombra y El Sueño," One Wound for Another/Una herida por otra:Testimonios de Latinas in the U.S. through Cyberspace (11 de septiembre de 2001 - 11 de marzo de 2002), eds. Claire Joysmith and Clara Lomas, CISAN-UNAM, Mexico,The Colorado College, Colorado Springs and Whittier College, CA, Prologue by Elena Poniatowska, 2005, p. 102.This cyberspace-project-turned-book originated at the CISAN, UNAM, Mexico, in October 2001, to (ad)dress 9-11-01 woundings.

Inner Struggles, Outer Change: Anzaldúa's Holistic Worldview/ *AnaLouise Keating* *

> The struggle is inner: Chicano, *indio,* American Indian, *mojado, mexicano,* immigrant Latino, Anglo in power, working class Anglo, Black, Asian-our psyches resemble the bordertowns and are populated by the same people. The struggle has always been inner, and is played out in outer terrains. Awareness of our situation must come before inner changes, which in turn come before changes in society. Nothing happens in the "real" world unless it first happens in the images in our heads. (*Borderlands/La Frontera* 109)

Whenever I teach *Borderlands/La Frontera* or other writings by Gloria Anzaldúa I am struck by the profound ways her words resonate with my students—not with all students, of course, but with a surprisingly wide range—including many who do not self-identify as Chicana/o, Latina/o, feminist, and/or queer. They are shocked by the intimacy of Anzaldúa's insights; they feel as if she's speaking directly to them, as if she's describing their own deeply buried secrets and beliefs. They acknowledge the many differences between their embodied locations and Anzaldúa's—differences including but not limited to her campesino upbringing in South Texas; the specific forms of alienation and oppression she experienced due to her color, gender, economic status, health, and sexuality; and her complex relationship to language. But when they read Anzaldúa they feel a sense of familiarity more intense than they feel with most other authors. By plunging so deeply into the depths of her own experiences and by exposing herself—raw and bleeding—to her readers, she externalizes her inner struggles and draws connections among multiple groups.

This ability to connect across differences illustrates Anzaldúa's inclusionary, holistic worldview—her belief that "every cell in our bodies, every bone and bird and worm has spirit in it" (*Borderlands* 58). Drawing on indigenous philosophies, Anzaldúa posits a type of fluid cosmic spirit/energy/force that embodies itself throughout—and *as*— all existence. She uses this spiritualized worldview to synthesize social activism with spiritual vision, creating what she elsewhere describes as *spiritual activism* (see her *Interviews/Entrevistas* and *this bridge we call home*, 540-78). Spiritual activism is a visionary yet practical form of activism based on the belief in our radical interconnectedness. Spiritual activism is spirituality employed in the service of social justice. Spiritual activists recognize the many differences among us yet insist that we share important commonalities. Using these commonalities as catalysts for transformation, spiritual activists develop specific actions designed to challenge individual and systemic racism, sexism, homophobia, and other social injustice. Unlike conventional forms of activism or religion, Anzaldúa's spiritual activism does not impose authority on individuals through external texts, standards, and/or leaders. Instead, spiritual activism locates authority within each individual and links inner transformation with outer change. Thus in the above epigraph, Anzaldúa insists on the complex interrelatedness of inner/outer, self/ other, body/spirit.

All too often, however, scholars ignore Anzaldúa's spiritual activism and focus on the more overtly political and theoretical dimensions of her work. As Anzaldúa notes,

> The "safe" elements in Borderlands are procreated and used, and the "unsafe" elements are not talked about. One of the things that doesn't get talked about is the connection between body, mind, and spirit-anything that has to do with the sacred, anything that has to do with the spirit. As long as it's theoretical, if it's about history or about borders, that's fine... But if you start talking about nepantla-this border between the spirit, the psyche, and the mind-they resist. (*Interviews/ Entrevistas* 159)

Given the academy's over-emphasis on rational thought, coupled with the mind/body oppositional dualisms pervading western cultures, this resistance to exploring the spiritual dimensions of Anzaldúa's work is not surprising. When we talk about spirit, soul, the sacred, and so forth, we risk accusations of escapism, essentialism, or other forms of apolitical, naive thinking. However, these accusations overlook the activist dimensions of Anzaldúa's holistic worldview.

To deny *Borderlands'* politics of spirit dismisses some of the text's most innovative elements as well as important tools for social change including (but not limited to) the following. First, Anzaldúa's holistic worldview enables her to develop a theory of relational selfhood that offers an important alternative to traditional forms of hyper-individualism. By defining each human being as part of a cosmic whole, Anzaldúa develops theoretical justification and motivation linking self-reflection and self-change with social transformation. And, by locating each individual within this larger context, she can forge commonalities that do not ignore the many differences among us. As I explain elsewhere (*EntreMundos/Among Worlds* 241-254), Anzaldúa's relational approach to commonalities and differences challenges identity categories based on simplistic understandings of gender, ethnicity/'race,' class, sexuality, and other social labels. It's this holistic concept of selfhood which enables Anzaldúa to achieve the sense of intimacy I described in my opening paragraph.

Second, Anzaldúa's spiritual-activist perspective shapes her theory of transformative writing, or what I call her *shaman aesthetics.* She maintains that "[t]he ability of story (prose and poetry) to transform the storyteller and the listener into something or someone else is shamanistic. The writer, as shape-changer, is a *nahual,* a shaman" (*Borderlands* 88). For Anzaldúa, writing offers a pathway to knowledge and individual/collective change. Because she believes that "[n]othing happens in the 'real' world unless it first happens in the images in our heads" (*Borderlands* 109), she uses a careful, deliberate writing process that relies on multiple revisions and extraordinary attention to image, metaphor, and individual word choice. Anzaldúa insists that people can and must change; she uses her words to facilitate transformation, on both personal and communal levels.

Borderlands is testament to Anzaldúa's spiritual activism. In poems like "Interface," "Letting Go," and "that dark shining thing," and in theories like mestiza consciousness, la facultad, the new mestiza, the Borderlands, and nepantla, Anzaldúa develops and enacts her holistic worldview. Interconnectivity is key and serves as her theoretical framework for social change. We are interdependent and interrelated with all existence. Anzaldúa draws on this radical interconnectivity as she develops new strategies for survival, resistance, and transformation. As she painfully/joyfully transforms her inner struggles into images and words, she creates points of connection with diverse readers and inspires us to change. She demonstrates that holistic, spirit-inflected perspectives can sustain and assist us as we work towards social justice.

*I dedicate this essay to Gloria. Thanks to Irene Lara for helpful comments on an earlier draft. February/March, 2007

Introduction to the Second Edition
by Sonia Saldívar-Hull

In the 12 years since the publication of Gloria Anzaldúa's foundational *Borderlands/La Frontera: The New Mestiza*, women's studies and Chicana/Latina studies have flourished in intellectual production if not in academic acceptance. Even in the face of growing backlash, most dramatically embodied in anti-affirmative action laws in California, the Hopwood Decision in Texas, and similar legislation under consideration in many other states, *Borderlands* is now in its second edition. This historically significant text continues to be studied and included on class syllabi in courses on feminist theory, contemporary American women writers, autobiography, Chicana/o and Latina/o literature, cultural studies, and even major American authors.

After my initial reading of Gloria Anzaldúa's *Borderlands* in the summer of 1987, I, like many other Chicana academics, found myself compelled to engage its New Mestiza hermeneutics. Anzaldúa spoke to me as a fellow *Tejana*, as a *mujer* boldly naming herself feminist as well as Chicana. Juxtaposed against other foundational texts on the Border, such as *With His Pistol in His Hand* by Américo Paredes and *Occupied America* by Rodolfo Acuña, *Borderlands* offered a view of our America through the lens of a woman-identified woman.[1] The feminism that *Borderlands* advocates builds on the gendered articulations of women like Marta Cotera and Ana Nieto Gomez, whose early feminist speculations appear in the anthology *Chicana Feminist Thought: The Basic Historical Writings*.[2] Chicanas were theorizing in the 1960s and 70s, and with Gloria Anzaldúa and Cherríe Moraga's interventions in *This Bridge Called My Back: Writings by Radical Women of Color*, a *transfronterista* (that is, a transnational feminist, a *transfrontera feminista*) consciousness built new coalitions with other U.S. Latinas and U.S. women of color.[3] *Borderlands*, a socio-politically specific elaboration of late twentieth-century *feminista* Chicana epistemology, signals movement towards coalitions with other *mujeres* across the U.S. México geopolitical border.

Borderlands focuses on a specific geographic locale, the U.S.-México border, and presents a specific history–that of Mexican origin U.S. Chicanas. But as a treatise that is "above all a feminist one" (106), it opens up a radical way of restructuring the way we study history. Using a new genre she calls *autohistoria*,[4] Anzaldúa presents history as a serpentine cycle rather than a linear narrative.[5] The *historia* she tells is a story in which indigenous icons, traditions, and rituals replace post-

Cortesian, Catholic customs. Anzaldúa reconfigures Chicana affinities with the Catholic *Virgen de Guadalupe* and offers an alternative image: *Coatlicue*, the Aztec divine mother. In 1987, few U.S. *mexicana* scholars had invoked that name.

Borderlands' first essay/chapter, "The Homeland, Aztlán/*El otro México*," introduces the reader to a topography of displacement. For the reader unfamiliar with Chicana/o history or the history of Northern Mexico's absorption by the United States in 1848, the text defines the border, politically and ideologically, as an "unnatural boundary" and hence posits a destabilizing potential in late twentieth-century Chicana cartography. She gives *mestizos* a genealogy that, as hybrid people, interpollates them as both native to the Americas and with a non-Western, multiple identity. The "lost land" she rediscovers or uncovers is always grounded in a specific material history of what was once northern Mexico. For the unschooled reader, she reviews the treaty of Guadalupe-Hidalgo, signed on Feb. 2, 1848, as the document that created a new U.S. minority: American citizens of Mexican descent. Anzaldúa's *testimonio*-like pedagogy offers knowledge that Anglo-centric schools tend to erase, interjecting a counter-narrative that tells of the appropriation of land by Anglo-Americans who did more than take territory: the process of absorption into the U.S. included the imposition of White Supremacy aided by the overt terrorist tactics of the Texas Rangers.[6]

The nation-building discourse in "Homeland, Aztlán" revisits the story that other Chicano/a foundational novels of the 1930s and 40s had previously fictionalized.[7] Like *Caballero*, by Jovita González, a recently recovered historical novel, *Borderlands* offers a critique of the process of incorporation of Mexicans during the Mexican American war of 1836.[8] Similarly, the multiple identities in *Borderlands* mirror Américo Paredes' *George Washington Gomez*, a novel in which the protagonist's hybrid identity is at war with itself.[9] While both of these historical fictions recover memory erased from the official story, Anzaldúa's *historia* offers a new way to write History. Like Paredes, Anzaldúa boldly aligns Chicana territorial history with the early twentieth century Mexico-Tejano resistance fighters, the Seditionists, who polemicized against the Anglo invaders in their political manifesto, the *Plan de San Diego*.[10] But history in this New Mestiza narrative is not a univocal discursive exercise–in this new genre, a moving personal narrative about her Grandmother's dispossession occupies the same discursive space as a dry recitation of historical fact, while lyrics from a *corrido* about "the lost land" butt up against a poetic rendition of an ethnocentric Anglo historian's vision of U.S. dominion over México.

Indeed, the *Borderlands* genre continually refuses stasis. Shifting from México-*tejana* History, to personal testimonial, the text moves restlessly onward to a history of a larger political family. As she concludes the opening essay, the New Mestiza narrator emphasizes class alliances with Mexican border-crossers who labor in unregulated border factories, the *maquiladoras*, and brings to light the dehumanization of those Mexican workers who cross over to the U.S. where the Border Patrol hunts them as vermin. The *mestizo* workers are then "caught between being treated as criminals and being able to eat" (34).

The New Mestiza chronicles much more than the history of a "third country" she calls the Border. The "closed country," as she also names it, is peopled with gendered undocumented crossers. Not only does Anzaldúa disrupt Anglo-centric nationalist histories, she interrupts the Chicano nationalist agenda as she engages feminist analysis and issues. Underpinned by feminist ideology, the women's stories relentlessly expand previous androcentric history texts.

Anzaldúa continues this process in the next section, "*Movimientos de rebeldia y las culturas que traicionan*" ("Rebellious Movements and Traitorous Cultures"), as she moves to confront the tradition of male dominance within her community. It opens with a long epigraph in untranslated Spanish, a passage which serves as a Chicana proclamation in face of the war–a proclamation of independence for the *mestizas* bound within a male-dominated culture. When Anzaldúa addresses the men and male-identified women in her community in Spanish, it is as if she is addressing the elders who refused to speak English. She appeals to those authorities as she declares:

> Those rebellious movements that we have in our Mexican blood surge like rivers overflowing in my veins. And like my people, who sometimes release themselves from the slavery of obedience, of silent acceptance, rebellion exists in me on the surface. Under my humble gaze an insolent face exists ready to explode. My rebellion was quite costly-cramped with insomnia and doubts, feeling useless, stupid, and impotent. I'm filled with rage when someone-be it my mother, the Church, the Anglo culture-tells me do this, do that without considering my desires. I argued. I talked back. I was quite the loudmouth. I was indifferent to many of my culture's values. I did not let the men push me around. I was not good or obedient. But I have grown. I no longer spend my life dumping cultural customs and values that have betrayed me. I have also gathered time proven customs and the customs that respect women. (37, my translation)

The passage ends in English, as if the language acquired as an adult is the language of feminist assertion: "But despite my growing tolerance, for this Chicana *la guerra de independencia* (the war for independence) is a constant" (37). This bilingual strategy implies that while the patriarchs of her youth may well be fluent English speakers, she will confront them directly in the language of her Chicana-*mexicana-tejana* traditions.

Dogmatic rules and assumptions prescribed Anzaldúa's life as a child and young woman in South Texas, but now she understands that "rules" are man-made and can be unmade with feminist logic. She offers specific examples of how she was restricted even from a life of the mind and recounts her rebellious resistance to incorporation by the family and community customs. Her *testimonio* relates the limitations placed on many subaltern women under the rule of fathers and male-identified mothers. The feminist rebel in her is the Shadow-Beast, "a part of me that refuses to take orders from outside authorities" (38). The Shadow Beast emerges as the part of women that frightens men and causes them to try to control and devalue female culture. Girls in the borderland are commonly taught to fear sexuality and learn that men value women's bodies only. Their individuality is devalued and selfishness is decried. (In the borderlands of Anzaldúa's youth, "selfishness" includes anything women want to do to improve their lives.) The New Mestiza consciousness—while it refuses static notions of the self—profoundly validates Chicana selfhood.

"Cultural Tyranny" in Anzaldúa's South Texas is metonymy for patriarchy—the manner in which traditional culture works against women. Taking up the figure of Malintzín, Anzaldúa contests her place in Mexican mythology as the fallen Eve who "betrayed" her people by becoming Cortes' mistress and the mother of *mestizaje*. By reclaiming and reconceptualizing Malintzín, she claims for women the mythical homeland of Chicano cultural nationalists, Aztlán. This new historian subtly prods Chicano males to understand feminist rebellion as twin to the racialized class rebellion advocated by the cultural nationalists. Anzaldúa redefines cultural identity through gender and sexuality. And the now-transformed nationalism and gendered Aztlán are rescripted as feminist theory and New Mestiza consciousness.[11]

Part of the work of that *mestiza* consciousness is to break down dualities that serve to imprison women. Her articulation of Chicana lesbian theory does just that, as she declares herself both male and female. Again, she uses *cuento* and *testimonio* to present theory as she recounts the young neighbor of her youth who was an outsider and labeled "one of the others," half woman, half man. Refusing the condemnation of the labels, however, she strategically takes a feminist-nationalist turn to indigenous "tradition" that views alterity as power. The ultimate rebellion for Chicanas is through sexuality, and in Anzaldúa's version of queer theory, this is specifically true for lesbians of color.

Similarly, Anzaldúa's claim of the Indian part of her *mestizaje* avoids simplistic appropriation. The *indigena* in the New Mestiza is a new political stance as a fully racialized feminist Chicana. She appeals to a history of resistance by subaltern Indian women of the Americas and in that shared history narrates strong political affiliation: "My Chicana identity is grounded in the Indian woman's history of resistance" (43). This political alliance further strengthens her internal critique of Chicano cultural practices that deny the indigenous part of the *mestizaje*. Claiming all parts of her identity, even those that clash, she escapes essentialist categories and envisions one provisional home where she can "stand and claim my space, making a new culture-*una cultura mestiza*-with my own lumber, my own bricks and mortar and my own feminist architecture" (44).

Armed with her feminist tools, Anzaldúa's narrator is prepared to "enter the serpent," as she does in the following section, to explore the legacy of indigenous forbears. In keeping with this new feminism, the New Mestiza dramatically reclaims the female cultural figures that were marked traitors to the community. The first betrayal-denying the Indian in the Chicano makes the second one easier to accept without question: the scripting of Malinali Tenepat (*Malintzín*) (44) and *la Llorona* (the woman who weeps for her lost or murdered children) into the whore of the *virgen*/whore dyad.[12]

By rewriting the stories of Malinali, *la Llorona* and the *Virgen de Guadalupe*, Anzaldúa is strategically reclaiming a ground for female historical presence. Her task here is to uncover the names and powers of the female deities whose identities have been submerged in Mexican memory of these three Mexican mothers. The New Mestiza narrates the pre-Cortesian history of these deities, and shows how they were devalued by both the Azteca-Mexica patriarchs and by the Christian conquerors. In presenting the origins of the Guadalupe myth, Anzaldúa offers new names for our studies-names that we must labor to pronounce: *Coatlicue, Cihuacoatl, Tonantsi, Coyolxauhqui.*

Significantly, Anzaldúa employs the language of the Spanish colonizers when she narrates the invention of Guadalupe by the Catholic Church. The well-known Juan Diego version of the Guadalupe story is told in poetic stanzas, a presentation that underlines the *historia's* fictive character. The feminist revision, written in prose, authorizes itself as legitimate history. Anzaldúa's narrative then returns to Aztlán and Aztec history before the conquest with a critique that consciously ruptures the male Chicano romanticization of a vague utopian indigenous past. The reader enters a conversation between the New Mestiza scribe and those unreconstructed Chicano nationalists who, even today, refuse to accept the possibility that the Aztecs were but one nation of many and that they enslaved surrounding tribes.

La Llorona is another part of the *virgen*/whore dyad the New Mestiza reclaims, naming her the heir of *Cihuacoatl*, the deity who presided over women in childbirth. I do not believe it a simple mistake that this powerful female figure is then transformed into a woman who murders children rather than one who guides them into life. The centrality of *la Llorona* in Chicana oral and written traditions emerges in literature written by other contemporary Chicana feminists. In cuentos like Helena Maria Viramontes' "The Cariboo Cafe," and "Tears on My Pillow," as well as in Sandra Cisneros' "Woman Hollering Creek," a Chicana feminist transformation of the powerless wailing woman resonates with Anzaldúa's revisionary project.[13]

Reclaiming and reinventing *Coatlicue*, Malintzín, and *la Llorona/Cihuacoatl* in New Mestiza narratives elaborates the constantly shifting identity formation of Anzaldúa's Chicana/*mestiza* feminist. In the next section, "*La herencia de Coatlicue*/The *Coatlicue* State," Anzaldúa turns to consider the implications of such a reclamation for the developing consciousness of her New Mestiza. In a powerful, dramatic incantatory poem, the search for the erased histories of female ancestors and the yearning for visibility follow the alien and alienated subject-in-process as she constructs provisional identities:

> She has this fear that she has no names that she has many names that she doesn't know her names She has this fear that she's an image that comes and goes clearing and darkening the fear that she's the dreamwork inside somebody else's skull. (65)

Rather than a reductive, essential self, the New Mestiza constantly migrates between knowing herself: "She has many names;" not knowing who or what she is: "the fear that she has no name;" and the fear of not owning who she is: a "fear that she's an image that comes and goes... the dreamwork inside somebody else's skull." She is all of the above, a woman without an official history and the woman who constructs her own historical legacy.[14] The *Coatlicue* State precedes a spiritual and political crossing through which one arrives at a higher spiritual and political consciousness. The transformation involves facing her fear of change as she "tremble[s] before the animal, the alien, the sub- or suprahuman, the me that . . . possesses a demon determination and ruthlessness beyond the human" (72). Once she accomplishes the personal inner journey, the New Mestiza relies on the "ruthlessness" she has acquired when she emerges from the *Coatlicue* State and takes on the struggle for social change. When she names all her names, once again she enacts the culmination of unearthing her multiple subjectivities: the "divine within, *Coatlicue-Cihuacoatl-Tlazolteotl-Tonantzin-Coatlalopeuh-Guadalupe*-they are one" (72). As scholar Norma Alarcón notes, the shifting identities, the multiple names are encapsulated in the New Mestiza's other name: Chicana.[15]

The recovery project that leads to the political, feminist social awareness Anzaldúa calls New Mestiza Consciousness emerges in her discussion of the language of the Borderers. Not until midway through the prose sections of *Borderlands*, in "How to Tame a Wild Tongue," does Anzaldúa begin to explain her use of multiple Chicana languages. The use of English/Spanish from the title page to the chapter headings and subheadings marks this new critical discourse. Throughout the text, in most of the chapter titles and subtitles, Spanish appears as casually as English. Readers who traverse these Borderlands are bound to face her strategy to reclaim the ground of multiple Mestiza languages. The multilingual text does not easily admit those who refuse full engagement with the linguistic demands of Border language.

New Mestiza Chicanas speak multiple Chicana tongues in order to enunciate their multiple names. Anzaldúa mixes Nahuatl, English and vernacular Spanish as a larger cultural critique of how the dominant group enforces domination through language. In "Wild Tongue," Anzaldúa focuses on how Chicanas are doubly punished for their illegitimate languages. Linguistic reclamation aside, her feminist point is that within the Chicana/o culture, language serves as a prison house for women, for whom not only assertiveness but the very act of speaking count as transgressions. She notes how males within the culture escape criticism for such transgressions.

She traces the origins of Chicano Spanish, a Border tongue, from sixteenth century usage: "Chicano Spanish is not incorrect; it is a living language" (07). Multiple Chicana languages allow for the multiple positionalities of *Coatlicue* and the subject she names New Mestiza. She claims eight languages, ending with *Caló, pachuco* Spanish, the "secret language" of the barrio, the vernacular. Chicana language is a *mestizaje* as well: it breaks down all dualisms. Deploying the language of warfare in the "Linguistic Terrorism" section, she stresses that there is no one Chicano language just as there is no one Chicano experience.

The discussion culminates with a feminist note: "I will no longer be made to feel ashamed of existing. I will have my voice: Indian, Spanish, white. I will have my serpent's tongue-my woman's voice, my sexual voice, my poet's voice. I will overcome the tradition of silence" (81).

The following chapter, "*Tlilli, Tlapalli* /The Path of the Red and Black Ink*," enacts the multilingual methodology of *mestiza* language. As Walter Mignolo tells us, Anzaldúa quotes a dialogue (in *Borderlands* 93) in Spanish from the *Colloquios y doctrina christiana*. The dialogue, which was initially recorded in Nahuatl and then translated into Spanish by Bernardino de Sahagún in 1565, "narrates," according to Mignolo, "the moment in which the Spanish noblemen refer to the Tlamatinime (the wise men, those who can read the black and the red ink written in the codices)." He continues:

> Anzaldúa's languaging entangles Spanish, English and Nahuatl (the first two with a strong "literary" tradition kept alive after the conquest; the third, which was and still is an oral way of languaging, was disrupted during and marginalized after the conquest), and her languaging invokes two kinds of writing: the alphabetic writing of the metropolitan center and the pictographic writing of pre-Columbian Mexican (as well as Mesoamerican) civilizations.[16]

Anzaldúa thus stages her writing within the larger context of the continent and its layered histories. When Anzaldúa deploys multiple languages as part of her New Mestiza methodology, she enunciates her writing as an act of self-creation within that context, a strategy she claims as a Nahuatl concept.

In the final prose section, "*La conciencia de la mestiza*," Anzaldúa brings together the work of the previous essays and offers a working definition of a New Mestiza Consciousness. Above all it is a feminist consciousness, one that goes beyond filiation—the ties of "blood." She moves beyond psychological examinations, leaping from "insecurity and indecisiveness," (100) traveling with "mental nepantilism;" accepting her interstitial material existence, to a life committed to social action. She risks exposing the "work the soul performs" (101) as she attains a "differential consciousness," to use Chela Sandoval's notion of this other consciousness.[17] Throughout the text, she labors to construct a new, activist subject who can re-inscribe Chicana History into the record, relegitimize Chicano multiple linguistic capacities, and trace the ethnic/racial origins of Mestiza *mexicano tejanas*. Paradoxically, it is only in that context that she can claim that "as a *mestiza* I have no country. . . as a lesbian I have no race," and that as a feminist she is "cultureless" (102).

"*El camino de la mestiza*/ The Mestiza Way," synthesizes the previous speculations and offers the requisite actions for the new subject, the New Mestiza, as she embarks on her life of action: "Her first step is to take inventory." She "puts history through a sieve"; she communicates "the rupture . . . with oppressive traditions" and "documents the struggle." Only after undertaking that process can she "reinterpret history and, using new symbols, ... shape new myths" (104). The text of the entire book is encapsulated here. She calls for a "new man" and reiterates: "the struggle of the mestiza is above all a feminist one" (106).

The second half of *Borderlands* reenacts dramatically the process of coming into (mestiza) consciousness and the practice of the mestiza way. The section, "*Mas antes en los ranchos*" [Long ago in the ranches], invokes the oral tradition and prepares the reader to enter the poetic dramatizations. In "White-wing Season," the South Texas hardscrabble lives of México tejanas serve as backdrop for the cuentito (vignette) of a farm woman who accepts money from "whitemen" (124), allowing them to shoot white wing doves on her land. Slaughtered white wing doves, which are sport for the hunters returning to the Midwest, are juxtaposed against the Mexican woman's need to accept the kill to feed her family. In "horse," which Anzaldúa dedicates to the pueblo of her childhood in Hargill, Texas, the Chicano community rejects the gringo money offered as compensation when the sons of the white community wantonly torture a horse. What may appear as passive acceptance by the mexicano is actually a wisdom exhibited by these men who know that justice is beyond their reach in the borderlands of Texas: "the mexicanos mumble if you're Mexican/ you are born old" (129).

"*La Perdida*" [The Loss], continues the practice of New Mestiza consciousness by chronicling workers' *historias*. "*Sus plumas el viento*" [Give Wind to Her Feathers] (138) records the everyday labor of subaltern women. A disturbing rape narrative like "We Call Them Greasers," "*Sus plumas el viento*" tells the story of Pepita, a woman who is raped by her boss in the field, against whom she has no recourse. The narrative is a reverie, a memory of a childhood spent in the farm fields witnessing Chicanas like Pepita submitting to the white field boss's sexual violence in order to keep their jobs. Further adding to her humiliation, Pepita also endures the Chicanos' contempt as they spit on the ground when she emerges from her ordeal. Now bearing the mark of *Malinche*, the traitor to her race, Pepita projects herself onto the figure of the *chuparrosa*, the humming bird. No longer the creature she remembers from the safe haven of her grandmother's garden, the hummingbird now appears to her, in the context of the fields, as an object of violence: "the obsidian wind/cut tassels of blood/from the hummingbird's throat" (139). The scribe longs to escape her class-mandated fate as manual laborer. She reads books; she searches for another possibility. The *pluma*, the hummingbird's feather, becomes the quill that helps liberate the New Mestiza from *las labores* [the fields]. She imagines the possibility of escape, "If the wind would give her feathers for fingers/she would string words and images together." But even nature conspires against her dreams: "*el viento sur le tiro su saliva/pa' 'tras en la cara*" [the southern wind blew her spit back in her face] (140).

The section "*Crossers y otros atravesados*" [and other mis-fits] focuses on the poetic sensibility, on lesbian sexuality, and on homophobic violence. "*Yo no fui, fue Tete*"(164), employs cholo speak, the barrio vernacular, as a gay man recounts a beating by his homophobic "brothers." He recognizes fear and hatred in those crazed faces that stab him and curse him with sexual epithets. His pain intensifies because "*mi misma raza*" [his own people] make him an orphan, reiterating Anzaldúa's assertion that like Chicana lesbians, this gay man is without a race (102). In contrast, "*Compañera, cuando amabamos*" [When We Loved] lyrically celebrates those muted afternoons when two women loved and made love: "When unscathed flesh sought flesh and teeth, lips/In the labyrinths of your mouths" (168, my translation).

"*Cihuatlyotl*, Woman Alone" celebrates the goddess, antecedent of *la Llorona*, Serpent Skirt, the sexual goddess of childbirth. The New Mestiza mythmaker links Saint Theresa in "Holy Relics," to other wailing women in "*En el nombre de todas las madres que han perdido sus hijos en la guerra*" [In the name of all the mothers who have lost their children in war]. Mestiza feminists take on the guise of the goddess in "*Cihuatlyotl*, Woman Alone" (195) as they are banished from traditional Chicano communities. The betrayal here is not by a female or by the multilingual Malintzín-the traitor is the community. The poem reenacts the New Mestiza's struggle to retain the "homeland" and yet negotiate multiple subject positions as well. The "Animas" section begins with "*La curandera*"(198), a dramatic allegory in which the traditional folk healer enters into the serpent and emerges with the knowledge, the healing *yerbitas* (herbs), which contribute physically, psychologically and intellectually to strong communities.

The final section, like the last section of the prose, is "*El Retorno*" [The Return]. "To live in the Borderlands Means You" (216) calls mestizas to action as they become aware of multiple positionalities, contradictions, and ambiguities. The mestiza with her hard-earned consciousness cannot remain within the self, however. The awareness of borderland existence spurs her to "fight hard" to resist stasis, "the gold elixir beckoning from the bottle," as well as to continue her resistance strategies in the other war where the "gun barrel" and "the rope crushing the hollow of your throat" still exist. Survival may signify that "you must live *sin fronteras* (without borders)" and "be a crossroads," but to do so requires activism and not simply being born a racialized, gendered mestiza in the borderlands.

While *estudios de la frontera* (border studies) certainly were not invented by Gloria Anzaldúa in *Borderlands*, this book signaled a new visibility for academic programs on the study of the U.S.-México border area. Discursive production on the border flourished with new anthologies and other academic publications bringing to light a remapped academic topography with the border as the organizing trope. In 1991, Hector Calderon and Jose Saldívar published the groundbreaking anthology, *Criticism in the Borderlands: Studies in Chicano Literature, Culture and Ideology*. Emily Hicks published *Border Writing: The Multi-dimensional Text* in 1991. And Ruth Bejar crossed generic and disciplinary borders in her study, *Translated Woman: Crossing the Border* with *Esperanza's Story* in 1993. Alfred Arteaga's anthology, *An Other Tongue: Nation and Ethnicity in the Linguistic Borderlands* was published in 1994, and Carl Gutierrez-Jones analyzed legal discourse in Chicano cultural production in *Rethinking the Borderlands* in 1995. Guillermo Gómez Peña published his genre-mixing *The New World Border* in 1996 and Jose Saldívar remapped American cultural studies in *Border Matters*, 1997.

This *transfrontera*, transdisciplinary text also crossed rigid boundaries in academia as it traveled between Literature (English and Spanish), History, American Studies, Anthropology and Political Science departments, and further illuminated multiple theories of feminism in Women's Studies and Chicana studies. It was—and remains—a defining statement on the inextricability of sexuality, gender, race and class for Chicanas and changed the way we talk about difference in sexuality, race/ethnicity, gender, and class in the U.S. Read within its historical context, *Borderlands* resists containment as a transcendant excursion into "otherness." With this second edition, *Borderlands/La Frontera* continues to offer a radical (re)construction of space in the Americas where political struggles and alliances are forged only after risking conflicts, appropriations, and contradictions in the face of power and domination.

February 1999

Notes

1 Américo Paredes, *With His Pistol in His Hand: A Border Ballad and Its Hero.* Austin: University of Texas Press. Reprint, 1971. Rodolfo Acuña, *Occupied America: A History of Chicanos.* Second Edition, 1981, Third Edition, 1988. New York: Harper Collins Publishers.

2 See for example, Marta Cotera, "Among the Feminists: Racist Classist Issues-1976" 213-20; and Anna Nieto Gomez, "*La Feminista*" 86-92 in *Chicana Feminist Thought: The Basic Historical Writings,* ed. Alma M. Garcia. NewYork: Routledge, 1997.

3 *This Bridge Called My Back: Writings by Radical Women of Color,* ed. Cherríe Moraga and Gloria Anzaldúa. 2nd Edition. New York: Kitchen Table: Women of Color Press, 1981. In the Foreword to the second edition, Moraga maps U.S. feminists' color political location within a global context. For a full discussion of this transnational impulse, see my *Feminism on the Border: Chicana Gender Politics and Literature.*

4 In the essay, "Border Arte: *Nepantla, El Lugar de la Frontera,*" Anzaldúa identifies border visual art as one that "supercedes the pictorial. It depicts both the soul of the artist and the soul of the *pueblo.* It deals with who tells the stories and what stories and histories are told. I call this form of visual narrative *autohistorias.* This form goes beyond the traditional self portrait or autobiography; in telling the writer/artists' personal story, it also includes the artist's cultural history" (113). She continues that when she creates art, such as an altar, she represents much more than herself, "they are representations of Chicana culture" (113). While her definition here targets visual artistry, I believe that it could well describe the *Borderlands* genre as well. In *La Frontera/The Border: Art About the México/United States Border Experience,* ed. Natasha Bonilla Martinez. San Diego: Centro Cultural de la Raza, Museum of Contemporary Art, 1993.

5 See Yvonne Yarbro-Bejarano, "Gloria Anzaldúa's *Borderlands / La Frontera: Cultural Studies,* 'Difference,' and the Non-Unitary Subject." *Cultural Critique,* Fall 1994, 5-28. My reading was greatly influenced by her comprehensive study and by our numerous discussions about Chicana feminism(s), *mestizaje,* and *Borderlands.*

6 Angie Chabram-Dernersesian's "On the Social Construction of Whiteness within Selected Chicana/o Discourses" offers a brilliant discussion of the construction of Aztlán by Chicano cultural nationalists and presents a reading of *Borderlands.* In *Displacing Whiteness: Essays in Social and Cultural Criticism,* ed. Ruth Frankenberg. Durham and London: Duke University Press, 1997, 107-64.

7 My interpretation of these early Chicana/o novels builds on Doris Sommer's observations about Latin American historical fiction, *Foundational Fictions:The National Romances of Latin America.* Berkeley: University of California Press, 1991.

8 *Caballero: A Historical Novel,* Jovita González and Eve Raleigh. College Station: Texas A & M University Press, 1996. This novel was originally written in the late 1930s but not "recovered" until recently. (There is some question about the extent to which Eve Raleigh participated in the actual writing of the text.)

9 Américo Paredes, *George Washington Gómez.* Houston: Arte Público Press, 1990. This is yet another novel of the 1930s that was not published until this decade.

10 For a discussion of the Seditionists and their manifesto, see Américo Paredes, *A Texas-Mexican Cancionero.* Urbana: University of Illinois Press, 1976, 33. See also Ramón Saldívar's discussion of the Seditionists and El Plan de San Diego in *Chicano Narrative:*

The Dialectics of Difference. Madison: University of Wisconsin Press, 1990, 28-31. For the text of the Plan de San Diego see *Literatura Chicana: Texto y Contexto*, ed. Antonia Castañeda Shuler, Tomás Ybarra-Frausto, and David Sommer. Englewood Cliffs, NJ: Prentice-Hall, 1982, 81-83.

11 Inderpal Grewal in "Autobiographic Subjects, Diasporic Locations," makes a similar point: "Anzaldúa's exploration of the 'borderland' consciousness powerfully asserts itself as feminist .... [it] reveal[s] different modes of multiple positioning and practices around issues of feminists and feminism" 235-6. In *Scattered Hegemonies: Postmodernity and Transnational Feminist Practices*, ed. Inderpal Grewal and Caren Kaplan. Minneapolis: University of Minnesota Press, 1994, 231-54.

12 For a comprehensive analyses of Malintzín Tenepal see Norma Alarcón's two essays: "Chicana's Feminist Literature: A Revision Through Malintzín/ Or: Malintzín: Putting Flesh Back on the Object," in *This Bridge Called My Back*, ed. Cherríe Moraga and Gloria Anzaldúa. New York: Kitchen Table: Women of Color Press, 1981, 182-90; and "Traddutora, Traditora: A Paradigmatic Figure of Chicana Feminism," in *Cultural Critique*, Fall 1989, 57-87. For one of the first Chicana feminist examinations of Malintzín, see Adelaida del Castillo, "Malintzín Tenepal: A Preliminary Look Into a New Perspective" in *Essays on La Mujer*, ed. Rosaura Sánchez and Rosa Martínez Cruz. Los Angeles: Chicano Studies Research Center Publications, University of California, Los Angeles, 1977.

13 "The Cariboo Cafe," in *The Moths and Other Stories*, Helena María Viramontes. Houston: Arte Público Press, 1985, 61-75. "Tears on My Pillow," Helena María Viramontes in *New Chicano/a Writing*. Ed. Charles Tatum. Tucson: University of Arizona Press, pp. 110-15. "Woman Hollering Creek," in *Woman Hollering Creek and Other Stories* by Sandra Cisneros. New York: Vintage Books, 1991, 43-56. For readings of *la Llorona* in the above stories see *My Feminism on the Border: Chicana Gender Politics and Literature*.

14 My reading of this passage is informed by Norma Alarcón's brilliant discussion, "Chicana Feminism: In the Tracks of 'The' Native Woman" in *Cultural Studies*, 1:3 (October 1990), 248-56.

15 In "Chicana Feminism," Alarcón explains: "the name 'Chicana,' in the present, is the name of resistance that enables cultural and political points of departure and thinking through the multiple migrations and dislocations of women of 'Mexican' descent. The name Chicana, is not a name that women (or men) are born to or with, as is often the case with 'Mexican,' but rather it is consciously and critically assumed..." (250). In the short story in the *Woman Hollering Creek* collection, "Little Miracles, Kept Promises," Sandra Cisneros also evokes those multiple Chicana/Mestiza identities.

16 Walter Mignolo, "Linguistic Maps, Literary Geographies, and Cultural Landscapes: Languages, Languaging, and (Trans)nationalism," 190-91. In *Modern Language Quarterly*, 57:2, June 1996, 182-96.

Interview

Interview with Gloria Anzaldúa
by Karin Ikas

Karin Ikas: In your life, particularly in your personal life but also in your writing career, you had to struggle a lot, as there was a lot of hardship and oppression to overcome right from the beginning. Can you tell us a bit more about that, about your childhood and how you were raised?

Gloria Anzaldúa: I grew up on a ranch settlement called Jesus Maria in the Valley of South Texas. At that time there were four or five of these ranches in that area. And on each of these ranch settlements there lived between two to four families. My mother and my father, who each lived on one of these adjoining ranches, met there and married while they were quite young. My mother had just turned 16 when I was born. Both of my parents had no high school education. Until I was eleven years old we lived in a ranching environment, and all of us had to participate in farm work like, for example, working in the fields, raising animals–cows and chickens, et cetera. Then we moved closer to a little town called Hargill, Texas. We had a little house and continued ranching there. However, until I turned ten we were continually changing places as we were working on different ranches and in different places as migrant workers. We had started out as migrant workers when I was about seven or eight. But I had missed so much school in the first years at elementary school that after a year my father decided he would just migrate by himself and leave us at home so that all of us children could go to school regularly. I first went to school permanently in Hargill, and I graduated there after eighth grade. Then we, my sister and I, were bused to school in Edinburgh, Texas. Although I stopped being a migrant laborer while I was still very young, I continued working in the fields of my home valley until I earned my B.A. from Pan American University in 1969. So I had learned the hardships of working in the fields and of being a migrant laborer myself, and that experience formed me. I have a very deep respect for all the migrant laborers, the so-called *campesinos*. That experience also reinforced me in my work with migrant kids. After I got my M.A. in English and Education from University of Texas, Austin in 1972 I became a high school teacher, and I taught a lot of migrant kids. For one summer I even traveled with the migrant families who were on their way from Texas to the Midwest. By doing so, I became a liaison between the migrant camps and the regular school teachers for one year. Later they hired me to be the bilingual and migrant director of the full state of Indiana. At that time I was already teaching. But I was mostly working with kids in South Texas migrant kids, emotionally disturbed and mentally retarded kids.

K.I.: Were these kids of different ethnic or racial background or were they mainly Chicano/as?

G.A.: Not all were Chicano/as. It depended on the kind of class I was teaching. The migrant kids' classes were all one hundred percent Mexican. But I was also teaching the so-called genius classes, ninth, tenth, eleventh and twelfth grade. And these genius classes were about fifty percent white. The Chicano/a enrollment in the schools of south Texas is, all together, about eighty percent. Then I started teaching bilingual five-year-olds. And I also taught emotionally disturbed and mentally retarded students who were ages seven to thirteen. Later I moved on to high school, where I taught English and literature at ninth, tenth, eleventh and twelfth grade. Afterwards I lived in Indiana for a while. After Indiana I became a Ph.D. candidate at the University of Texas at Austin. While I was in Austin I was also a lecturer in Chicano studies. So I was teaching while I was going to school myself. I did a keynote speech in Austin this last spring, and a former student of mine showed up, telling me, "You know we read *Borderlands* in your class back then, and you haven't changed since then. You sound just like you sounded first in *Borderlands*."

K.I.: Would you agree that you haven't changed since *Borderlands*?

G.A.: No, not at all. I very much feel that I have changed. Their interpretation of me through the writing influenced their memories, because I wasn't as political and feminist in the beginning. I was always rebellious and political when it came to the cultural stuff, but not to the same degree that I was later when I wrote *Borderlands*. So they read *Borderlands*, which was published in 1987, but most of which I already wrote from 1984 to 1986. In *Borderlands* I was much more extreme, political and angry than I was before when I was teaching at UT, Austin. But what many people do is that they just take *Borderlands* as the way to figure out how I am in general and how I must have been ten years before. However, yes, I was always angry, and I am still angry. And in my teaching I keep telling those Chicano kids about how women are so much considered to be inferior and how that has happened.

K.I.: Did you also participate in the Chicano Movement then?

G.A.: Yes, I did. Actually, I started out with MECHA, a Mexican American youth organization. Also I was involved with different farm worker activities in South Texas and later in Indiana. When I became more recognized as a writer, I started articulating a lot of these feminist ideas that were a kind of continuation of the Chicano Movement. But I call it, *"El Movimiento Macha."* A *marimacha* is a woman who is very assertive. That is what they used to call dykes, *marimachas*, half-and-halfs. You were different, you were queer, not normal, you were *marimacha*. I had been witnessing all these Chicana writers, activists, artists and professors who were very strong and therefore very *marimacha*. So I named it, *"El Movimiento Macha"* as the Chicano Civil Rights Movement kind of petered out. And there were women like myself, many Chicanas, who were already questioning, having problems with the guys who were ignoring women's issues. Therefore, in the eighties and nineties, there are all these women-Chicana activists, writers and artists around, and I listen to them, read them and reflect their influence on my life as well. What you could say is that in the sixties and the early seventies the Chicanos were at the controls. They were the ones who were visible, the Chicano leaders. Then in the eighties and nineties, the women have become visible. I see a lot of Chicanas when I travel. They come up to me, and while we are talking I ask them about their role models. They mention names like Cherríe Moraga, Gloria Anzaldúa and other Chicana authors. It is, and will continue to be, women that they are reading, that they respect. Not the guys. So it—the Chicano Movement—has shifted into the *Movimiento Macha*.

K.I.: What motivated you in particular to edit *This Bridge Called My Back*?

G.A.: One motivation for doing *This Bridge Called My Back* was that when I was at UT I wanted to focus my dissertation on feminist studies and Chicana literature and soon realized that this seemed to be an impossible project. The advisor told me that Chicana literature was not a legitimate discipline, that it didn't exist, and that Women's Studies was not something that I should do. You know, this was back then in 1976-77. If you were a Chicana at a university, all you were taught were these red, white and blue American philosophies, systems, disciplines, and ways of knowledge. They didn't consider ethnic cultural studies as having the impact or weight needed to enter the academy. And so in a lot of these classes I felt silenced, like I had no voice. Finally I quit the Ph.D. program at UT and left Texas for California in 1977. When I moved to San Francisco, I participated in the Women's Writers' Union, where I got to know Susan Griffin, Karen Brodine, Nellie Wong and Merle Woo, among others. Also I joined the Feminist Writers' Guild, which was a little bit less radical. This is where I met Cherríe Moraga, whom I asked a few months later to become my co-editor for *This Bridge Called My Back*. Anyway, I found that this little community of feminist writers in San Francisco, Oakland and Berkeley, this Feminist Writers' Guild, was very much excluding women of color. Most of the white women I knew were part of that organization. I did meet Luisah Teish there, though. She is an AfroAmerican woman from Louisiana who has all those books on spirituality and practices all that in her own life, so you can call her a *santería*. Every two weeks we would have our meetings and everybody would talk about the white problems and their white experiences. When it was my turn to talk, it was almost like they were putting words into my mouth. They interrupted me while I was still talking or, after I had finished, they interpreted what I just said according to their thoughts and ideas. They thought that all women were oppressed in the same way, and they tried to force me to accept their image of me and my experiences. They were not willing to be open to my own presentation of myself and to accept that I might be different from what they had thought of me so far. Therefore one of the messages *of This Bridge Called My Back* is that gender is not the only oppression. There is race, class, religious orientation; there are generational and age kinds of things, all the physical stuff, et cetera. I mean, somehow these women were great. They were white and a lot of them were dykes and very supportive. But they were also blacked out and blinded out about our multiple oppressions. They didn't understand what we were going through. They wanted to speak for us because they had an idea of what feminism was, and they wanted to apply their notion of feminism across all cultures. *This Bridge Called My Back*, therefore, was my sweeping back against that kind of "All of us are women so you are all included and we were all equal." Their idea was that we all were cultureless because we were feminists; we didn't have any other culture. But they never left their whiteness at home. Their whiteness covered everything they said. However, they wanted me to give up my Chicana-ness and become part of them; I was asked to leave my race at the door.

K.I.: So *This Bridge Called My Back* was your response to all that?

G.A.: Yes, exactly. Some of the things that I said in "*La Prieta*" and "*El Mundo Zurdo*/The left-handed world" were all introductions, the foreword and the essay to what I said in "Speaking in Tongues" in *This Bridge Called My Back*. And I was the only woman of color doing that at that time, that is, speaking against this silencing from the outside by getting our work published. However, after several months of struggling with *This Bridge* on my own, and trying to convince other women of color that they really have a voice worth being listened to and being published, I asked Cherríe Moraga to become a co-editor and support me with this project that had become too overwhelming for me alone.

K.I.: How did Chicanas then receive your next book, *Borderlands/La Frontera*?

G.A.: Well, when Chicanas read *Borderlands*, when it was read by little Chicanas in particular, it somehow legitimated them. They saw that I was code-switching, which is what a lot of Chicanas were doing in real life as well, and for the first time after reading that book they seemed to realize, "Oh, my way of writing and speaking is okay" and, "Oh, she is writing about *La Virgen de Guadalupe*, about *la Llorona*, about the *corridos*, the gringos, the abusive, et cetera. So if she [Gloria Anzaldúa] does it, why not me as well?" The book gave them permission to do the same thing. So they started using code-switching and writing about all the issues they have to deal with in daily life. To them, it was like somebody was saying: You are just as important as a woman, as anybody, from another race. And the experiences that you have are worth being told and written about.

K.I.: How do you feel about the critical reception of *Borderlands*?

G.A.: Critics are more open towards it right now. For some reason or other I got lucky in that they still teach my book at school and university. They teach it as a way of introducing students to cultural diversity. However, some of the writing is glossed over as, particularly, white critics and teachers often pick just some parts of *Borderlands*. For example, they take the passages in which I talk about *mestizaje* and borderlands because they can more easily apply them to their own experiences. The angrier parts of *Borderlands*, however, are often ignored as they seem to be too threatening and too confrontational. In some way, I think you could call this selective critical interpretation a kind of racism. On the other hand, I am happy that the book is read at all. For us, it is not always easy to have people read our work or deal with our art. If the work is not interesting or entertaining enough, forget it. So I have to keep all these different issues regarding the reception of my work in mind and try to compromise. For example, if I had made *Borderlands* too inaccessible to you by putting in too many Chicano terms, too many Spanish words, or if I had been more fragmented in the text than I am right now, you would have been very frustrated. So there are certain traditions in all the different genres—like autobiography, fiction, poetry, theory, criticism—and certain standards that you have to follow. Otherwise you are almost naked. It is like when you write a dissertation: there are certain rules you have to apply; otherwise they won't pass you. My whole struggle is to change the disciplines, to change the genres, to change how people look at a poem, at theory or at children's books. So I have to struggle between how many of these rules I can break and how I still can have readers read the book without getting frustrated. These are the things that have to happen first. I need other people who deepen my fears, like professors, critics, the students. They do have to somehow like and approve what I am writing and accept it.

K.I.: The task, therefore, is to keep the traditional approaches in mind somehow but don't stay there, right?

G.A.: Yes, that's it. It is the same kind of struggle *mestizas* have living at the borders, living in the borderlands. How much do they assimilate to the white culture and how much do we resist and risk becoming isolated in the culture and ghettoized? This issue applies to everything.

K.I.: So do you think intercultural understanding is possible and can be enhanced by writing?

G.A.: I do. I believe that both inter- and intracultural understanding can be enhanced. "Intracultural" means within the Chicano culture and Mexican culture. "Intercultural" is about how we are related with other cultures like the Black culture, the Native American cultures, the white culture and the international cultures in general. I am operating on both perspectives as I am trying to write for different audiences. On the one hand, I write for more of an international audience that came across from one world to the other and that has border people. Actually, more and more people today become border people because the pace of society has increased. Just think about multimedia, computers and World Wide Web, for example. By the Internet you can communicate instantly with someone in India or somewhere else in the world, like Australia, Hungary or China. We are all living in a society where these borders are transgressed constantly.

K.I.: How do you see this intercultural situation with regard to the Chicano culture and the Anglo-American influence?

G.A.: In that context, one particular image comes into my mind: the Banyan Tree. It is a tree that is originally from India but which I saw in Hawaii first. It looks like a solid wall. When the seeds from the tree fall, they don't take root in the ground. They take root in the branches. So the seeds fall in the branches, and it is there, above the earth, where the tree blooms and forms its fruits. And I thought, that is where we are getting it. Instead of going to the roots of our Hispanic or Chicano culture we are getting it from the branches, from white dominant culture. I mean, it is not that I reject everything that has to do with white culture. I like the English language, for example, and there is a lot of Anglo ideology that I like as well. But not all of it fits with our experiences and cultural roots. And that is why it is dangerous not to know about your own cultural heritage at all, because then you don't have the chance to choose and select.

I also want Chicano kids to hear stuff about *la Llorona*, about the border, et cetera, as early as possible. I don't want them to wait until they are eighteen or nineteen to get that information. I think it is very important that they get to know their culture already as children. Here in California I met a lot of young Chicanos and Chicanas who didn't have a clue about their own Chicano culture. They lost it all. However, later on, when they were already twenty, twenty-five or even thirty years old, they took classes in Chicano studies to learn more about their ancestors, their history and culture. But I want the kids to already have access to this kind of information. That is why I started writing children's books. So far I have had two bilingual books published, and I am writing the third one at the moment. This is going to be more for juvenile readers, little boys and girls who are like ages eleven to twelve. Next I want to write a book for young adults who are about fifteen to sixteen years old as well. With my children's books I want to provide them with more knowledge about their roots and, by doing so, give them the chance to choose. To choose whether they want to be completely assimilated, whether they want to be border people, or whether they want to be isolationists.

K.I.: How about your ties with Mexico? Do you still feel some close connections with Mexico and Mexican culture itself?

G.A.: I am a seventh generation American and so I don't have any real "original Mexican" roots. So this is what happened to someone living at the border like me: My ancestors have always lived with the land here in Texas. My indigenous ancestors go back twenty to twenty-five thousand years and that is how old I am in this country. My Spanish ancestors have been in this land since the European takeover which pulled migration from Spain to Mexico. Texas was part of a Mexican state called Tamaulipas. And Texas, New Mexico, Arizona, and part of California and Colorado, were part of the northern section of Mexico. It was almost half of Mexico that the U.S. cheated Mexico out of when they bought it by the Treaty of Guadalupe-Hidalgo. By doing so they created the borderlands. The Anzaldúas lived right at the border. Therefore the ones of our family who ended up north of the border, in the U.S., were the Anzaldúas with an accent, whereas the ones that still lived in Mexico dropped their accent after a while. As the generations then went by, we lost contact with each other. Nowadays the Anzaldúas in the United States no longer know the Anzaldúas in Mexico. The border split my family, so to speak.

K.I.: You started as a writer in 1974, but you didn't get started by focusing on just one particular genre. You were concentrating on several, is that right?

G.A.: *Sí*. I wrote the first poem, the first story, the first creative non-fiction and a rough draft for my first novel, all at the same time. So I didn't start writing just one genre over the years. I started out with all of them at the same time. The only thing that I have added since then is the children's literature.

K.L.: Was this starting with all genres at the same time a way of trying to figure out what you like and/or master best?

G.A.: Well, I think it was because I am interested in multiple projects. I have an incredible hunger to experience the world. And I can best experience the world by writing about it, thinking about it or making little drawings about it. I always want to do a thorough job. So when I start out with an idea like that of *Nepantla* or border crossing, for example, I want to be able to unravel it for different readers for the academic professors and students as well as for children and the average person. I want to do it through different media, through poetry, fiction and through theory because each of these genres enriches the others. For example, a lot of the adult books I am writing have impact on the children's books and vice versa. It all provides me with this rich, rich field in which to work. Therefore I would never accept any genre boundaries in my work. Every now and then people say to me, "Why don't you do just one thing and finish that?" Like, for example, the "*La Llorona*" sequel of *Borderlands*—the reading, writing and speaking. Why don't you just perfect one chapter and then go to the other?" And my answer always is: "I don't work that way." For example, the bridge idea I tried in anthologies, in the theoretical work, in poetry and in fiction. So there is always the person who is a bridge to other cultures. Connections between different cultures, between different generations and so on.

K.I.: How do you develop your ideas?

G.A.: The way that I originate my ideas is the following: First there has to be something that is bothering me, something emotional so that I will be upset, angry or conflicted. Then I start meditating on it, sometimes I do that while I am walking. Usually I come up with something visual of what I am feeling. So then I have a visual that sometimes is like a bridge, sometimes like a person with fifty legs, one in each world; sometimes *la mano izquierda*, the left-handed world; the *rebollino*, et cetera, and I try to put that into words. So behind this feeling there is this image, this visual, and I have to figure out what the articulation of this image is. That's how I get into the theory. I start theorizing about it. But it always comes from a feeling.

K.I.: So first there is the feeling, then a vision or visual and then comes the writing?

G.A.: *Sí*. For example the feeling of not belonging to any culture at all, of being an exile in all the different cultures. You feel like there are all these gaps, these cracks in the world. In that case I would draw a crack in the world. Then I start thinking: "Okay, what does this say about my gender, my race, the discipline of writing, the U.S. society in general and finally about the whole world?" And I start seeing all these cracks, these things that don't fit. People pass as though they were average or normal; however, everybody is different. There is no such thing as normal or average. And your culture says: "That is reality!" Women are this way, men are this way, and white people are this way. And you start seeing behind that reality. You see the cracks and realize that there are other realities. Women can be this or that, whites can be this or that. Besides physical reality there might be a spiritual reality. A parallel world, a world of the supernatural. After having realized all these cracks, I start articulating them and I do this particularly in the theory. I have stories where these women, these *prietas*—they are all *prietas*—actually have access to other worlds through these cracks. So I take these major things, I just go with it and work it out as much as I can. I bring the concept of borders and borderlands more into unraveling all that, too. And I now call it *Nepantla*, which is a Nahuatl word for the space between two bodies of water, the space between two worlds. It is a limited space, a space where you are not this or that but where you are changing. You haven't got into the new identity yet and haven't left the old identity behind either-you are in a kind of transition. And that is what *Nepantla* stands for. It is very awkward, uncomfortable and frustrating to be in that *Nepantla* because you are in the midst of transformation.

K.I.: The *Nepantla* concept—is it somehow a sequel to *Borderlands*?

G.A.: No, it is not a continuation of *Borderlands*. It is a completely new book. The title is *La Prieta, The Dark One*, and I deal with the consequences of *Nepantla* as well as with the *la Llorona* figure in all its chapters. *La Prieta* is about my being a writer and how I look at reality, how reality gets constructed, how knowledge gets produced and how identities get created. The subtext is reading, writing and speaking. So *Nepantla* is a way of reading the world. You see behind the veil and you see these scraps. Also it is a way of creating knowledge and writing a philosophy, a system that explains the world. *Nepantla* is a stage that women and men, and whoever is willing to change into a new person and further grow and develop, go through. The concept is articulated as a process of writing: it is one of the stages of writing, the stage where you have all these ideas, all these images, sentences and paragraphs, and where you are trying to make them into one piece, a story, plot or whatever it is all very chaotic. So you feel like you are living in that mist of chaos. It is also a little bit of an agony you experience. My symbol of that is Coyolxauhqui, the moon goddess, who was dismembered by her brother Huitzilopochtli. The art of composition, whether you are composing a work of fiction or your life, or whether you are composing reality, always means pulling off fragmented pieces and putting them together into a whole that makes sense. A lot of my composition theories are not just about writing but about how people live their lives, construct their cultures, so actually about how people construct reality.

K.I.: If you think about people and philosophies that influenced you in your writing and your writing philosophy, so to speak, who or what in particular had a major influence on you in that regard?

G.A.: I started out being born into a culture that philosophizes very much. All Mexicans have all these stakes in realities, and they are always very likely to start philosophizing about their lives. Then when I was a little girl my way of escaping through a lot of the pain I suffered was through reading. Some of my pain was cultural in origin—you know about being Mexican—some of it was because of my gender, so about being this girl, who wasn't supposed to be as important as my brothers, even though I was older. Part of this suffering was related to the fact that I was in pain most of the time because I was born with a hormonal imbalance, which meant that I went into puberty very early on. I remember that I was always made to feel ashamed because I was having a period and had breasts when I was six years old. Then I also was this freak who was very sensitive. My way of dealing with the world was to read, to escape through reading. I would read everything. Very early on I started reading Nietzsche. Also I was reading Schoppenhauer, Sartre, Kafka and most of those heavy duty guys. Then I turned more to the women that were philosophers, like Jeffner Allen and Maria Lugones, the Latina philosopher.

K.I.: How would you describe your own philosophy?

G.A.: I would describe it the way I describe my spirituality. My spiritual reality I call spiritual *mestizaje*, so I think my philosophy is like a philosophical *mestizaje* where I take from all different cultures—for instance, from the cultures of Latin America, the people of color and also the Europeans.

K.I.: I would like to talk a bit more about your spiritual reality and religion in general. How does it look exactly? Could you also tell us a bit more about your experiences with the Catholic Church which has a very strong hold among the Mexicans and Mexican Americans in general?

G.A.: The grounding of my spiritual reality is based on indigenous Mexican spirituality, which is *Nahualismo*, which loosely translates as "shamanism." But the *Nahual* was a shapeshifter, a shaman that could shift shapes, that could become a person or an animal. The philosophy that I am now trying to unravel also goes back to Mexican indigenous times where I use the words like *Nepantla*, like *conocimiento*, so things that come from the indigenous, the Mexican or the Chicano. And then I try to philosophize about that. With the spiritual *mestizaje* there is a component of folk Catholicism in it. But very early on—beginning with the death of my father and my *desencanto*, my disillusionment with traditional Catholicism—I rebelled. The Catholicism that Mexicans in south Texas participate in is more of a folk Catholicism, as it has a lot of indigenous elements in there. But on top of the indigenous elements are put the Catholic scenes. Therefore underneath all those Catholic saints and the Virgin Mary there are all these native American figures, these indigenous Mexicans like *Tonantzin*.

K.I.: Is it more an ethnic-based problem you have with Catholicism and traditional religion, then, and not so much a gender-related issue?

G.A.: Oh no, gender is an important issue, too, as in most of the major religions in the world—like Christianity, Hindi and Islam—women are second-place and inferior. Women are regarded as nothing and often treated worse than cattle. In all these religions there is that attitude underneath. But yes, Christianity has cleaned up a lot of that. However, if you look at all the violence towards women, women are battered, molested, raped or killed—for example, one out of every three women in this country gets molested—there is a deep hatred and fear of women. So, yeah, the white culture emphasizes that we are all equal, men and women. However, underneath all that there is this violence against women, all this negative stuff about women. So if you can see through that illusion, through those cracks, you can see to that reality—of Protestantism, Christianity, Judaism, Hindi, Islam and Moslem, the major religions in the world—that they still have that negative attitude towards women as they continue to regard and treat them as inferior beings.

K.I.: How did you build up your own spiritual reality?

G.A.: When you go through a heavy difficult time, and you don't have the resources, you can't go to anybody in the society or in the community, you finally fall back on yourself. What I did was that I started breathing. I had to like breathing and to start meditating in order to get through the pain and that whole difficult period. And all that reconnected me with nature, from which I had gotten away. So this is why I like to live at the ocean, like I do now here in Santa Cruz. You know, to live near the ocean means that you just go there and then get another infusion of energy. All the petty problems you have fall away because of the presence of the ocean. It therefore is a real spiritual presence for me. I feel that way with some trees, the wind, serpents, snakes, deserts, too. So in the periods that I was going through, my very darkest times when there was nobody there for me, I realized that at least I had to be there for me. So I started to access that part of me, of my personality and of something that is connected to something else. You know, like that *"Antigua mi diosa"* I tell about in *Borderlands. "Antigua mi diosa"* is a figure I connected with when I was in a lot of isolation and frustration in Brooklyn, where I didn't really want to be anyway. I didn't feel comfortable in that city at all. I had to reach for something to comfort me and *"Antigua mi diosa"* was both an agitator who made me suffer but also a comforter; it is like a double-edged figure. It can be turned into a goddess. Therefore it can be incorporated in your own personality. It could become the spiritual part of you or you can make it into a double. In my writing I call her the watcher. It is like: here you are, the person writing, the author, but in the back of the head there is somebody else out there, so it is like someone else looking on the scene. One notion would be Gloria Anzaldúa as the author writing this piece. Then there is the narrator, who is also Gloria Anzaldúa, and within that there is then maybe also a character, a protagonist which is based on me. So you have three frames. And behind all these frames there is some other power that is more than just a conscious ego. That's what I call the double or the watcher. Then there is the *antigua*, somebody who is a greater figure, more of a divine presence. I think this is my connection with *Coatlicue*, the serpent woman, with *la Virgen de Guadalupe*, with what people call "goddesses." However, I personally don't like the word goddess. To me these are figures which embody an awareness that is divine. A divine consciousness to which people just have given different names. If you are a santera there is all that *santería*, which, for example, the *Orishas* have, like *Yemaya* and Oya (goddess of the wind). If you are Native American there is a figure called the white buffalo woman, if you are Chinese there is Quan Yin, if you are Indian there are other names, et cetera. Therefore people just give it different names. So what I want to do is to leave all that as awareness or as a consciousness. Because what happens if you give these forces a human figure and a name is you start limiting them and their power. Therefore I just call them cultural figures, like *la Llorona*, *Coyolxauhqui*, the moon goddess and *la Virgen*. They are all cultural figures, and what's important is their consciousness and the things they are aware of.

K.I.: How do you feel about the contemporary relation between Chicano writers and Chicana writers on the one hand and lesbian Chicana writers versus heterosexual Chicano/a writers on the other hand? Do you feel that these are first of all two separate blocks without any connections or is border crossing happening here as well?

G.A.: Well, I agree with you in that there are different groups or categories. For example, there is the old vanguard, with old male Chicano writers like Rolando Hinojosa-Smith, Rudolfo Anaya and all the other writers and professors that grew up during those times where they were reading the guys. They are very fearful of the women, and they feel very threatened by us because we are blasting them with their sexism and we are questioning and challenging them. Then there is the younger generation of Chicanos. I don't know if Francisco Lomelí [University of California at Santa Barbara] is part of this, Hector Torres [University of New Mexico at Albuquerque] certainly is. A lot of these critical writers, as well as the creative writers, are part of the younger generation. We were their models. So they are open to us. The same thing is true for the women. The older category of women, who were very staunch straight Chicanas who supported their men, feel a little bit uncomfortable around the lesbians and the strong feminists. These older women are only lately becoming part of the feminist ranks. But back then, during the times when I was trying to publish, they turned their backs against me. They wouldn't publish me and no one else in the Chicano/a community would publish me either. I had to go to the Jewish and the white communities instead. Now there are these younger generations around, these kids, who are a little bit more open and who are reading us. They are in a way more broadminded. However, you still get the traditional blocks. For example, every now and then it happens that I go to a university and some guy says, "Oh I love *Borderlands*," but then he realizes that I am queer. He is shocked, although he shouldn't be because if you know my other books you already know that I am queer. Sometimes, those who find out later want to hate me, but they can't quite hate me because they have already liked me before. The queer stuff is still a problem with the guys, and it is still a major barrier to their reading me.

K.I.: What about other Chicana writers and critics? Do you feel that there might be a "generational gap" between established Chicana writers like yourself, Ana Castillo or Sandra Cisneros, who started writing in the 1980s and the younger generation of Chicana writers who just got started in the 1990s like Josefina López for example?

G.A.: I don't think so. One of the things that I have noticed is how charitable, warm and generous we are to each other. Sandra Cisneros, for example, is very supportive of my work. Then there is Antonia Castañeda, Emma Pérez, Chela Sandoval and Norma Alarcón. We are all dealing with each other's work. Norma Alarcón based all of her work on critiquing Chicanas. Two essays of hers which she has written about me came out just last year, for example. Or Tey Diana Rebolledo of the University of New Mexico in Albuquerque—she is another example. In general I would say that the professors, the academic Chicanas are very generous. There is a little bit more rivalry with the creative writers. But I think that I am out of it because they look at me as a *gente grande*, somebody who is older and maybe somebody who's already got more experience.

K.I.: *Borderlands/La Frontera* is often regarded by critics as an example of Chicana post-colonial writing. How do you feel about that?

G.A.: Well, there are two ways of spelling post-colonial, one with the dash in-between, the other one without the dash. The ones that use the term without the dash are a little bit more 'us-them' based and the ones that use the dash, of which I am one, we are more or less in each other's pockets. So it goes both ways: it is more an exchange between both sides. I have a term that is called *nos-otras*, and I put a dash between the *nos* and the *otras*. The *nos* is the subject "we," that is the people who were in power and colonized others. The *otras* is the "other," the colonized group. Then there is also the dash, the divide between us. However, what is happening, after years of colonization, is that all the divides disappear a little bit because the colonizer, in his or her interaction with the colonized, takes on a lot of their attributes. And, of course, the person who is colonizing leaks into our stuff. So we are neither one nor the other; we are really both. There is not a pure other; there is not a pure subject and not a pure object. We are implicated in each other's lives.

K.I.: How do you feel about post-colonialism in general, as the Chicana situation is quite a bit different from the post-colonial experience of the former colonies of the British Empire?

G.A.: Most of the post-colonial intellectuals are writing about their being in exile from one country or the other. Some of the work I am doing now looks at us Chicanas and the way we are internal exiles within our own country. But there is a difference with regard to post-colonialism, and I am trying to articulate that in the writing. In academic circles there is prejudice against that. It is okay to listen to a black man like Homi Bhaba from Britain—import him to the United States and listen to him and his thoughts about post-coloniality—rather than take somebody from California who is a Chicano/a and who has experienced some other things. If you are very exotic, like being from Australia, Africa, India, et cetera, this legitimates you more than being an internal exile. We still don't receive much attention and often aren't listened to at all.

K.I.: What are you working on right now and what future projects do you have in mind?

G.A.: First I would like to finish *La Prieta, The Dark One,* which will be about 24 stories. All characters in these stories were *prietas,* however *prietas* that were different from each other, with different first names, different experiences, different ages, et cetera. I started writing a couple of these stories as early as 1978. So this whole collection of stories went through different stages of development. About six years ago I realized that I didn't know how to write fiction. What I was writing until then was something like my memoirs, sort of my autobiography. What was keeping me back was that I was trying to stay with the truth, with the experiences that actually happened. Then I realized that to do fiction you have to be free, imagine things, exaggerate—whatever you need to do in order to convey the kind of reality that you are trying to transmit. I began to listen to people and talk with them about their writing and their methods. In order to learn how to write these stories, I was making notes about my process and I called the notes

Writing Outside La Prieta. It tells about my ideas for the stories, where I was having problems, how I did the research, et cetera. This was very interesting for me because I ended up having two parts actually: *La Prieta*, the fiction, on the one hand and then on the other, the notes that tell about how I did it. After *La Prieta*, I plan to do the sequel to *Borderlands*—theoretical pieces, a lot of which tie into the fiction.

Anyway, after *La Prieta, The Dark One* is finished, I want to focus on reading, writing and speaking for a while. While I am in that process I want to work on *Prietita and the grave robber*, a middle-grade school book for kids. Once I get all that out of the way, I am going to put out a manual, a guide for writers and artists. I am already very excited about that manual in particular; I would really like doing something like that.

Then I have another series of stories for another collection which I intend to publish. The title for that is *Fic Nineteen*. It was going to be *Fiction Nineteen* originally, but I had to cut it down to *Fic Nineteen* because you can't have big names for computer files. The stories of *Fic Nineteen* are more experimental, more way out, more wild. They demonstrate that I can free myself a little bit more. I also am writing poetry at the moment. I'm working on two books of poems, one is called *Nightface* and the other one *Tres Lenguas del Fuego* ("Three Tongues of Fire").

Another project I am working on is a book about myself and my relationship with my mom. It is going to be called *Myself and (m) other*. Also I would like to put together all the interviews that were conducted with me in one book. And then I have a Chicana dictionary in mind. I've already started collecting entries. It is going to be like an encyclopedia that focuses on Chicanas and their culture.

Oh, and then I almost forgot to mention that I am writing a novel right now as well. I have already started plotting it. I don't have an exact title yet. So far I just call it The Novel. It is gonna be way down the road. The protagonist is a woman named Dolores, and I am modeling her on my sister, whose name is Hilda. She is like the antithesis to me in every regard. But I want to make her the protagonist and I want to deal with Hargill, the little town in Texas where we grew up, and fictionalize it.

Finally, in addition to all these projects, at some point I want to do a fourth anthology. And the fourth anthology is going to be just Chicanas or Latinas rather than all the women of color.

K.I.: So there are a lot of books and works to be expected from you in the coming years. I am looking forward to that very much.

G.A.: I know it is a lot of work, and I will probably die before I have finished or realized all my plans and projects. You know, with my diabetes you never know, because with people who suffer from diabetes mortality is very unsure. But I hope I am lucky and get as much done as possible.

Selected Bibliography

Selected Bibliography*

Adams, Kate. "Northamerican Silences: History, Identity, and Witness in the Poetry of Gloria Anzaldúa, Cherríe Moraga, and Leslie Marmon Silko." *Listening to Silences: New Essays in Feminist Criticism*. Ed. Elaine Hedges and Shirley Fisher Fishkin. New York: Oxford UP, 1994. 130-45.

Aigner-Varoz, Erika. "Metaphors of a Mestiza Consciousness: Anzaldúa's *Borderlands/La Frontera.*" *MELUS* 25.2 (2000): 47-64.

Alarcón, Norma. "Anzaldúa's Frontera: Inscribing Gynetics." *Displacement, Diaspora, and Geographies of Identity*. Ed. Smadar Lavie and Ted Swedenburg. Durham, NC: Duke UP, 1996. 41-53.

Alcoff, Linda. "The Unassimilated Theorist." *PMLA* 121.1 (2006): 255-65.

Aldama, Arturo J. "Toward a Hermeneutics of Decolonization: Reading Radical Subjectivities in *Borderlands/La Frontera: The New Mestiza* by Gloria Anzaldúa." *Disrupting Savagism: Intersecting Chicana/o, Mexican Immigrant, and Native American Struggles for Self-representation*. Durham, NC: Duke UP, 2001. 95-128.

Alvarez, Maria Antonia. "Chicana Deconstruction of Cultural and Linguistic Borders." *Interactions: Aegean Journal of English and American Studies/Ege Ingiliz ve Amerikan Incelemeleri Dergisi* 14.1 (2005): 49-59.

Andersen, Corrinne. "Beyond Border Thinking: Gloria Anzaldúa's *Borderlands/La Frontera* and the Mexican-American Diaspora." *Detroit Monographs in Musicology* 40 (2004): 117-24.

Andrist, Debra D. "La Semiotica de la chicana: La escritora de Gloria Anzaldúa." *Mujer y literatura mexicana y chicana: Culturas en contacto II*. Ed. Aralia López González, Amelia Malagamba, and Elena Urrutia. Tijuana: Colegio de Mexico, Colegio de la Frontera Norte, 1990. 243-47.

Arteaga, Alfred. "Heterotextual Reproduction." *theory@buffalo* (Fall 1996): 61-85.

Bastian, Michelle. "the contradictory simultaneity of being with others: exploring concepts of time and community in the work of Gloria Anzaldúa." *Feminist Review* 97 (2011): 151-167.

Barnard, Ian. "Gloria Anzaldúa's Queer Mestisaje." *MELUS* 22 (1997): 35-53.

Belasteguigoitia Rius, Marisa. "Limits and Borderlands: Border-Crossing

Pedagogy and Transdiscipline in Gloria Anzaldúa's Writings." *Estudos Feministas* 17.3 (2009):755-767.

Berila, Beth. "Reading National Identities: The Radical Disruptions of *Borderlands/La Frontera.*" *EntreMundos* Keating 121-28.

—. "Unsettling Calls for National Unity: The Pedagogy of Experimental Multiethnic Literatures." *MELUS* 30.2 (2005): 31-47.

Bernal, Dolores Delgado. "Learning and Living Pedagogies of the Home: The Mestiza Consciousness of Chicana Students." *International Journal of Qualitative Studies in Education* 5 (2001): 623-39.

Bickford, Susan. "In the Presence of Others: Arendt and Anzaldúa on the Paradox of Public Appearance." *Feminist Interpretations of Hannah Arendt*. Pennsylvania: Pennsylvania State UP, 1995.

Blanchard, Mary Loving. "Reclaiming Pleasure: Reading the Body in 'People Should Not Die in June in South Texas.'" Keating *EntreMundos* 29-40.

Blom, Gerdien. "Divine Individuals, Cultural Identities: Post-Identitarian Representations and Two Chicana/o Texts." *Thamyris: Mythmaking from Past to Present* 4 (1997): 295-324.

Bobel, Chris, et al. "This Bridge We Are Building: 'Inner Work, Public Acts.'" *Human Architecture: Journal of the Sociology of Self-knowledge* 4 (2006): 333-38.

Bornstein-Gómez, Miriam. "Gloria Anzaldúa: Borders of Knowledge and (re)Signification." *Confluencia* 26.1 (2010): 46-55.

Bowery, Anne-Marie. "Voices from Within: Gloria Anzaldúa, bell hooks, and Roberta Bondi." *The Gift of Story: Narrating Hope in a Postmodern World*. Ed. Emily Griesinger and Mark Eaton. Waco, TX: Baylor UP, 2006. 51-68.

Branche, Jerome. "Anzaldúa: El ser y la nación." *Entorno* 34 (1995): 39-44.

Browdy De Hernandez, Jennifer. "Mothering the Self: Writing the Lesbian Sublime in Audre Lorde's *Zami* and Gloria Anzaldúa's *Borderlands/La Frontera.*" *Other Sisterhoods: Literary Theory and U.S. Women of Color*. Ed. Sandra Kumamoto Stanley. Urbana, IL : U of Illinois P, 1998. 244-62.

—. "On Home Ground: Politics, Location, and the Construction of Identity in Four American Women's Autobiographies." 22.4 *MELUS* (1997): 21-38.

—. "The Plural Self: The Politicization and Form in Three American Ethnic Autobiographies." *Memory and Cultural Politics: New*

Approaches to American Ethnic Literatures. Ed. Amritjit Singh, Joseph J. Skerret, and Robert E Hogan. Boston: Northeastern UP, 1996. 41-59.

Bundy, Mark. "'Know Me Unbroken': Peeling Back the Silenced Rind of the Queer Mouth through the Works of Gloria Anzaldúa." Keating *EntreMundos* 139-46.

Calderón, Héctor. "Literatura fronteriza tejana: El compromiso con la historia en Américo Paredes, Rolando Hinojosa y Gloria Anzaldúa." *Mester* 22-23.2-1 (1993): 41-61.

—. "Texas Border Literature: Cultural Transformation and Historical Reflection in the Works of Americo Paredes, Rolando Hinojosa and Gloria Anzaldúa." *Dispositio: Revista Americana de Estudios Comparados y Culturales* 16.41 (1991): 13-27.

Candelaria, Cordelia. "Una vela por Gloria/A Candle for Gloria." *Frontiers* 25.3 (2004): 1-3.

Cantú, Norma E. "Comparative Perspectives Symposium: Gloria E. Anzaldúa, an International Perspective." *Signs* 37.1 (2011) : 1-5.

—. "Gloria Anzaldúa and Transnational Contemporary Concerns." *30th Annual National Women's Studies Association Conference (NWSA 2009)* Sheraton Hotel, Atlanta, Georgia. November 2009.

—. ed. et al. *El Mundo Zurdo*. San Francisco: Aunt Lute Books, 2010.

Capetillo-Ponce, Jorge. "Exploring Gloria Anzaldúa's Methodology in *Borderlands/La Frontera—The New Mestiza*." *Human Architecture* 4. Special Issue (2006): 87-94.

Caputi, Jane. "Shifting the Shapes of Things to Come: The Presence of the Future in Gloria Anzaldúa." Keating *EntreMundos* 185-93.

Carrasco, Davíd and Roberto Lint Sagarrena. "The Religious Vision of Gloria Anzaldúa: *Borderlands/La Frontera* as a Shamanic Space." *Mexican American Religions: Spirituality, Activism, and Culture.* Ed. Gastón Espinosa and Mario T. García. Durham, NC: Duke UP, (2008): 223-241.

Castillo, Debra A. "Anzaldúa and Transnational American Studies." 121.1 *PMLA* (2006): 260-65.

Concannon, Kevin. "The Contemporary Space of the Border: Gloria Anzaldúa's *Borderlands* and William Gibson's *Neuromancer*." *Textual Practice* 12 (1998): 429-42.

Corbin, Michelle. "Facing Our Dragons: Spiritual Activism, Psychedelic Mysticism, and the Pursuit of Opposition." *Human Architecture* 4 (2006): 239-47.

Cota-Cárdenas, Margarita. "The Faith of Activists: Barrios, Cities, and the Chicana Feminist Response." *Frontiers* 14.2 (1994): 241-59.

Cruz, Cindy. "Toward an Epistemology of the Brown Body." *Qualitative Studies in Education* 14.5 (2001): 657-669.

Davis-Undiano, Robert Con. "Mestizos Critique the New World: Vasconcelos, Anzaldúa, and Anaya." *LIT* (2000): 117-42.

Delgadillo, Theresa. *Spiritual Mestizaje: Religion, Gender, Race, and Nation in Contemporary Chicana Narrative.* Durham, NC. Duke UP Books, 2011.

Disch, Estelle. "Nurturing the Nepantlera Within: Working in the Borderlands of Our Prejudices." *Human Architecture* 4 (2006): 123-30.

Donadey, Anne. "Overlapping and Interlocking Frames for Humanities Literary Studies: Assia Djebar, Tsitsi Dangarembga, Gloria Anzaldúa (Transnational Feminist Writers)." *College Literature* 34.4 (2007): 22-42.

el Moncef, Salah. "Übermenschen, Mestizas, Nomads: The Ontology of Becoming and the Scene of Transnational Citizenship in Anzaldúa and Nietzsche." *Angelaki* 8.3 (2003): 41-57.

Embry, Marcus. "Cholo Angels in Guadalajara: The Politics and Poetics of Anzaldúa's *Borderlands/La Frontera.*" *Women & Performance* 8 (1996): 87-108.

Espinosa-Aguilar, Amanda. "Radical Rhetoric: Anger, Activism, and Change." Keating *EntreMundos* 227-32.

Espinoza, Dionne. "Women of Color and Identity Politics: Translating Theory, Haciendo Teoría." *Other Sisterhoods: Literary Theory and U.S. Women of Color.* Ed. Sandra Kumamoto Stanley. Urbana, IL: U of Illinois P, 1998. 44-62.

Esquibel, Catrióna Rueda. "Shameless Histories: Chicana Lesbian Fictions Talking Race/Talking Sex." *Tortilleras: Hispanic and U.S. Latina Lesbian Expression.* Ed. Lourdes Torres. Philadelphia: Temple UP, 2003. 258-75.

Fast, Robin Riley. "Borderland Voices in Contemporary Native American Poetry." *Contemporary Literature* 36.3 (1995): 508-36.

Fishkin, Shelley Fisher. "The Borderlands of Culture: Writing by W.E.B. Du Bois, James Agee, Tillie Olsen, and Gloria Anzaldúa." *Literary Journalism in the Twentieth Century*. Ed. Norman Sims. New York. Oxford UP, 1990.

Fowlkes, Diane. "Moving from Feminist Identity Politics to Coalition Politics through a Feminist Materialist Standpoint of Intersubjectivity in Gloria Anzaldúa's *Borderlands/La Frontera:The New Mestiza*." *Hypatia* 12 (1997): 105-24.

Franklin, Cynthia G. "Another 1981." *Writing Women's Communities: The Politics and Poetics of Contemporary Multi-Genre Anthologies*. Madison: University of Wisconsin Press, 1997. 31-55.

Freedman, Diane P. "Living on the Borderland:The Poetic Prose of Gloria Anzaldúa and Susan Griffin." *Women and Language* 12.1 (1989): 1-4.

Gagnier, Regenia. "Review Essay: Feminist Autobiography in the 1980's." *Feminist Studies* 17.1 (1991): 135-48.

Garber, Linda. "'Caught in the Crossfire Between Camps': Gloria Anzaldúa." *Identity Poetics: Race, Class, and the Lesbian-Feminist Roots of Queer Theory.*" New York, Columbia UP, 2001. 146-75.

—. "Spirit, Culture, Sex: Elements of the Creative Process in Gloria Anzaldúa's Poetry." Keating *EntreMundos* 213-26.

Garcia-Serrano, Maria Victoria. "Gloria Anzaldúa y la politica de la identidad." *Revista Canadiense de Estudios Hispánicos* 19.3 (1995): 479-94.

Gaspar de Alba, Alicia. "Crop Circles in the Cornfield: Remembering Gloria E. Anzaldúa (1942-2004)." *American Quarterly* 56.3 (2004): iv-vii.

Gentile, Brigidina. "Gloria Anzaldúa y la travesia transgresiva de las fronteras de la escritura." *Latino Studies* 2 (2004): 322-27.

Gil-Gomez, Ellen M. "Performing 'La Mestiza': Lesbians of Color Negotiating Identities." *Journal of Lesbian Studies* 4.2 (2000): 21-38.

Gomez Hernandez, Adriana. "Gloria Anzaldúa: Enfrentando el desafio." *Cuadernos Americanos* D.F. Mexico. 59 (1996): 57-63.

Gonzalez, Deena J. "Chicana Identity Matters." *Aztlán* 22.2 (1997): 123-38.

González-López, Gloria. "Epistemologies of the Wound: Anzaldúan Theories and Sociological Research on Incest in Mexican Society." *Human Architecture: Journal of the Sociology of Self-knowledge* 4 (2006): 17-24.

Grewal, Inderpal. "Autobiographic Subjects and Diasporic Locations: *Meatless Days* and *Borderlands*." *Scattered Hegemonies: Postmodernity and Transnational Feminist Practices*. Ed. Inderpal Grewal and Caren Kaplan. Minneapolis: U of Minnesota P, 1994. 231-54.

Gounari, Panayota. "How to Tame a Wild Tongue: Language Rights in the United States." *Human Architecture: Journal of the Sociology of Self-knowledge* 4 (2006): 71-77.

Hall, Lynda. "Writing Selves Home at the Crossroads: Anzaldúa and Chrystos (Re)Configure Lesbian Bodies." *Ariel* 30 (1999): 99-117.

Hames-Garcia, Michael. "How to Tell a Mestizo from an Enchirito© Colonialism and National Culture in the Borderlands." *Diacritics* 30.4 (2000): 102-122.

Hartley, George. "The Curandera of Conquest: Gloria Anzaldua's Decolonial Remedy." *Aztlán* 35.1 (2010): 135-161.

—"'Matriz sin tumba': The Trash Goddess and the Healing Matrix of Gloria Anzaldúa's Reclaimed Womb." *MELUS* 35.3 (2010): 41-61.

Hedley, Jane. "Nepantilist Poetics: Narrative and Cultural Identity in the Mixed-Language Writings of Irena Klepfisz and Gloria Anzaldúa." *Narrative* 4 (1996): 36-54.

Hedrick, Tace. "Queering the Cosmic Race: Esotericism, Mestizaje, and Sexuality in the Work of Gabriela Mistral and Gloria Anzaldúa." *Aztlán* 34.2 (2009): 67-98.

Henríquez-Betancor, María. "Gloria Anzaldúa in the Canary Islands." *Signs* 37.1 (2011): 41-46.

Herrera-Sobek, María. "Gloria Anzaldúa: Place, Race, Language, and Sexuality in the Magic Valley." 121.1 *PMLA* (2006): 266-71.

Hill, Simona J. "Teaching la Conciencia de la Mestiza in the Midst of White Privilege." Keating *EntreMundos* 29-38.

Ingenschay, Dieter. "Pepsicoatl, Nation of Aztlán und New World Border:

Problematisierung, Hybridisierung und Überwindung der mexicanidad im Lichte der Kultur der chicans." *Grenzen der Macht-Macht der Grenzen: Lateinamerika im globalen Kontext*. Ed. Ottmar Ette et al. Frankfurt, Germany: Vervuert, 2005. 77-101.

Jacobs, Glenn. "Finding the Center: Constructing the Subaltern Master Narrative." *Human Architecture* 4 (2006): 79-86.

Jagose, Annamarie. "Slash and Suture: The Border's Figuration of Colonialism, Phallocentrism, and Homophobia in *Borderlands/La Frontera: The New Mestiza.*" *Lesbian Utopics.* New York: Routledge, 1994. 137-58.

Joysmith, Claire. *"Ya se me quitó la vergüenza y la cobardía. Una plática con Gloria Anzaldúa." Debate Feminista,* (4, 8, September 1993) Mexico City, pp. 15-16.

Karrer, Wolfgang. "Gender and the Sense of Place in the Writings of Gloria Anzaldúa and Rolando Hinojosa." 237-45.

Kaup, Monika. "Crossing Borders: An Aesthetic Practice in Writings by Gloria Anzaldúa." *Cultural Difference and the Literary Text: Pluralism and the Limits of Authenticity in North American Literatures.* Iowa City: U of Iowa P, 1996. 100-11.

Keating, AnaLouise. "Back to the Mother? Feminist Mythmaking with a Difference." *Feminist Interpretations of Mary Daly.* Ed. Marilyn Frye and Sarah Lucia Hoagland. New York: SUNY P, 2000.

—.ed. *Bridging: How Gloria Anzaldúa's Life and Work Transformed Our Own.* Ana Louise Keating and Gloria González-López. Austin: University of Texas P., 2011.

—. "(De)Centering the Margins? Identity Politics and Tactical (Re) Naming." *Other Sisterhoods: Literary Theory and U.S. Women Writers of Color.* Ed. Sandra Kumamoto Stanley. Urbana: University of Illinois P, 1998. 23-43.

—. ed. *EntreMundos/AmongWorlds: New Perspectives on Gloria E. Anzaldúa.* New York: Palgrave, 2005.

—. "From Borderlands and New Mestizas to Nepantlas and Nepantleras: Anzaldúan Theories for Social Change." *Human Architecture* 4 (2006): 5-16.

—. "'I'm a Citizen of the Universe': Gloria Anzaldúa's Spiritual Activism as Catalyst for Social Change." *Feminist Studies* 34.1/2 (2008): 53-69

—. "Myth Smashers, Myth Makers: (Re)Visionary Techniques in the Works of Paula Gunn Allen, Gloria Anzaldúa, and Audre Lorde." *Journal of Homosexuality* 26 (1993): 73-95.

—. "Reading 'Through the Eyes of the Other': Self, Identity, and the Other in the Works of Paula Gunn Allen, Gloria Anzaldúa, and Audre Lorde." *Readerly/Writerly Texts: Essays on Literature, Literary/Textual Criticism, and Pedagogy* 1 (1993): 139-65.

—. "Risking the Personal: An Introduction." *Interviews/Entrevistas.* Gloria E. Anzaldúa. Ed. AnaLouise Keating. New York: Routledge, 2000. 1-15.

—. *Women Reading Women Writing: Self-Invention in Paula Gunn Allen, Gloria Anzaldúa and Audre Lorde.* Philadelphia: Temple University Press, 1996.

—. "Writing, Politics, and las Lesberadas: Platicando con Gloria Anzaldúa." *Frontiers* 14 (1993): 105-150.

Koshy, Kavitha. "Nepantlera-Activism in the Transnational Moment: In Dialogue with Gloria Anzaldúa's Theorizing of Nepantla." *Human Architecture* 4 (2006): 147-61.

Kynclová, Tereza. "Constructing Mestiza Consciousness: Gloria Anzaldúa's Literary Techniques in *Borderlands/La Frontera—The New Mestiza.*" *Human Architecture* 4 (2006): 43-55.

Lara, Irene. "Daughter of Coatlicue: An Interview with Gloria Anzaldúa." Keating *EntreMundos* 41-55.

Leland, Dorothy. "La formación de la identidad en *Borderlands/ La Frontera*, de Gloria Anzaldúa." *La seducción de la escritura: Los discursos de la cultura hoy.* Ed. Rosaura Hernandez Monroy and Manuel F. Medina. Mexico City: Mexico, 1997.

Levine, Amala. "Champion of the Spirit: Anzaldúa's Critique of Rationalist Epistemology." Keating *EntreMundos* 171-84.

Levy-Navarro, Elena. "'So Much Meat': Gloria Anzaldúa, the Mind/Body Split, and Exerting Control over My Fat Body." Keating *EntreMundos* 163-69.

Lopez, Tiffany Ana with Phillip Serrato. "A New Mestiza Primer: Borderlands Philosophy in the Children's Books of Gloria Anzaldúa." *Such News of the Land: U.S. Women Nature Writers.* Ed. Thomas S. Edwards and Elizabeth A. De Wolfe. Hanover, NH: University Press of New England, 2001. 204-216.

Lugones, María. "From within Germinative Stasis: Creating Active Subjectivity, Resistant Agency." Keating *EntreMundos* 85-100.

—. "On *Borderlands/La Frontera*: An Interpretive Essay." *Hypatia* 7.4 (1992): 31-37.

—. "On Complex Communication." *Hypatia* 21.3 (2006): 75-85

Mahraj, Katy. "Dis/locating the Margins: Gloria Anzaldúa and Dynamic Feminist Learning." *Feminist Teacher* 21.1 (2010):1-20.

Majewska, Ewa. "La Mestiza from Ukraine? Border Crossing with Gloria Anzaldúa." *Signs* 37.1 (2011): 34-41.

Maracle, Lee. "This Is Personal: Revisiting Gloria Anzaldúa from within the Borderlands." Keating *EntreMundos* 207-12.

Martinez, Jacqueline M. "*La Conciencia De La Mestiza*: Intra- and Intersubjective Transformations of Racist and Homophobic Culture." *Phenomenology of Chicana Experience and Identity*. Lanham, MD: Rowman & Littlefield Publishers, Inc., 2000. 81-101.

Martinez, Theresa A. "The Double-Consciousness of DuBois and the 'Mestiza Consciousness' of Anzaldúa." *Race, Gender, & Class* 9 (2002): 158-176.

—. "Making Oppositional Culture, Making Standpoint: A Journey into Gloria Anzaldúa's Borderlands." *Sociological Spectrum* 25.5 (2005): 539-70.

Martinot, Steve. "Social Justice Movements as Border Thinking: An Anzaldúan Meditation." *Human Architecture: Journal of the Sociology of Self-knowledge* 4 (2006): 163-76.

McMaster, Carrie. "Negotiating Paradoxical Spaces: Women, Disabilities, and the Experience of Nepantla." Keating *EntreMundos* 101-06.

Medina, Ruben. "Mestizaje across the Border: Vasconcelos and Anzaldúa." Spanish-language. *Mexican Studies - Estudios Mexicanos* 25.1 (2009): 101-123.

Mignolo, Walter. "Linguistic Maps, Literary Geographies, and Cultural Landscapes: Languages, Languaging and (Trans)Nationalism," *Modern Language Quarterly* 57.2 (1996): 181-96.

McRuer, Robert. *The Queer Renaissance: Contemporary American Literature and the Reinvention of Lesbian and Gay Identities*. New York: New York UP, 1997.

Murphy, Patrick. "Grandmother Borderland: Placing Identity and Ethnicity." *Isle* 1 (1993): 35-41.

Neely, Carol Thomas. "Women/Utopia/Fetish: Disavowal and Satisfied Desire in Margaret Cavendish's *New Blazing World* and Gloria Anzaldúa's *Borderlands/La Frontera*." *Heterotopia: Postmodern Utopia and the Body Politic*. Ann Arbor: U of Michigan P, 1995. 58-95.

Negrón-Muntaner, Frances. "Bridging Islands: Gloria Anzaldúa and the Carribean." *PMLA* 121.1 (2006): 272-278.

Neile, Caren S. "The 1,000-Piece Nights of Gloria Anzaldúa: Autohistoria-teoría at Florida Atlantic University." Keating *EntreMundos* 17-27.

Neitz, Mary Jo. "*2008 Associaton for the Sociology of Religion Presidential Address* Encounters in the Heartland: What Studying Rural Churches Taught Me about Working across Differences." *Sociology of Religion* 70.4 (2008): 343-361.

Nelson, Linda. "After Reading *Borderlands/La Frontera* by Gloria Anzaldúa." *Trivia* 14 (Spring 1989): 90-101.

Norton, Jody. "Transchildren, Changelings, and Fairies: Living the Dream and Surviving the Nightmare in Contemporary America." *this bridge we call home: radical visions for transformation.* Ed. Gloria E. Anzaldúa and AnaLouise Keating. New York: Routledge, 2002. 145-154.

Ohmer, Sarah. "Gloria Anzaldúa's Decolonizing Ritual of Knowledge." Spanish-language. *Confluencia* 26.1, (2010): 141-153.

Oliver-Rotger, Maria Antònia. "Gloria Anzaldúa's Borderless Theory in Spain." *Signs* 37.1 (2011): 5-10.

Ortega, Mariana. "Apertures of In-Betweeness, of Selves in the Middle." Keating *EntreMundos* 85-100.

Palczewski, Catherine Helen. "Bodies, Borders, and Letters: Gloria Anzaldúa's 'Speaking in Tongues: A Letter to 3rd World Women Writers.'" *The Southern Communication Journal* 62.1 (1996): 1-16.

Perez, Domino Renee. "Words, Worlds in Our Heads: Reclaiming La Llorona's Aztecan Antecedents in Gloria Anzaldúa's 'My Black *Angelos.*'" *Studies in American Indian Literatures* 15 (2003): 51-63.

Pérez, Laura E. "Spirit Glyphs: Reimagining Art and Artist in the Work of Chicana *Tlamatinime.*" *MFS* 44.1 (1998): 36-76.

Perry, Yaakov. "The Homecoming Queen: The Reconstruction of Home in Queer Life-Narratives." *A-B:-Auto-Biography-Studies* 15.2 (2000): 193-222.

Peterson, Carla L. "Borderlands in the Classroom: Meeting Point of Two or More Cultures." *American Quarterly* 45.2 (1993): 295-300.

Pope, Barbara. "Texts of Difference and Ways of Knowing: On Teaching Patricia Hill Collins, Gloria Anzaldúa, and Trinh Minh-ha." *Transformations* 11 (201): 73-79

Premo, Cassie. "Mutual Recognition and the Borders within the Self in the Writing of Cherríe Moraga and Gloria Anzaldúa." *Critical Studies on the Feminist Subject*. Ed. Giovanna Covi. Trento, Italy: Università degli Studi di Trento, 1997. 229-43.

Radlwimmer, Romana. "Searching for Gloria Anzaldúa: A Fictional Dialogue on Realities Somewhere Between Austria and Spain." *Signs* 37.1 (2011): 18-23.

Raiskin, Judith. "Inverts and Hybrids: Lesbian Rewritings of Sexual and Racial Identities." *The Lesbian Postmodern*. Ed. Laura Doan. New York: Columbia UP, 1994. 156-72.

Ramirez, Arturo. "El feminismo y la Frontera: Gloria Anzaldúa." *A Ricardo Gullón: Sus discípulos*. Ed. Adelaida Lopez de Martinez. Erie, PA: Pub de la Asociación de Licenciados y Doctores Españoles en Estados Unidos, 1995. 203-9.

Ramlow, Todd R. "Bodies in the Borderlands: Gloria Anzaldúa's and David Wojnarowicz's Mobility Machines." *MELUS* 31.3 (2006): 169-90.

Ramsdell, Lea. "Language and Identity Politics: The Linguistic Autobiographies of Latinos in the United States." *Journal of Modern Literature* 28.1 (2004): 166-76.

Rebolledo, Tey Diana. "'Prietita y El Otro Lado': Gloria Anzaldúa's Literature for Children." *PMLA*. 121.1(2006): 279-284.

Reti, Irene. "House of Nepantla." Keating *EntreMundos* 57-59.

Reuman, Ann E. "'Wild Tongues Can't Be Tamed': Gloria Anzaldúa's (R)evolution of Voice." *Violence, Silence, and Anger: Women's Writing as Transgression*. Ed. Deidre Lashgari. Charlottesville: U of Virginia P, 1995. 305-19.

Ricard, Serge. "'La Fiancée de Frankenstein' aux pays des Aztèques: La nouvelle métisse selon Gloria Anzaldúa." *Accra* 20 (1995): 143-55.

Rochel, Perles and Juan Antonio. "Revisiting the Borderlands: A Critical Reading of Gloria Anzaldúa's *Borderlands/La Frontera:* Towards a New Mestiza." *Evolving Origins, Transplanting Cultures: Literary Legacies of the New Americans*. Ed. Antonia Dominguez Miguela. Huelva, Spain: Universidad de Huelva, 2002. 229-35.

Rotger, Ma-Antónia Oliver. "'Sangre Fértil'/Fertile Blood: Migratory Crossings, War and Healing in Gloria Anzaldúa's *Borderlands/La Frontera*." *Dressing Up for War: Transformations of Gender and Genre in the Discourse and Literature of War*. Ed. Aránzazu Usandizaga and Andrew Monnickendam. Amsterdam, Netherlands: Rodopi, 2001. 189-211.

Saldívar-Hull, Sonia. *Feminism on the Border: Chicana Gender Politics and Literature*. Berkeley: U of California P, 2000.

—. ed. et al. *El Mundo Zurdo 2*. San Francisco: Aunt Lute Books, 2012.

—. "Feminism on the Border: From Gender Politics to Geopolitics." Ed. Héctor Calderón and José David Saldívar. *Criticism in the Borderlands: Studies in Chicano Literature, Culture, and Ideology*. Durham: Duke UP, 1991. 203-20.

—. "Introduction to the Second Edition." *Borderlands/La Frontera: The New Mestiza*. Gloria Anzaldúa. San Francisco: Spinsters/Aunt Lute, 1999.

Sandoval, Gabriela. "On Skin As Borderlands: Using Gloria Anzaldúa's New Mestiza to Understand Self-Injury among Latinas." *Human Architecture* 4 (2006): 217-24.

Schotten, C. Heike. "Revolutionary Futures: Nietzsche, Anzaldúa, and Playful 'World'-Travel." *Human Architecture* 4 (2006): 303-19.

Schweitzer, Ivy. "For Gloria Anzaldúa: Collecting America, Performing Friendship." *PMLA* 121.1 (2006): 285-291.

Short, Kayann. "Coming to the Table: The Differential Politics of *This Bridge Called My Back*." *Genders* 20 (1994): 3-44.

Sieber, Tim. "Knowledge, Learning, and Teaching: Striving for Conocimiento." *Human Architecture* 4 (2006):355-358.

Spitta, Silvia. "The Contingencies of Life and Reading: Para Gloria (Gloria Anzaldúa)." *PMLA* 121.1 (2006): 292-294.

Smith, Sidonie. "Autobiographical Manifestoes." *Subjectivity, Identity, and the Body: Women's Autobiographical Practices in the Twentieth Century*. Bloomington: Indiana UP, 1993. 153-82.

Steele, Cassie Premo. "Leading from 'You' and 'I' to 'We': Contemporary American Women's Poetry of Witness." *Leadership Journal: Women in Leadership—Sharing the Vision* 2 (1998): 67-80.

—. *We Heal From Memory: Sexton, Lorde, Anzaldúa, and the Poetry of Witness*. New York: Palgrave, 2000.

Suyemoto, Karen L. "Processes of Emergence and Connection: Interrelations of Past, Present, and Future in Journeying for Conocimiento." *Human Architecture* 4 (2006): 339-45.

Tamdgidi, Mohammad H. "Anzaldúa's Sociological Imagination: Comparative Applied Insights into Utopystic and Quantal Sociology." *Human Architecture* 4 (2006): 265-85.

—. "'I Change Myself, I Change the World':Gloria Anzaldúa's Sociological Imagination in *Borderlands/La Frontera: The New Mestiza.*" *Humanity and Society* 32.4 (2008): 311-335.

Torres, Hector A. *Conversations with Contemporary Chicana and Chicano Writers.* Albuquerque: University of New Mexico P, 2007.

Torres, Lourdes. "The Construction of Self in U.S. Latina Autobiographies." *Third World Women and the Politics of Feminism.* Ed. Chandra Talpade Mohanty, Ann Russo, and Lourdes Torres. Bloomington: Indiana UP, 1991. 271-87.

Torres, Mónica. "Doing Mestizaje: When Epistemology Becomes Ethics." Keating *EntreMundos* 195-203.

Vargas-Monroy, Liliana. "IV Knowledge from the Borderlands: Revisiting the Paradigmatic Mestiza of Gloria Anzaldúa." *Feminisim & Psychology* 0.0 (2011): 1-10.

Velasco, Juan. "La construccion de la mexicanidad en la narrativa chicana contemporanea: la estetica de la/s frontera/s." *Aztlán* 21.1-2 (1992): 105-23.

Vásquez, Edith M. "La Gloriosa Travesura de la Musa Que Cruza/The Misbehaving Glory(a) of the Border-Crossing Muse: Transgression in Anzaldúa's Children's Stories." Keating *EntreMundos* 63-75.

Watts, Brenda. "Aztlán As a Palimpsest: From Chicano Nationalism Toward Transnational Feminism in Anzaldúa's *Borderlands.*" *Latino Studies* 2 (2004): 304-21.

Wiederhold, Eve. "What Do You Learn from What You See? Gloria Anzaldúa and Double-Vision in the Teaching of Writing." Keating *EntreMundos* 107-20.

Wright, Melissa. "Maquiladora Mestizas and a Feminist Border Politics: Revisiting Anzaldúa." *Hypatia* 13.3 (1998): 114-31.

Yarbro-Bejarano, Yvonne. "Gloria Anzaldúa's *Borderlands/La Frontera*: Cultural Studies, 'Difference,' and the Non-Unitary Subject." *Cultural Critique* 28 (Fall, 1994): 5-28.

—. "The Lesbian Body in Chicana Cultural Production." *Entiendes? Queer Readings, Hispanic Writings.* Ed. Emilie L. Bergmann and Paul Julian Smith. Durham: Duke UP, 1995. 181-97.

Ybarra, Priscilla Solis. "Borderlands as Bioregion: Jovita González, Gloria Anzaldúa, and the Twentieth-Century Ecological Revolution in the Rio Grande Valley." *MELUS* 34.2 (2009):175-189.

Zaccaria, Paola. "Translating Borders, Performing Trans-Nationalism." *Human Architecture: Journal of the Sociology of Self-knowledge* 4 (2006): 57-70.

Zaytoun, Kelli. "New Pathways towards Understanding Self-in-Relation: Anzaldúan (Re)Visions for Developmental Psychology." *EntreMundos/Among Worlds: New Perspectives on Gloria E. Anzaldúa*. Ed. AnaLouise Keating. New York: Palgrave Macmillan, 2005. 147-59.

—. "Theorizing at the Borders: Considering Social Location in Rethinking Self and Psychological Development." *NWSA Journal* 18.2 (2006) 52-72.

Zimmerman, Bonnie. *The Safe Sea of Women: Lesbian Fiction 1969-1989*. Boston: Beacon, 1990.

Zita, Jacquelyn N. "Anzaldúan Body." *Body Talk: Philosophical Reflections on Sex and Gender*. New York: Columbia UP, 1998. 165-83.

Zygadło, Grażyna. "'Where the Third World Grates Against the First': Teaching Gloria Anzaldúa from a Polish Perspective." *Signs: Journal of Women in Culture & Society*. 37.1 (2011): 29-34.

Contributors

Norma Alarcón is a professor of Comparative Ethnic/Indigenous Studies at the University of California at Berkeley, and she is the founder and publisher of Third Woman Press.

Julia Alvarez is a poet, fiction-writer and essayist. She is the author of *How the García Girls Lost Their Accents, In the Time of the Butterflies,* and *Saving the World.*

Paola Bacchetta is an associate professor in Gender and Women's Studies at the University of California at Berkeley, and the author of *Gender in the Hindu Nation: RSS Women as Ideologues* and co-editor of *Right-Wing Women: From Conservatives to Extremists around the World.*

Rusty Barcelo is the Vice President and Vice Provost for Equity and Diversity at the University of Minnesota, and a national consultant for diversity in higher education.

Norma Cantú is a professor of English at the University of Texas at San Antonio. She is the author of *Canícula Snapshots of a Girlhood en la Frontera* and co-editor of *Chicana Traditions: Continuity and Change.*

Ana Castillo is a poet, novelist, and essayist whose works include the novels *So Far from God* and *Watercolor Women/Opaque: A Novel in Verse,* and the collection of essays *Massacre of the Dreamers.*

Sandra Cisneros is a poet and fiction writer whose works include *The House on Mango Street, Woman Hollering Creek, Loose Woman,* and *Caramelo, or, Puro Cuento.*

T. Jackie Cuevas is pursuing her Ph.D. in English at the University of Texas at Austin. She is the author of a chapbook, *Otherhood U.S.A.,* and is currently writing a collection of short stories called *Selena Don't Live Here Anymore: Tex-Mex Stories.*

Aída Hurtado is Professor of Psychology at the University of California at Santa Cruz. She is the author of *The Color of Privilege: Three Blasphemies on Race and Feminism* (1996) and *Voicing Chicana Feminisms: Young Chicanas Speak Out on Sexuality and Feminism* (2003).

Karin Ikas is the author of *Chicana Ways: Conversations with Ten Chicana Writers* and co-editor (with Francisco Lomelí) of *U.S. Latino Literatures and Cultures: Transnational Perspectives.*

Claire Joysmith teaches and researches at the Universidad Nacional Autónoma de México, and is the editor of *Las formas de nuestras voces: Chicana and Mexican Writers in Mexico.*

AnaLouise Keating is a professor of Women's Studies at Texas Woman's University and the author of *Women Reading Women Writing: Self- Invention in Paula Gunn Allen, Gloria Anzaldúa, and Audre Lorde* and editor of *EntreMundos/ Among Worlds: New Perspectives on Gloria Anzaldúa.*

Sonia Saldívar-Hull is a professor of English at the University of Texas at San Antonio and the author of *Feminism on the Border: Chicana Gender Politics and Literature.*

Gloria Anzaldúa was born September 26, 1942, in Raymondville, Texas, to Amalia and Urbano Anzaldúa. The eldest of four children, she moved with her family to work on different ranches in South Texas until she was eleven, when the family settled in Hargill, Texas to give the children more educational opportunities. She received her B.A. from Pan American University. As an openly lesbian Chicana writer and activist, one of very few at the beginning of her career, most of Gloria's life work involved creating cultural and political space for the voices of women of color. In addition to writing *Borderlands/La Frontera: The New Mestiza*, a book named by Library Journal as one the 38 best books of 1987 and by *The Hungry Mind Review* as one of the 100 most important books of the twentieth century, Gloria co-edited (with Cherríe Moraga) *This Bridge Called My Back: Writings by Radical Women of Color* (1981); edited *Making Face/Making Soul: Haciendo Caras* (1990); wrote three children's books; and (with AnaLouise Keating) co-edited the anthology *this bridge we call home,* and published *Entrevistas/Interviews*, a collection of interviews.

Among several other awards, Gloria received a Before Columbus American Book Award for *This Bridge Called My Back*, the Lesbian Rights Award, and the American Studies Association Lifetime Achievement Award. Gloria did graduate work at the University of Texas at Austin and the University of California at Santa Cruz. She had just completed her dissertation when she died, on May 15, 2004, from diabetes-related complications. She was awarded her PhD posthumously in June of 2004.

Aunt Lute Books is a multicultural women's press that has been committed to publishing high quality, culturally diverse literature since 1982. In 1990, the Aunt Lute Foundation was formed as a non-profit corporation to publish and distribute books that reflect the complex truths of women's lives and to present voices that are underrepresented in mainstream publishing. We seek work that explores the specificities of the very different histories from which we come, and the possibilities for personal and social change.

Please contact us if you would like a free catalog of our books or if you wish to be on our mailing list for news of future titles. You may buy books from our website, by phoning in a credit card order, or by mailing a check with the catalog order form.

Aunt Lute Books
P.O. Box 410687
San Francisco, CA 94141
415.826.1300

www.auntlute.com
books@auntlute.com

This book would not have been possible without the kind contributions of the Aunt Lute Founding Friends:

Anonymous Donor	Diana Harris
Anonymous Donor	Phoebe Robins Hunter
Rusty Barcelo	Diane Mosbacher, M.D., Ph.D.
Marian Bremer	Sara Paretsky
Marta Drury	William Preston, Jr.
Diane Goldstein	Elise Rymer Turner